MW00860513

Language, Nation, and Identity in the Classroom

Studies in the
Postmodern Theory of Education

Shirley R. Steinberg
General Editor

Vol. 456

The Counterpoints series is part of the Peter Lang Education list.
Every volume is peer reviewed and meets
the highest quality standards for content and production.

PETER LANG
New York • Bern • Frankfurt • Berlin
Brussels • Vienna • Oxford • Warsaw

David Hemphill and Erin Blakely

Language, Nation, and Identity in the Classroom

Legacies of Modernity and Colonialism in Schooling

PETER LANG
New York • Bern • Frankfurt • Berlin
Brussels • Vienna • Oxford • Warsaw

Library of Congress Cataloging-in-Publication Data

Hemphill, David.
Language, nation, and identity in the classroom: legacies of modernity
and colonialism in schooling / David Hemphill, Erin Blakely.
p. cm. — (Counterpoints: studies in the postmodern theory of education; vol. 456)
Includes bibliographical references and index.
1. Education—Social aspects. 2. Critical pedagogy. 3. Postmodernism and education.
4. Language and education. I. Blakely, Erin. II. Title.
LC191.H42   306.43—dc23   2014005852
ISBN 978-1-4331-2372-6 (hardcover)
ISBN 978-1-4331-2371-9 (paperback)
ISBN 978-1-4539-1343-7 (e-book)
ISSN 1058-1634

Bibliographic information published by **Die Deutsche Nationalbibliothek**.
Die Deutsche Nationalbibliothek lists this publication in the "Deutsche
Nationalbibliografie"; detailed bibliographic data are available
on the Internet at http://dnb.d-nb.de/.

The paper in this book meets the guidelines for permanence and durability
of the Committee on Production Guidelines for Book Longevity
of the Council of Library Resources.

© 2015 Peter Lang Publishing, Inc., New York
29 Broadway, 18th floor, New York, NY 10006
www.peterlang.com

All rights reserved.
Reprint or reproduction, even partially, in all forms such as microfilm,
xerography, microfiche, microcard, and offset strictly prohibited.

Printed in the United States of America

This book is dedicated to my wife, Jennifer, my daughters, Lydia and Bizzy, and my late parents, Robert and Elizabeth. It is also dedicated to multiple generations of graduate students in the Graduate College of Education at San Francisco State University who helped work through the ideas presented here–*David Hemphill*

For Troy, with gratitude–*Erin Blakely*

Table of Contents

1 Narratives of Progress and the Colonial Origins of Schooling

In the West and regions influenced by the West, educators operate within a system structured by modernity and colonialism, though the history and legacies of both remain largely unrecognized and ignored in the field. Despite the fact that schooling is a primary forum for the transmission of language, citizenship, and culture, it is rare in recent decades for teacher preparation programs and schools of education to address the historical origins or cultural specificity of learning and identity. This absence of theory and history contributes to the wide pendulum swings that often occur within the field from: phonics to whole language reading instruction; bilingualism to English-only mandates; portfolio assessments to pencil-and-paper tests; or US national policies like the No Child Left Behind legislation to the Common Core Standards. Each generation of new teachers comes into the profession with little access to knowledge of what has gone before and without the theoretical resources to move beyond two-sided debates in order to investigate how language, nation, and identity unfold in their classrooms.

Many seemingly natural or commonsense policies and practices within the field of education—the age-graded organization of students, the chronological division of history from prehistoric to modern civilizations, and the exploration of regions and cultures one at a time, with sequential units, for example, on Native Americans or China—may appear inevitable or neutral to educators. Yet these patterns are implicated in the distribution and normalization of social hierarchies and systems of difference that privilege certain forms of knowledge (abstract, decontextualized, or scientific) and certain communities (Western, developed, or "civilized").

A modernist paradigm has dominated Western thought since its development around the time of the European Enlightenment in the 18th and 19th centuries. Primary elements of modernism include:

- a privileging of logic, rationality, science, and observable evidence as the most reliable, legitimate paths to truth and knowledge;
- an emphasis on overarching metanarratives—theories that seek to "explain everything," like the narrative of progress that organizes history in an ever-upward march towards advanced civilization;
- a reliance on form over content that, for example, focuses on research procedures and not context in the scientific method, or emphasizes process in legal proceedings;
- a tendency to see things as binaries (either/or), such as mind/body, rational/irrational, science/humanities, male/female, White/Black, or self/Other; and
- a conceptualization of subjectivity that defines the individual as being of primary importance, and characterizes the "normal" adult self as rational, stable, autonomous, fully transparent to itself, and responsible for its actions.

The main tenets of modernism are so thoroughly embedded in the conceptual frameworks, languages, and socioeconomic systems operating in the West that they seem natural and timeless. Countering Western social hierarchies and systems of difference requires unpacking the normative binaries in Western discourse and articulating how the tenets of modernism undergird Western institutions like schools.

The Invention of Childhood and "Developmentally Appropriate" Curriculum

Before Western industrialization, age was not the primary criterion for ordering lives. Children were not segregated from the full range of adult activities and work, but labored alongside their relatives at home or on a farm. The separation of the workplace from the home that accompanied industrialization led to the development of age-graded, child-focused bureaucratic institutions, such as pediatrics and compulsory schooling, which began to monitor, organize, and define childhood. From these institutions a discourse emerged that imagined childhood as an innocent, vulnerable, and transient stage, requiring a range of protective services. Though now widely considered a "natural" stage of life, childhood is an historical invention and product of modernist binaries—work/home, child/adult, and mature/immature. The naturalization of these binaries and the modernist conceptualization of subjectivity has rendered childhood essentially separate from adulthood. This naturalization has created a hierarchical relationship between adults, who are presumed to be stable, rational, and fully transparent to themselves, and children, who have yet to achieve this state. Institutions like schools, as a result, are required to promote the advancement of children.

Children in the West are described almost without exception in terms of a linear narrative of progress. Childhood is delineated into many stages, where children are viewed as advancing in sequential stages from the primitive scrawls of a preschooler through mastery of advanced skills. A narrative of progress underlies many of the hierarchies that operate within school systems. The pay scales of instructors, for example, where preschool teachers are paid the least and university professors the most, reflect the inherent assumption that the pedagogical requirements for teaching the youngest students are less than the requirements for teaching the most "advanced, rigorous" courses.

This narrative of progress has been operationalized in schools, particularly through the division of students into grade-levels and the adherence to age-based stage theories that promote "developmentally appropriate" instruction. This curricular direction for young children leads to the constant measurement of children's progress and hyper-assessment based on a mythical norm. Examples of the broad range of stage theories that have influenced Western education include: Jean Piaget's stages of cognitive development; Lawrence Kohlberg's stages of moral development; Abraham Maslow's hierarchy of needs; Erik Erikson's stages of psychosocial development; and Daniel Levinson's stages of adult development, among others.

The widely cited Swiss developmental researcher Jean Piaget suggests that there are four sequential, fixed stages of human cognitive development: sensorimotor; pre-operational; concrete-operational; and formal-operational. Through these stages, Piaget charts how a child moves from initially acquiring information through sensory experiences to eventually employing deductive, abstract reasoning. The majority of curricula adopted in the US and other Western countries are based on Piaget's developmental theories, which are generalized to all ages and cultures, though they were developed from only observations of his own children. The *Ages & Stages* evaluations and learning activities used by Head Start and many other public and private preschool programs in the US go even further than Piagetian research claims; they break down activities and instructional strategies into four-month micro-increments for children aged one month through five years. "Developmentally appropriate" curriculum assumes that there is consistent development and progress even over short spans of time. It assumes that children will be able to perform the same in any setting—and at any time—when assessed. This type of bureaucratization is a pervasive practice in education that amplifies uncritical universalization of Western norms.

Descriptions of childhood in educational, social work, and psychological literature almost without exception present stage-based models of youth and of identity, marking the transition to adulthood as a moment of identity crisis. Adolescents, for instance, are considered to be in a deficit state of "becoming"; it only has meaning in relation to the rational adult they are expected to become. The binary division of youth from adulthood and the corresponding deficit-based model of adolescence is not, however, an objective developmental state. As youth development theorists Sunaina Maira and Elisabeth Soep note, the idea of "youth-as-transition" is culturally constructed. This division is neither natural nor universal, but exists for historical and cultural reasons; it is, they argue, "necessary to the division of labor and the hierarchy of material relations specific to various forms of the capitalist state" (2005, p. xxiii).

In the West, the prevailing image of adolescents is one of hormonally-driven individuals, highly subject to peer pressure, impulsivity, and a desire to rebel or separate themselves from their adult caretakers. This unquestioned image shapes the disciplinary and surveillance systems that schools put in place and the kinds of intervention programs they offer, from self-esteem workshops to drug and gang intervention programs, sex education, and parent support groups. These interventions are widely accepted as necessary and inevitable, often without any recognition of the history, norms, or national and commercial interests that underlie the Western "storm and stress" model of adolescence.

The storm and stress depiction of adolescence was originally advanced by psychologist G. Stanley Hall in response to a perceived growth of juvenile delinquency during rapid urbanization at the turn of the 20th century in the US. Hall, who was an early leader in American psychology and the first president of the American Psychological Association (APA), argued that child development is akin to the history of human evolution—the ascent from savagery to civilization. Based on this narrative of progress, Hall claimed that reasoning with children was a waste of time. Public education, he thought, should not be about intellectual attainment, but about indoctrinating obedience to authority and devotion to the state. He disapproved of open discussions or critical thinking exercises, and supported corporal punishment. Though many of Hall's ideas are now unthinkable in the field of education, his depiction of the storm and stress of adolescence and its three major features—conflict with parents, mood disruptions, and risky behavior—continue to be tacitly accepted.

With the emergence of psychology as a scientific discipline in the 1950s, Hall's storm and stress model became a universal depiction of youth. The

1950s marked the triumph of psychology over religion as the preferred system for understanding behavior. As sociologists Gary Alan Fine and Jay Mechling argue, "The prestige of scientific psychology received a boost from the Progressive Era's worship of expertise and the subsequent marriage of behaviorism and 'scientific management' in American industry and bureaucracy" (1993, p. 123). Psychology, and the social sciences in general, served the war effort "from analysis of propaganda to the treatment of the traumas of war" and by the late 1940s had "established its credentials with the American public, who looked increasingly to experts for advice on rearing children" (Fine & Mechling, 1993, p. 123). Many American parents, for instance, began to look to "experts" like Dr. Spock as sources of child-rearing wisdom, discounting the knowledge of their own parents or forbearers. Psychology supplanted and often discounted traditional perspectives on childhood, leading to the idealization of childhood and play and fostering notions of childhood as a time of innocence, with the primary aims of "having fun" and "fitting in."

Beginning with the proliferation of TV sets in the 1950s, middle and upper class youth were also exposed daily to mass media that modeled their lives. Inundated with televised versions of themselves in *Father Knows Best, The Adventures of Ozzie and Harriet,* or *Leave It to Beaver,* the middle class came to believe in the universality of their family organization and norms. This "typical" family was, however, an aberration or a new invention: "Middle class parents and their baby-boomer children believed they were the normal American family, and it is the 1950s' family that became the benchmark for judging 'threats' to the family over the next four decades" (Fine & Mechling, 1993, p. 123).

What emerged alongside the 1950s construction of the "normal" child was its "threatening alternative: the juvenile delinquent" who was linked to the working class. Undesirable behaviors were blamed on the influence of mass media and popular culture practices like rock and roll and the decline of the traditional family. Rock and roll, originating in African American rhythm and blues (R&B), emerged as a major threat to the traditional American family. One psychiatrist, writing for the *New York Times*, in the early 1950s branded rock as "a cannibalistic and tribalistic form of music" (Altschuler, 2003, p. 17). "Brewed in the hidden corners of Black American cities," wrote another media commentator, "its rhythms infected White Americans, seducing them.... Rock and roll was elemental, savage, dripping with sex; it was just as our parents feared" (Altschuler, 2003, p. 8). Rock and roll was also a threat to the established popular music industry, still invested in big bands. Crooner Frank Sinatra, disavowing the riots of swooning bobbysoxers at his own performances a decade earlier, pronounced this self-serving verdict on rock: "It smells phony and false. It is sung, played, and written for the most part by cretinous goons, and by means of its almost imbecilic reiteration and sly, lewd, in plain fact dirty lyrics it manages to be the martial music of every side-burned delinquent on the face of the earth" (Palmer, 1995, pp. 135–136).

The 1950s version of the typical family and its juvenile delinquent counterpart lingers and continues to frame discussions of youth identity and understandings of "at-risk" youth. In educational and psychological discourses, exposure to mass media and popular culture remains a primary threat for youth, leading to interventions that limit gaming, cell phone use, and media consumption, or policies to ban contemporary music forms. Hip-hop is censored, in the same pattern as 50s rock and roll, for its suggestive lyrics and blamed for contributing to youth delinquency and violence. The prestige of psychological and scientific discourses that describe and define youth, along with the hierarchical division of cultural products into high culture and low or popular culture, promotes the criminalization of youth identities and the disproportionate labeling of minority or low-income youth as "at-risk." The effect of applying storm and stress models, invariant linear stage theories, and related categories leads to a focus in education and psychological discourses on adolescent problems, the dominance of remedial and intervention programs for youth, and the maintenance of Western knowledge hierarchies and systems of difference.

The Spread of Formal Education

The narrative of progress that underlies the age-graded, developmental conceptions of the individual also organizes an understanding of society's historical development. Time, in the West, is imagined as a progressive, forward movement of "humanity from slouching deprivation to erect, enlightened reason" (McClintock, 1995, p.9). The organization of history into an inevitable and unceasing linear path of development began in the era of the Enlightenment—also called the Age of Reason—in 17th- and 18th-century Europe when newly emerging academic disciplines developed "rational and scientific" understandings of the past and present. History was then organized as a chronological tale of progress from prehistoric times to the modern era of advanced civilization. The idea of progress and perfectibility is "the grand idea of the twentieth century," observed the poet Charles Baudelaire (qtd. in McClintock, 1995, p. 10).

The idea of progress is an enduring legacy of modernism that has become a metanarrative or overarching theory that seeks to explain everything.

This metanarrative of progress describes all of history as a constant forward movement, ever upward towards greater economic, political, social, technological, spiritual, and personal development and achievement. Though taken for granted as a universal, "objective" means of structuring time, the linear metanarrative of progress represents but one way to view historical movement. Other cultures have conceived of history quite differently: as a process of rise and fall; as a continuous decline; or as in Chinese history, a series of cyclical repetitions.

In the West, it is unquestioningly accepted that the spread of formal schooling is the product of advancing progress, democracy, and enlightenment. This rational, linear account, however, obscures the national and commercial interests behind the development of formal schools. Public schools were not set up exclusively to promote democracy or other enlightenment goals, but rather to meet the increased knowledge requirements of industrialized labor, assimilate new immigrants, and meet the growing need to build consumer markets. The rise of industrialization and capitalism compelled the development of widespread common or public schools in Europe, the US, and across the colonies of the West.

Before the 1800s the educational system in the US, for example, was highly localized, available only to elites, and generally focused on religious instruction. The General Court of the Massachusetts Bay Colony decreed in 1647 that every town with 100 families or more should have a Latin school to ensure that Puritan children learned to read the Bible and understand Calvinist principles. In the early 1800s the aim of schooling shifted to support the growing need for factory labor; in 1805 the New York Public School Society was established by wealthy businessmen to provide education for poor children. The schools employed a "Lancasterian" or monitorial model, where a single master taught hundreds of students, employing older students to pass lessons down to younger pupils with an emphasis on rote skill building, discipline, and hierarchical obedience (Tyack, 1974).

In the US and many other parts of the world, schooling was also developed to assimilate native-born, as well as newcomer or immigrant children, into an imagined cultural norm. The influx of immigrants from Ireland and other places in Europe in the mid-1800s, along with the annexation of Utah, Nevada, Wyoming, and California from Mexico, led to the development of formal schools in the US to assimilate immigrants and "civilize" native peoples. In 1864, Congress made it illegal, for example, for Native Americans to be taught in their native languages, establishing Bureau of Indian Affairs (BIA) off-reservation boarding schools where children from ages four and up were taken with the aim, as one BIA official said, to "kill the Indian in him and save the man" (Pratt, 1973, p. 260). By the end of the 19th century, public education was available throughout the US; all states by 1918 had laws in place requiring children to attend elementary school. The turn of the 20th century saw a renewal of deep concern in the US that the newly arriving immigrants, clustered in urban enclaves, would diminish or mongrelize American culture. Mandating schooling became the answer to such fears. The pledge of allegiance was invented in 1892 and mandated to start the school day. Schooling became the primary way to Americanize Irish, Germans, Italians, and many other primarily European immigrant groups into America's imagined cultural "melting pot" (Gu, 2001).

In addition to nation-building, curriculum and schooling have been organized historically to shape knowledge and student identities to comply with economic interests. According to economic historians Samuel Bowles and Herbert Gintis, one of the primary aims for expanding schooling is to prepare children "for adult work rules, by socializing people to function well, and without complaint, in the hierarchical structure of the modern corporation" (1976, p. 21). The need to create a stable, skilled workforce remains a central, frequently stated, and well-accepted purpose of schooling in many nations. Business community concerns continue to shape both the structure and content of schooling. The need for a workforce that can navigate technological advances and globalized markets have led to many 21st-century curriculum reform movements in Western nations. School districts across the US, for instance, worked in the early 21st century to align their curriculum to meet the demands of the new globalized economy, as articulated in the Common Core State Standards. State and federal laws and funding stipulations require each local school district to standardize and assess the technical, mathematical, and abstract reasoning skills that are intended to help students compete in this global marketplace. Behind this policy, and prior standards-based instruction movements like the No Child Left Behind policy, is the key argument that "the main purpose of schooling is bolstering the US economy and its national sovereignty and security" (Sleeter & Stillman, 2005, p. 31). The history of formal education is thus intertwined with the history of nation-building and the rise of industrialization, capitalism, and imperialism.

Nation-Building, Ideology, and Hegemony in the Classroom

The tacitly accepted metanarrative of progress in Western discourse defines nation-states as the logical evolutionary development from tribal cultures or "primitive" societies, which are represented as living in backward simplicity and deprivation. Nation-states are represented in school curriculum (geography, social studies, and history lessons) as the uncontested, inevitable organization of the globe. Nation-states are not, however, a neutral means of organization, argues historian Anne McClintock: "Rather than expressing the flowering into time of the organic essence of a timeless people, nations are contested systems of cultural representation that limit and legitimize peoples' access to resources of the nation-state" (1995, p. 353). Nations are not organized through natural physical, geographical divisions, nor are they simply the default entities of historical evolution. They are a specific cultural invention, intended to structure social relations. The nation, anthropologist Katherine Verdery suggests, needs to be treated as "a symbol, and any given nationalism as having multiple meanings offered as alternatives and competed over by different groups maneuvering to capture the symbol's definition and its legitimating effects" (1996, p. 228).

The global legitimacy of the nation-state as the political unit that exercises power over territory was first established in the 18th and 19th centuries by European and later North American global powers. When nation-states replaced the Church as the defining authority, a new discourse was needed to stabilize the nation-state and legitimize the emerging hierarchical structure of social relations. Historian Stephen Toulmin describes this shift:

> The new European system of states, built around absolute claims to nationhood... depended on stable systems of social relations within each nation. Given a historical situation in which feudalism could no longer provide a general mode of social organization, fashioning the new system of Nation-States meant inventing a new kind of class society... In the 16th and 17th centuries, the clear threat to social stability and loyalty was seen as the growing number of 'masterless men' not merely vagrants, but those people (e.g., printers, charcoal burners) whose ways of life did not attach them securely to the vertical chains of reciprocal obligation that had been constitutive of traditional society (1990, p. 96).

"None of this happened overnight," continues Toulmin, "it took time for a fresh pattern of relations, within and among nation-states and between states and their churches, to settle down, become familiar, and shape 'commonsense' attitudes" (1990, p. 91). This common sense and "everyday rationality" is produced through institutions, like schools, which maintain the class-based systems of the nation-state and normalize specific kinds of citizenship through various educational, medical, and psychological discourses (Foucault, 1973, 1977).

Political theorist Benedict Anderson (1991) refers to nations as "imagined communities," in the sense that they are systems of cultural representation through which people come to imagine a shared experience of identification with an extended community. These imagined communities are created by inventing cohesive national narratives that portray a shared history, common purpose, and unifying national interest. Schools serve as a primary setting for the creation and distribution of this shared past and common national interest. Nation-building—defining and assimilating citizens—is a key task of schooling in most parts of the world. In the US, educational researcher Wan Shun Eva Lam suggests,

> This assimilationist process is found in the cultural literacy propaganda that aims to deal with difference by eradicating it—all Americans should read from the same largely white, Western canon and adopt a common set of values and linguistic conventions (2006, p. 1).

The transition to the Common Core Standards reflects this nation-building agenda, where the adoption of nationwide standards is intended to provide teachers and parents with a common understanding of what students are expected to learn. As written on the Common Core website,

> Consistent standards will provide appropriate benchmarks for all students, regardless of where they live. These standards define the knowledge and skills students should have within their K-12 education careers so that they will graduate high school able to succeed in entry-level, credit-bearing academic college courses and in workforce training programs (Common Core State Standards Initiative, 2012).

The production of "good citizens" is a central aim of schooling, as described a century ago as "factories in which the raw products (children) are to be shaped and fashioned into products to meet the various demands of life" (Beyer & Liston qtd. in Sleeter & Stillman, 2005, p. 44). Assimilation and the production of "good citizens" occurs primarily through the mandating of English in the US public school system, where resources are deployed to help English Language Learners (ELLs) catch-up to their monolingual peers. School measures often classify ELLs as at-risk or isolate them in lower-level remedial classes, measuring their progress in English-only tests that dismiss or ignore multilingual proficiencies.

Assimilation occurs not only through language instruction, but also through citizenship education. Starting in kindergarten, citizenship education and patriotism are the main goals of social studies and history instruction. The California Social Studies and History content standards for public schools, for example, begin as follows: "1.0) Students understand that being a good citizen involves acting in certain ways." The standards go on to name the important elements of a shared national knowledge, defining American identity in particular terms: "Learn examples of honesty, courage, determination, individual responsibility, and patriotism in American and world history from stories and folklore." By the end of kindergarten, students are expected to recognize national and state symbols and icons such as the national and state flags, the bald eagle, and the Statue of Liberty... [and] know the triumphs in American legends and historical accounts through the stories of such people as Pocahontas, George Washington, Booker T. Washington, Daniel Boone, and Benjamin Franklin (California Department of Education, 1998).

Historical narratives that permeate the US educational system, including the classic American legends of Johnny Appleseed, Paul Bunyan, Casey Jones, or John Henry, function, not only to craft a shared past, but also to produce specific kinds of citizen-consumers who support the socioeconomic systems of the nation-state. Standard narratives presented in large publishing-house textbooks mandated across the US (and reproduced in commercial media products, such as "Disney's American Legends") include stories that define American identity and forge patterns of consumption, often without recognition of the actual historical events behind them. The legend of Johnny Appleseed, for instance, tells the story of how a pioneer named Johnny Chapman spread apple trees from Pennsylvania to Indiana, helping to build the nation. Excluded from the school-based and Disney-sanitized version of this tale is the fact that Chapman planted apple trees in order to bring hard cider alcohol to the frontier (Disney Studios, 2001).

Worried that Prohibition would ruin alcohol sales in the early 1900s, apple growers reinvented the apple as a healthy, central component of the American diet, creating the marketing slogan, "An apple a day keeps the doctor away." The shiny red apple perched on a teacher's desk is now a ubiquitous symbol of wholesomeness, schooling, and childhood in the US. This image is, however, the product of a discursive, market-driven reinvention to promote specific national and commercial interests. The histories behind curriculum and schooling structures are often hidden, rendering current narratives and images like the red apple for teachers as natural and neutral.

The use of schools to promote nationalism and the production of specific kinds of patriotic citizen-consumers is not limited to the US. As curriculum theorists Kristen Buras and Paulino Motter note, "Since their inception, state education systems have been charged with the responsibility of cultivating 'common' values and creating national identity" (2006, p. 257). It is a common sight in public schools in China, for example, to see entrance walls covered with patriotic slogans and images. In one middle school in Guangzhou, a large shining metallic plaque states, "The mother country is at the center of my heart." Also pictured are a set of patriotic flags and an image of Beijing's Tiananmen Square with rays of light emanating outward. Chinese students uniformed in red kerchiefs start the day by marching onto the playground in military formation while singing patriotic songs. Similar nation-building activities, such as flag displays, posted images of national leaders or heroes, and patriotic, often martial, rituals and assemblies are commonplace in schools across the globe.

Curriculum authorities in many nation-states place their nation at the center of history or geography, or impose an imagined national history of a glorious recent or distant past in school textbooks. The Japanese Education Ministry, for example, has proposed controversial textbook screening standards that "require the inclusion of nationalist views of World War II-era history" (Fackler, 2013, p. 2). The Ministry's unwillingness to recognize in school history texts the atrocities of Japanese military forces in World War II China and Southeast Asia is a continuing source of friction between Japan and other East Asian countries. Similar instances of politically edited history curricula can be seen in the Chinese government's failure to provide any references to the Tiananmen Square massacres in 1989. Likewise, the current Russian government has worked to fashion a post-Soviet history curriculum that emphasizes Russian imperial cultural heritage, tradition, and patriotism while de-emphasizing the previous Soviet era. These examples, taken together, suggest that schooling and the production of knowledge are contested—never neutral—domains that are inextricably entangled with nation-building.

The notion that knowledge production and institutions, like schools, are not neutral stems from the conception of ideology first introduced by German philosopher Karl Marx and his colleague Friedrich Engels in the late 19th century. Marx argued that the logic of capitalism underlies the historical organization of institutions, maintaining the dominance of a ruling class and the exploitation of a working class. The ruling class, according to Marx, reproduces itself through a political state, employing both physical force and a system of ruling ideas and culture. Marx described ideology as a set of ideas, representations, and actions that influence social relationships in an often distorted way that reinforces and reproduces inequality.

Critical educational theorists Michael Apple, Henry Giroux, and Peter McLaren use Marx's conception of ideology to call into question the notion that schools are value-free institutions. They see common sense educational policies and value-neutral educational research as masked ideologies. In Apple's view, schooling "makes the ideological forms seem neutral" (1979, p. 11). He investigates how schools simultaneously promote and conceal dominant ideologies, asking:

> 1) How [do] the basic day-to-day regularities of schools contribute to students learn-
> ing these ideologies? 2) How [do] the specific forms of curricular knowledge both in

the past and now reflect these configurations? 3) How [are] these ideologies... reflected in the fundamental perspectives educators themselves employ to order, guide, and give meaning to their own activity? (1979, p. 14).

Building on Marx's conception of ideology, Italian theorist Antonio Gramsci investigated how power is maintained through cultural and social forces as much as—or more than—through physical force. Writing from prison in the late 1920s, Gramsci developed the concept of hegemony to describe how cultural values and norms, promulgated by a dominant or elite class, are taken for granted and disseminated even though they are not in the interests of all who adopt them. Social power, Gramsci believed, derives from the ability of leaders to frame problems and offer solutions in a way that taps popular sentiment and thus achieves widespread support. Hegemonic processes, he argues, often act to make subordinated groups complicit in their own exploitation by persuading them to accept existing conditions of inequity as the status quo. Hegemonic forces are at work, for example, when people who are marginalized or exploited by the marketing and production practices of large corporations consume uncritically the media and products of these same corporations.

In schools, hegemony is at work when some students accept that the gap in their academic performance is a product of a natural lack of skill, intelligence, or effort rather than institutionalized forms of racism or limited resources. The belief that high-achieving, elite students attain their status through competing in a fair and open system ignores that "being elite" requires a whole portfolio of signs (attending the right schools, wearing the right clothes, and having a designated set of possessions, degrees, trips, and experiences). Poststructuralist Jean Baudrillard argues that signs are increasingly detached from any reality they are meant to signify. This means that academic designations, such as "at-risk" or "ELL" may have less to do with a student's reading level or language proficiency, than with the portfolio of signs that accompany this identity—minority status, participation in the free or reduced price school lunch program, or accent.

To illustrate how institutions assign and maintain deficit identities, linguistic researcher Guadalupe Valdés offers the story of a young immigrant Latina student named Elisa, who worked hard in middle school and high school to escape what Valdés calls the "ESL ghetto." She even changed school districts to register for mainstream, college-bound classes where her ESL record would not follow her; during her senior year she took the ACT and SAT and prepared for college. When Elisa moved to another state, however, and took the regular English placement test at a local community college, she was told that she could not take mainstream classes and would have to register for ESL writing. As Valdés observes,

> The tiny flaws in [her written] English... were too much for the sensitivities of community college teachers. Elisa was told that she will not be eligible for enrollment in credit-bearing, college-level instruction in the regular English sequence until she finishes the sequence of ESL courses (2001, p. 145).

Educational institutions create and maintain identities, like ELL designations, through the assessments and policies that aim to assimilate students and standardize learning outcomes and expectations.

Schools construct and maintain, often without recognition, the symbolic boundaries of the nation, policing who is and who is not a member of the nation-state and who has access to its resources. They evoke "the ideal national," an invented identity, with an often corresponding ethnicity that represents the nation-state. As social theorist Sallie Westwood puts it,

> Racisms are part of the complex which organizes the imaginary of the nation— producing homogeneity, organized through the state, which defines, through the legal/military complex, the borders of the nation, not only in terms of territory but also in terms of the geographies of exclusion that constitute citizens and aliens (2000, p. 31).

Cultural Invisibility, Cultural Capital, & White Privilege

The hegemonies and racisms of the nation-state are produced and distributed in schools through curriculum, where historical narratives, often distorted and partial renderings of the past, are validated. In the true/false and multiple-choice testing regimes schools employ, the responses that fit the national narratives (such as "Columbus discovered America") are marked correct. For students who "know a different reality (Columbus was lost and thought he had discovered the continent of India)... to answer true means the youngster... 'sells out'. To answer 'false' is to get the answer wrong" (Sue, 2004, p. 766). The role schools play in perpetuating national hegemonies and racisms has been addressed to some extent in the field of education, primarily through multicultural education reforms that seek to add perspectives to the curriculum (such as Native American viewpoints on Columbus' arrival). These additions are inadequate, though, as the hegemonies of the nation-state are also distributed in less visible ways, through institutional norms, classroom routines, and other forms of knowledge construction. These routinized schooling practices comprise what Giroux and Penna call the "hidden curriculum": "The unstated values and beliefs that are transmitted to students through the underlying structure of meaning in both the formal content as well as the social relations of school and classroom life" (1979, p. 22).

Anthropologist Renato Rosaldo uses the term "cultural invisibility" to describe how people in dominant positions frequently fail to recognize the nature of their own culture, or that they even have a culture, since their beliefs, language, practices, and worldviews are constantly reinforced by the institutions, people, and media that surround them. Rosaldo suggests that acculturation, often carried out in the schools, especially through language instruction, acts to "produce postcultural citizens of the nation-state" or "people without culture." Rosaldo elaborates:

> Full citizenship and cultural visibility appear to be inversely related.... Full citizens lack culture, and those most culturally endowed lack full citizenship.... Upward mobility appears to be at odds with a distinctive cultural identity. One achieves full citizenship in the nation-state by becoming a culturally blank slate (1989, pp. 199, 201).

Cultural invisibility operates, argues Rosaldo, to make privileged White communities believe that they are "without culture." He offers the example of the homogenous retirement community of Sun City, Arizona, where,

> the men are by and large retired professionals.... Most of the women were housewives.... Most Sun Citians are Protestants.... Politically, they are conservative and vote Republican. Yet the sources of this uniformity remain largely invisible to Sun Citians. To themselves, Sun Citians appear to be so many self-made, rootless nomads whose social origins are quite diverse. For them, their current circumstances have produced their cultural transparency (1989, p. 143).

As cognitive psychologist Barbara Rogoff further describes, "The cultural practices, traditions, values, and understandings of middle-class European American communities may be less visible to people of this heritage precisely because people from a dominant majority often take their practices for granted as the norm" (2003, p. 85).

"Whiteness is transparent," clinical psychologist Derald Wing Sue echoes,

> precisely because of its everyday occurrence. It represents institutional normality, and White people are taught to think of their lives as morally neutral, average, and ideal.... [Schools are the] gateway to knowledge construction, truth and falsity, problem definition, what constitutes normality and abnormality, and ultimately, the nature of reality (2004, pp. 764, 766).

Teachers, embedded in Western paradigms, tend to view the social and language practices of schools as standard or normal, since their existing worldviews generally match the demands of schooling. Educators, notes sociolinguist James Gee, "are often so deeply embedded in their social practices that they take the meanings and values of the texts associated with those practices for granted in an unquestioning way" (2003, pp. 29–30). The monoculturalism of schools keeps educators from recognizing the ethnocentrism inherent in their values and assumptions.

Cultural invisibility often leads to pathologizing cultural values that are outside the mainstream. This occurs, for example, when teachers are directed to call local child and family service (CFS) agencies on the suspicion of sexual abuse after discovering that a sister shares a bed with her two brothers, or a middle-school age child sleeps together in the same room with his parents. The handout, "Guidelines to Determine Reasonable Suspicion," often provided to teachers at the beginning of a school year, includes lists of questions to help determine whether a student experiences sexual abuse: "Do you like it when people hug you? Where do you sleep? Where do others in your house sleep?" Teachers, embedded in Western, middle-class childrearing practices, may assume that these questions are universally valid, yet what constitutes "abuse" or "neglect" varies widely according to the childrearing practices of particular cultures or families. Failure to consider the economic circumstances that might lead a family to share a single bed or the family's views on co-sleeping can lead to the unwarranted criminalization of families. Rogoff notes how "folk wisdom" in middle-class communities portrays the nighttime separation of adults and children, especially older children, as essential for healthy psychological development and acquisition of independence. This is a relatively uncommon practice, however, from a global and historical perspective. As Rogoff writes,

> Communities that practice co-sleeping include both highly technological and less technological communities. Japanese urban children have usually slept next to their mother in early childhood and continued to sleep with another family member after that. Space considerations appear to play only a minor role (2003, p. 198).

Upon hearing about the US custom of placing children alone in their own room, Mayan and East African parents were shocked, finding it unthinkable to leave children alone. Rogoff observes: "This shock at others' cultural practices parallels the disapproval often shown by European American middle class adults over the idea of children sleeping with their parents" (2003, p. 198).

According to social theorist Pierre Bourdieu, the sense that one's own culture is universal "ignores the social-historical conditions which have established a particular set of... practices as dominant and legitimate" (1991, p. 5). Teachers' expectations for how students behave and communicate (how they tell stories, initiate discussion, raise questions, wait for a turn in conversation, or signal paying attention) are all culturally mediated practices that may be unknown, awkward, or unwelcome practices for students in varying degrees given their congruence with home practices. Children from middle-class, Western cultural backgrounds may arrive at school already adept at the social and linguistic patterns necessary for academic success. They have practice in taking turns in conversation, focusing their attention on a single object or task, telling stories following a linear sequence, and responding to known-answer questions. As Rogoff recounts,

> Even before attending school, children in some communities where schooling is central begin to participate with their family in the sort of discourse that often occurs in tests and schools. Middle-class European American parents often play language games with their toddlers that involve test questions in the same format as the known-answer questions used by teachers and testers (such as 'Where is your belly button?'). Familiarity with questions that serve as directives to perform in specific ways can make a difference in whether children respond as expected by the tester [or teacher], creatively play with the materials, or warily try to figure out what is going on (2003, p. 247).

Bourdieu refers to the knowledge and skills necessary to successfully navigate cultural institutions, like schools, as cultural capital. He applies Marx's notion of economic capital, or concentrated wealth, to the cultural realm, arguing that there is certain cultural knowledge that has substantial economic value. Schooling often serves as the gatekeeper for attaining cultural capital. As Apple writes: "Not only is there economic property, there also seems to be symbolic property—cultural capital—which schools preserve and distribute." (1979, p. 3). This distribution of cultural capital is not limited to student competencies, but includes parental knowledge about how to navigate the school system, advocate for students, or understand school and teacher expectations.

In addition to cultural capital, Bourdieu identifies two other forms of capital—symbolic capital, meaning the accumulation of prestige, celebrity, or honor, and linguistic capital. Bourdieu uses the term linguistic capital to describe the capacity to produce expressions that are suitable for particular contexts. When there is congruence between linguistic knowledge and the demands of particular social settings such as schools or workplaces, one can "reap symbolic benefits by speaking in a way that comes naturally" (Bourdieu, 1991, p. 21). However, when a community's language practices do not match with the language demands of a particular institution or setting, then their language is assigned a limited value. As Bourdieu notes, "Obligatory on official occasions and in official places (schools, public administrations, political institutions, etc.), this state language becomes the theoretical norm against which all linguistic practices are objectively measured" (1991, p. 45). Entering school with a set of congruent social and language practices is one part of what scholars call "white privilege," defined as "the unearned advantages and benefits that accrue to White people by virtue of a system normed on the experiences, values, and perceptions of their group" (Sue, 2004, p. 764).

Broadening Bourdieu's original definition, several scholars argue that the possession of cultural capital is not limited to dominant groups. Educational ethnographer Luis Moll introduces the concept of "funds of knowledge" as a way to describe the cultural resources that minority language groups possess and use. He defines funds of knowledge as "the essential cultural practices, and bodies of knowledge and information that households use to survive, to get ahead, and to thrive" (Moll & Greenberg, 1990, p. 321). Critical race theorist Tara Yosso identifies an array of cultural knowledge, skills, abilities and contacts that often go unrecognized and unacknowledged in traditional definitions of cultural capital. These various forms of capital, Yosso argues, include: aspirational, navigational, social, linguistic, familial, and resistant capital. Yosso maintains that her work and the related work of other scholars, "expose[s] the racism underlying cultural deficit theorizing and reveal[s] the need to restructure US social institutions around those knowledges, skills, abilities and networks—the community cultural wealth" (2005, p. 82; Franklin, 2002; Morris, 2004; Solórzano & Solórzano, 1995).

Most educators and "most Americans," argues Sue, "believe in equity and fairness," but their failure to deconstruct Western institutional norms and forms of knowledge construction makes them "unwittingly complicit in maintaining unjust social arrangements... [T]he inability to deconstruct... [Western norms and practices] allows society to continue unjust actions and arrangements.... Making the 'invisible' visible is the major challenge" (2004, pp. 761, 762, 764).

Case in Point: "Universal" Educational Truths: Class Size and Classroom Management Practices

The cultural invisibility of schooling practices leads to the assumption that Western educational policies and practices are standard or universal, applicable to all classrooms and students. Two current widely universalized educational "truths" are: (1) that smaller class sizes are always preferable to larger classes; and (2) that positive reinforcement and encouragement of individual expression are always preferable to punishment and authoritarian control. Studies conducted in Chinese cultural settings (China, Taiwan, and Hong Kong), however, suggest that these are neither universally accepted nor always valid truths (Cortazzi & Jin, 2001).

Researchers Martin Cortazzi and Lixian Jin report that in China, class sizes average 50 students, and in some instances as many as 70 or more. In part, the large class sizes are due to sheer demographics, but many schools in China that could reduce class size still choose not to. When teachers in China are asked to enumerate the greatest educational barriers they face, they list teacher preparation and quality of teachers and instruction ahead of class size. The larger class sizes enable teachers to teach fewer lessons per week, allowing them more time to prepare their lessons and conduct peer observations, lesson study, and group lesson planning activities.

Despite Western incredulity over the idea of large class sizes, the academic performance of Chinese students frequently eclipses the performance of students from many Western nations in international measures, such as Trends in International Mathematics and Science Study (TIMMS) and Program for International Student Assessment (PISA). In observations of Chinese classes, researchers find many instances of interactive activities, despite the expected difficulty of maintaining student interactions in large classes. The lessons are teacher-controlled, but often involve learners quite heavily, depending on explicitly taught grouping routines that structure learning interactions and reduce transition time. Chinese teachers present tightly organized lessons, packaged in terms of preparation, timing, pacing, brevity of activity, and efficient transitions.

Standard discipline practices in Chinese schools also raise doubts about the universality of Western approaches to classroom management. Researcher Irene Ho found that in Chinese societies influenced by Confucian culture, teacher authority and suppression of individuality have historical roots. Ho suggests that student discipline in Confucian collectivistic cultures is based on several principles: (a) expectations of conformity; (b) teachers' moral responsibility for student guidance; and (c) strict measures in discipline. While Western concepts of authority are set against the background of the concept of the free, autonomous individual, Chinese teachers' authoritarian and competitive approach reflects, in their cultural context, care for the student. Chinese teachers in one study, for example, saw student detention not solely as punishment, but as an opportunity to spend out-of-class time with students on a one-on-one basis. While Western teachers often view punishment as a deterrent, Chinese teachers see it as a re-assertion of behavioral norms—a declaration of the system (Ho, 2001).

Orientalism and the "Othering" of Non-Western Cultures

Cultural invisibility renders the products and practices of the West as normative, universal or "without culture," while simultaneously "othering" or "exoticizing" non-Western cultural products and practices. "One of [the West's] deepest and most recurring images of the Other," argues postcolonial theorist Edward Said, "is the Orient... The Orient has helped to define Europe (or the West) as its contrasting image, idea, personality, experience (1979, p. 1). "The emergence," adds cultural theorist Aníbal Quijano,

> of the idea of the 'West' or of Europe is an admission of identity—that is, of relations with other cultural experiences, of differences with other cultures.... [T]hose differences were admitted primarily above all as inequities in the hierarchical sense. And such inequalities are perceived as being of nature: only European culture is rational, it can contain 'subjects'—the rest are not rational, they cannot be or harbor 'subjects'. As a consequence, the other cultures are different in the sense that they are unequal, in fact inferior, by nature. They only can be 'objects' of knowledge or/and of domination practices. From that perspective, the relation between European culture and the other cultures was established and has been maintained, as a relation between 'subject' and 'object' (2007, p. 174).

From the mid-1800s to the present, British, French, and American colonial institutions objectified the Orient by documenting its flora and fauna and describing its peoples and traditions in literature, scientific journals, and anthropological works. Said refers to this produced body of knowledge or discourse as "Orientalism," which he further defines,

> as the corporate institution for dealing with the Orient—dealing with it by making statements about it, authorizing views of it, describing it, teaching it, settling it, ruling over it: in short, Orientalism is a Western style for dominating, restructuring, and having authority over the Orient (1979, p. 3).

The West's depiction of the East was used to demonstrate Western superiority over the Orient. "Eurocentrism maps the world," communication theorists Ella Shohat and Robert Stam argue,

> in a cartography that centralizes and augments Europe and North America and 'belittles' other nations or continents. It bifurcates the world into the West and the Rest and organizes everyday language into binaristic hierarchies implicitly flattering to Europe: our nations, their tribes; our religions, their superstitions; our culture, their folklore; our defense, their terrorism (2003, p. 8).

In the common sense division of the world into West/East or North/South, K–12 social studies, geography, and history lessons produce the hegemonies that maintain the West's centrality and superiority. For example, in McGraw-Hill's *World Atlas for Intermediate Students*, the focus of the text is the US; maps of this region take up the first 30 pages of the 71-page world atlas. The US is also categorized with only one of its North American neighbors—Canada. Mexico, though also a part of North America, is divided from the US in the text and is instead included in the four-page section on Latin America (McGraw Hill, 2000).

In addition to promoting its own centrality, Western hegemonies also represent their cultural accomplishments as pure products. The contributions of non-Western cultures are obscured and dismissed in Western accounts, denying the hybridity of European and American cultural products. Marching bands, to take one example, have come to represent All-American schools and the US nation-state with little to no acknowledgment of their roots in Turkish Ottoman culture. Western military marching bands, which symbolized Western military might in the 19th century and now embody American culture at football games and Fourth of July parades, are actually a hybrid product originating in the *Janissary* army bands of the Turkish Ottoman Empire in the 14th century. The Turks were the first to integrate metal and woodwind instruments with loud percussion—cymbals, massive bass drums, bells, triangles, and whistles—into large, imposing ensembles; Turkish families still dominate cymbal manufacturing today. Performance techniques now widely used in Western marching bands—juggling drumsticks, twirling batons, marching in menacing, close formations, and so forth—were all part of the original Turkish *Janissary* band spectacle (Appell & Hemphill, 2005).

Standard Western historical accounts further obscure and dismiss non-Western cultures by configuring history to align with the West's narrative of progress, representing, philosopher Enrique Dussel explains, a "pseudo-scientific division of history into: a) Antiquity; b) the Medieval Age; and c) the Modern Age.... [that] is an ideological and deforming organization of history" (1998, pp. 175–176). This organization of history highlights Western inventions and scientific achievements, while dismissing non-Western forms of research and knowledge, presenting the rise of power in the East as the "Dark Ages." The science, math, and other cultural developments in China, South Asia, and the Islamic World are ignored or reattributed to the West. As law professor Shad Saleem Faruqi writes in the opinion pages of *The Star*, the major English-language newspaper in Malaysia:

> Everyone knows about the Gutenberg printing press. Very few know that Pi Sheng developed one in 1040. In science, Galileo, Newton, and Einstein illuminated the firmament, but not much is known about Al-hazen and Nasir al-Din al-Tusi.... Cultural and scientific renaissance flourished in the East long before the European renaissance.... Arabic was at one time the lingua franca of science and technology. A large number of texts written in Arabic were translated into Latin without acknowledgment (2011, p. 2)

"Eastern ideas and institutions are viewed," Faruqi argues further, "through Western prisms and invariably regarded as primitive and in need of change. The imperatives of globalization have further tilted the balance in favor of the Anglo-American worldview" (2011, p. 1). Said echoes this argument, writing:

> the world has become immediately accessible to a Western citizen living in the electronic age, the Orient too has drawn nearer to him... Television, the films, and all the media's resources have forced information into more and more standardized molds. So far as the Orient is concerned, standardization... [has] intensified the hold of the nineteenth century academic and imaginative demonology of the "mysterious Orient" (1979, p. 26).

Thus, the residue of 19th-century Orientalism has seeped into "everyday language and media discourses, engendering a fictitious sense of the axiomatic superiority and universality of Western culture" (Shohat & Stam, 2003, p. 8).

The metanarratives of progress that lead to the tacit assumption that Western forms of knowledge and practices (science, capitalism, individualism, written modes of communication) are more advanced further entail the consideration of "Others" as deficient and in need of intervention or remediation. "Other societies or groups," writes Sue, are construed

> as less developed, uncivilized, primitive, or even pathological. The group's lifestyles or ways of doing things are considered inferior... This perception means that people of color, for example, are prone to being seen as less qualified, less capable, unintelligent, inarticulate, unmotivated, lazy, and as coming from broken homes (2004, p. 765).

The power of the West is thus not limited to its capacity to destroy, but is exercised, perhaps now most fully, in its hegemonic capacity to produce knowledge, images, and common sense worldviews. Europe did not destroy African artwork, for example, but deprived it of "legitimacy and recognition in the global cultural order dominated by European patterns. [African artwork] was confined to the category of 'exotic'" (Quijano, 2007, p. 170). African art serves, Quijano argues, as the starting point or inspiration for European art, but "not as a mode of artistic expression on its own, of a rank equivalent to the European norm. And that exactly identifies a colonial view" (2007, p. 170). The roles schools play in producing depictions of Others and maintaining the common sense disciplines and hierarchies of Western knowledge are thus implicated in the imperialist projects of the West.

Schooling and Colonial Logic

Historically, Western expansion has been legitimized by both the developmental narrative of progress that describes the maturation of individuals from childhood to adulthood and the historical narrative of progress that organizes the past into a linear chronology of ever-advancing civilizations. To legitimize imperial projects, Westerners infantilized the people they colonized and imagined that traveling to distant lands was moving backwards through time. In this colonial logic, Western colonizers depicted the people they "discovered" as primitive savages in need of salvation or advancement. As historian Arif Dirlik notes,

> By the end of the nineteenth century EuroAmericans had more or less conquered the whole world, and proceeded to produce ideological legitimations for the conquest, as a cultural orientation Eurocentrism itself is a hindsight invention of the Europe/Other binary, not the other way around (1999, p. 12).

In history and social studies curriculum, maps and timelines that divide the world into developed/developing nations or First/Third World binaries are provided to students as authoritative accounts; yet these seemingly neutral tools of chronology and geography represent a hegemonic framing of world history. The historical account presented to US students casts colonialism as the spread of reason and democracy, generally ignoring the loss of indigenous lives and lands. Students begin to learn about colonialism in fourth- and fifth-grade California history through a study of explorers and English settlements in North America. Seventh graders study "the Age of Exploration to the Enlightenment." Tenth grade includes the study of the worldwide expansion to fuel the demands of industrial nations for natural resources. In this progress-driven history of colonialism, there is no mention of the colonization of Puerto Rico, the Philippines, or islands in the Pacific and Caribbean, and very limited study of US relationships with indigenous peoples.

Education and scholarship have long been a part of colonial endeavors, as a means of establishing sovereignty over new territories and extending the hierarchical relationships that render colonized people in need of "fixing," development, and modernization. The first modern colonial project of the Enlightenment, Napoleon Bonaparte's invasion of Egypt from 1798 to 1801, for instance, included scholars and scientists along with soldiers. Anthropologists, biologists, botanists, geologists, engineers, mathematicians, chemists, and artists were sent to capture the flora and fauna and document the physical, social, and economic basis of the country. They were organized by Napoleon into the *"Institut d' Égypte."* According to historian Paul Strathern,

Central to Napoleon's dream was to be the creation of an Institute of Egypt *[Institut d' Égypte]* in Cairo. This was to be modeled upon the Institute of France in Paris, of which Napoleon was so proud to have become a member that even in Egypt he still headed his dispatches "Member of the Institute and Commander-in-Chief"—in that order. Indeed, it is his pride on becoming a member of the Institute in Paris that may well have crystallized his vision of himself as more than just a general, more even than a conqueror of foreign countries; rather as a bringer of civilization (2009, p. 191).

The stated objectives of the *Institut* were:

1) Progress and the propagation of enlightenment in Egypt; 2) Research, study and the publication of natural, industrial and historical facts concerning Egypt; 3) To give advice on different questions on which its members will be consulted by the government (Strathern, 2009, p. 191).

Modern colonial projects were therefore not solely about military and economic domination; they included the domination of knowledge, research, ideas, and social relationships. The *Institut* consisted of 48 scholars organized into four sections, reflecting dominant academic disciplinary codifications of the Enlightenment era: mathematics, physics and natural history, political economy, and literature and arts. The scholars held weekly seminars with Napoleon and his generals in order to share scientific findings and plan for the "improvement" of Egypt once the French military had completely subdued the country—an event that never fully transpired; Napoleon's hubristic military and cultural mission in Egypt ultimately ended in failure. The subsequent Western anthropological, medical, and psychological writings of the late 19th and early 20th centuries, however, continued to depict the cultures and civilizations of the colonizers—the "scientific observers"—in binary opposition to the "primitive" colonized subjects under observation. This distinction was categorized in racial terms, where advanced civilization was marked as White. "Imperialism," argues McClintock, "is not something that happened elsewhere—a disagreeable fact of history external to Western identity. Rather, imperialism and the invention of race were fundamental aspects of Western, industrial modernity" (1995, p. 5; Said, 1979; Strathern, 2009).

"The objective of colonial discourse," according to cultural theorist Homi Bhabha, "is to construe the colonized as a population of degenerate types on the basis of racial origin, in order to justify conquest and to establish systems of administration and instruction" (1994, p. 70). An American schoolteacher upon arrival in the Philippines in the early 20th century, for example, described herself as: "one of an *army* of enthusiasts enlisted to instruct our little brown brother, and to pass on the torch of occidental knowledge several degrees east of the international date line" (Fee qtd. in Rogoff, 2003, p. 345). US colonial discourse produced and reinforced racialization of Filipinas/os as racially black, and by implication, less-developed than White Americans. This racial depiction of Filipinas/os legitimized colonial endeavors to create a new labor force. Accordingly, the vocational education that was designed for African Americans in the southern US served as a template for schools in the Philippines, where students were instructed in agriculture, handicrafts, and housekeeping. The aim of US schooling in the Philippines in the early 20th century was thus to support progress by providing Filipina/os a model for Western cleanliness and order, to motivate the development of a Protestant work ethic, and desire for the new products of the West. As cultural theorist Roland Sintos Coloma notes,

> The implementation of the manual-industrial curriculum worked well with the economic interest of the United States to export Philippine goods for foreign interest and consumption.... The US colonial government was invested in 'prepar[ing] boys and girls in a practical way for the industrial, commercial, and domestic activities in which they are later to have a part' (2009, pp. 512–513).

Though the period from the 1500s through the 1900s marked the height of European colonialism, physical and symbolic colonialism continues without formal colonies. US colonial projects, for example, continue with disputes over the sovereignty of Native American reservations and indigenous lands in Hawaii, Puerto Rico, Guam, the US Virgin Islands, and American Samoa. There are also lingering forms of colonization in many regions across the Middle East, Asia, and Africa where imposed colonial borders and modern nation-state divisions conflict with historical ethnic or cultural boundaries.

The global diffusion of modern institutions and the increasing presence of multinational corporations and media conglomerates, along with the increasing displacement of people from colonized countries and regions, have created new colonial arrangements and a growing "Third World" diaspora within the boundaries of the "First World." Schools are one of many institutions positioned to bring the Third World into the First. The education of the Third World is shaped largely on what are presumed to be universal, modernizing imperatives; "closing the achievement gap," for instance, is implicated in the homogenizing processes of Western colonization. Contemporary vehicles of colonialism include the spread of English language use as the unquestioned medium of business and intellectual exchange, as well as the exportation of Western products, media, and institutions globally. The colonialism of the West comprises the physical taking of lands and controlling of economies, as well as the colonization of knowledge, research, ling of economies, as well as the colonization of knowledge, research, language, social relationships, and subjectivities.

Bringing the Third World into the First or achieving educational equity through the erasure of differences may seem like a laudable equity initiative, but when the goal of education is homogeneity—equal opportunity and equal access—it means adherence to a national identity or norm that perpetuates the same hierarchical systems of difference. English-only mandates or the prohibition of state-sanctioned bilingual instruction in US public schools devalue many possible forms of language and knowledge, reflecting a kind of linguistic colonization. Assimilation practices in general constitute what social theorist Robert Blauner terms "internal colonialism." Difference in educational policy is often taken to imply inferiority; thus, policymakers and educators define "minority, immigrant, or Third World" students as "at-risk" and in need of "First World" intervention. Tutoring, ESL classes, counseling, and parent education programs designed to "close the gap" or help "at-risk" students and families catch up are all part of this colonizing project (Blauner, 1969).

In general, Western forms of knowledge are perceived as more advanced than non-Western forms. There is substantial evidence of this in higher education, for example, where universities across the globe privilege Western knowledge and institutions. In Thailand's most prestigious university, Chulalongkorn, for instance, almost the entire faculty of the College of Education in the early 2000s have their PhDs from US universities, and the few that do not, have their degrees from British or Australian institutions. The professional worldview and research agendas of Thai teachers are thus imported from the West, often without regard to their relevance to local schools or communities. Almost all foreign language teacher training at Chulalongkorn, for example, focuses on English, French and German; a new program in Chinese is struggling to become established despite intense interest in learning Chinese among Thai students, and its importance as a global language of commerce. As Faruqi writes of Malaysia,

> The expatriate lecturers and external examiners are mostly from the North Atlantic countries. Asian books, Asian theories and Asian scholars are generally not regarded as fit for such recognition. This is despite historical evidence that Chinese, Indian and Persian universities predated universities in Europe and provided paradigms for early Western education (2011, p.2).

Non-Western educational systems are often dismantled and replaced with Western models. As a condition of receiving foreign aid, Latin America and Africa, for example, have had to dismantle their existing educational structures in order to implement Western educational policies. These global educational reform projects impose Western systems of education under the assumption that they are improvements to "less advanced" local systems, even though many of the imported practices are disputed and problematic in their countries of origin (Apple, 2001; Carnoy, 2000; Torres, 2002).

The reforms frequently demanded by agencies such as the International Monetary Fund (IMF) or the World Bank require exporting, for example, standardized testing, scripted curriculum, and market-driven business models of educational administration. Although many of these educational practices have not been particularly successful in the US or other Western nations, the fact that they are newly developed implies that they are "progressive," and thus appropriate to impose on developing nations. Western educational systems continue to prevail despite the evidence in international assessment comparisons, where nations such as Korea, Singapore, Japan, Hong Kong, and Taiwan routinely outperform the US and other Western-influenced nations, employing educational policies and practices that differ markedly from Western norms. Importing Western educational practices, thus, cannot guarantee outcomes (Barber & Mourshed, 2007; Darling-Hammond, 2010).

Counter to the metanarrative of progress, importing Western educational policies often exacerbates problems, proving at times more costly and less effective than past, local solutions. The Inter-American Development Bank (IADB), for example, began to work directly with the coffee industry in Colómbia to promote global marketing measures in education. Small rural schools were funded to provide instruction in entrepreneurship, specifically the growing and selling of coffee. One of the school's teachers, however, considers the mandates of the school's curriculum as,

> nothing more than fieldwork slavery.... Our older students arrive at school at six... and immediately begin working in the field. When and if they arrive in the class-room they are either too tired to learn, hungry, or simply uninterested in simply reading and answering questions in a workbook about the history of coffee (Nuñez, 2006, pp. 54–55).

Despite the promise of ten coffee plants upon graduation, the students have little hope of viable economic gain from their schooling given the local violence, difficulty of securing land, failing coffee industry, and the narrow-ness of their educational background. As one school counselor reports,

> If what these students see every day is math problems dealing with coffee sales, chemical compounds found in coffee from their science class, and Juan Valdez read-ings in language class, how can they obtain a university license in nursing... or any-thing else for that matter? (Nuñez, 2006, p. 42).

The idea of becoming coffee farmers is rejected by many of the students. As one student relates, "To them, all I am is a poor person from the *campo* who learns about coffee in school and harvests coffee at home. But I'm not that. I'm not a coffee farmer" (Nuñez, 2006, p. 45). Local conditions or any past educational practices of Third World nations are not only disregarded in the market-driven, colonial logic of the IMF, IADB, and other similar funding agencies, they are also automatically assumed to be inferior to the imported Western practices. The assumption that the presence of Western educational structures is a sign of democratic or economic advancement is a legacy of the modernist metanarrative of progress that upholds the West's colonial projects.

2 Deconstructing Modernity

When new research, instructional practices, or technologies are presented, educators generally make the assumption that they are better than past forms. There is a related presumption in education that knowledge continues to accumulate seamlessly toward ever-improving outcomes. The pendulum swings in educational curriculum and policy, despite polarizing debates that often ensue, take place within a fairly narrow theoretical range. They adhere to modernist notions of a presumed universal order of development, the rational, self-actualizing subject, and binary conceptual structures.

Binary constructions, in particular, remain an accepted means of classification across the swings of educational policy and practice. Learners are constructed as White/Other, male/female, proficient/at risk, literate/illiterate, and obedient/delinquent. Families, likewise, are viewed in mutually exclusive, dichotomous terms, as educated/uneducated, high income/low income, or involved/absent. These binaries collapse complex realities and identities into simplistic categories of analysis, homogenizing them. The either/or structure of modernist thinking denies the permeability of each side of the binary and the ways identity is multiply constituted. Inherent within these binaries is also a hierarchy; one side is naturally assumed to be "less than" the other.

Deconstructing binaries and other legacies of modernism is key, argue transnational feminists Inderpal Grewal and Caren Kaplan, since "models predicated upon binary oppositions cannot move us out of the paradigms of colonial discourse, nor can they provide us with accurate maps of social relations" (1994, p.9). These binaries persist, in part, because of the atheoretical and ahistorical nature of administrator and teacher preparation. Examining the history of these binary constructions (objective/subjective; rational/irrational; abstract/contextualized knowledge; and high culture/popular culture) can disrupt the perpetuation of culturally invisible hegemonies, which maintain the tacit hierarchical systems that shape language, nation, and identity in the classroom.

Enlightenment Origins

The beginning of modernity is generally placed in the early 17th century, when Enlightenment thinkers emphasized rational methods of inquiry. The desire for intellectual certainty emerged at a time of seeming crisis in Europe. There were political, civil, and religious conflicts across the region in the period from 1619 to 1622, including: the Thirty Years' War, a religious conflict among most of the Protestant and Catholic states of Europe that was one of the most destructive conflicts in European history; an economic depression; a decline of international trade; a rise in unemployment; and a climate shift that preceded an outbreak of plagues. The context of the time created a great sense of uncertainty. This sense of crisis was exacerbated by accumulating evidence from astronomers Galileo Galilei and Nicolaus Copernicus that the Earth was not the center of the universe: "the more vigorously Galileo advocated the new Copernican System... the more pressing was the need for a full renovation" (Toulmin, 1990, pp. 82–83). Long-accepted belief systems about the very nature of existence were being undermined.

In response, the West adopted a more controlled, structured system in sharp contrast to the Renaissance humanism of the prior century. Renaissance philosophers Michel de Montaigne, Desiderius Erasmus, and other humanists had been tolerant of "uncertainty, ambiguity, and diversity of opinion, [but]... by the mid-17th century most Enlightenment thinkers "were more dogmatic than the 16th-century humanists had ever been" (Toulmin, 1990, p. 44). The shape of Western Enlightenment that followed the Renaissance could thus be characterized as a time of gradual intellectual constraint, rather than the flowering of intellectual freedom, as it is often portrayed in traditional historical accounts of the West's narrative of progress.

Many Enlightenment thinkers contributed to the development of the West's grand narrative of progress, including: John Locke's social contract; Adam Smith's evolutionary argument of capitalism as survival of the fittest; David Hume's theory of rationality in social affairs; and Jean-Jacques Rousseau's argument that "good men" are a result of society's presence since the state of nature is brutish and without law or morality. Metanarratives were employed throughout the 19th century as well in the work of Charles Darwin, whose observations on natural selection were developed into a theory to explain not only the evolution of species, but of organizations—

corporations, institutions, even nation-states. Likewise, Marx generated a metanarrative from economic analysis that explains all forms of human exploitation in terms of class structure. This same kind of system-level, mechanistic analysis was employed by Max Weber, who argued that all nation-states could best be managed through a system of rationalized organizational structures, which he named bureaucracies. The political systems of Europe began to reorganize into nation-states, and these new state authorities sought scientific measures rather than force or religion to evaluate and enforce behavioral norms.

From approximately 1860 to 1950, Western modernity shifted from a primarily intellectual project to become a geopolitical force, which reshaped global economies. All of the sweeping new theories that emerged from the Enlightenment became grand narratives—or metanarratives—that functioned to legitimate modern institutions and practices. Philosopher Jean-Francois Lyotard defines as modern "any science that legitimates itself with reference to a metadiscourse of this kind making an explicit appeal to some grand narrative," following the logic that "that the whole is determinable" (1999, pp. xxiii, xxiv). This logic leads to the hubristic belief that everything can be understood from a single, rational methodological system or a single observed instance. He suggests that metanarratives are a hallmark of Western modernity, defining them as, "the stories that cultures tell themselves about their own practices and beliefs in order to legitimate them. They function as a unified story that purports to legitimate or found a set of practices, a cultural self-image, discourse, or institution" (qtd. in Peters, 1999, p. 2).

Modernist metanarratives were used to legitimate educational institutions, which in turn maintain and reinforce these metanarratives through their curriculum, disciplinary practices, and policies. "[E]ducation," as educational theorists Michael Peters and A.C. (Tina) Besley observe,

> is not merely one of the institutions that have been shaped or legitimated by the dominant metanarratives; at the lower levels, it has been instrumentally involved with their systematic reproduction, elucidation, and preservation, and at the higher levels, it has been concerned with their ideological production, dissemination, and refinement (2006, p. 42).

The modernist reliance on metanarratives to legitimate institutions and practices is not exclusive to the West; Hindu and Buddhist narratives of karma and the Chinese Confucian metanarrative of family obligation and filial piety, for instance, function in similar ways. In the West, however, these metanarratives are universalized, operating as if they apply to all times, places, and cultures. "The cultural complex known as European modernity/rationality was being constituted," writes Quijano, "[d]uring the same period as European colonial domination was consolidating itself"; Western knowledge was both used to legitimate EuroAmerican colonization and aided in turning it into "a universal paradigm of knowledge" (2007, pp. 171–172).

Enlightenment rationalists sought empirical, mathematical proof or certainty to derive abstract, universal laws that could be independent of historical context. Isaac Newton, for example, developed the field of calculus and derived laws of motion and gravity. Francis Bacon codified the scientific method, blending inductive and deductive reason to formulate a "universally valid" method for acquiring new knowledge. Enlightenment thinkers thus pursued scientific methods to develop metanarratives that could "explain everything." René Descartes, for instance, attempted to chart existence systematically in two dimensions; he developed the X/Y axis, the foundational structure that naturalizes binary thinking. Descartes further divided the world into material and nonmaterial things, articulating an essential division between the mind (nonmaterial) and the body (material). This subject/object dichotomy reifies the modernist notion that there is an external world outside the mind of the individual subject that can be empirically known, measured objectively, and fully understood.

The view of Western knowledge as scientific or rational enabled its proponents to elevate it above other prior forms of irrational, humanistic, or subjective knowledge. Modernity, Lyotard argues further, legitimates itself by "making an explicit appeal to some grand narrative [that] is cast in terms of... unanimity between rational minds: this is the Enlightenment narrative, in which the hero of knowledge works toward a good... end" (1999, p. xxiii). Modernism thus created a context where Western forms of knowledge were thought to comprise the most advanced, rational, objective, universal system, rather than a contingent, historical product tied to a particular time and place.

Even from the start of modernist thinking, however, some philosophers questioned the possibility of universal principles that could be rationally verified, or whether scientific methods could serve as the sole grounding of knowledge. Philosopher David Hume was skeptical of empiricist claims, arguing in contradiction to other thinkers of the time, that the senses and all forms of reasoning were imaginative and based on custom rather than reality. He questions the forms of inquiry that search for causation and cautions against looking for any "ultimate principles." He warns against the propensity to be "positive and certain" about particular points, which can only be surveyed in particular instances.

It was not until the 20th and 21st centuries that modernist metanarratives were called into question on a broader scale. The economic and cultural transformations of the 20th and 21st centuries began to destabilize the nation-state and many modernist institutions. New forms of circulation of capital through multinational corporations and the emergence of a consumer society shifted power away from the nation-state. Globalized information technology, media, and service industries replaced manufacturing as the major economic force. Further transformations included: the emergence of transnational corporations; the development of global information and telecommunications technologies; the substitution of transnational capital for labor in the global industrial economy; the decentering of the West; the expansion of diasporic flows; the commodification of everyday life; the collapse of distinctions between high and popular culture; and the growth of youth cultures. "The nature of knowledge can not," Lyotard argues, "survive unchanged within this context of general transformation" (1999, p. 4).

Postmodern Critiques

In the latter decades of the 20th century, a body of scholarship appeared in response to the purported neutrality and universalizing claims of Western modernist metanarratives. From multiple disciplines emerging within the humanities and the social sciences, a perspective known as postmodernism began to form. The term "postmodern" was first applied to architecture, then to art, where it was used to represent a new epoch or style, and subsequently to literature, history, and other social sciences. Historically and philosophically, postmodernism denotes a period or ethos that is a radical shift away from the system of values and practices of modernity. This shift, particularly in its departure from the metanarrative of science as the foundation of all knowledge, is also referred to or sometimes conflated with French poststructuralism. The meaning of both has changed historically without any "definitional closure"; each term remains contested.

Some accounts of postmodernism attribute its genesis to the philosopher Friedrich Nietzsche, who suggested metaphorically that "God is dead." "That is to say," philosopher Martin Heidegger explains,

> [the] "Christian God" [that]... stands for the "transcendent" in general in its various meanings—for "ideals" and "norms," "principles," and "rules," "ends" and "values," which are set "above" the being, in order to give being a whole, a purpose, and order... (qtd. in Peters & Besley, 2006, p. 40).

Nietzsche's statement became a starting point for a reassessment of values, but this reassessment resisted the temptation to substitute new metanarratives for God (such as humanity, reason, or science) as guarantees of morality or certainty. "Incredulity toward metanarratives" is one of the most often-cited definitions of postmodernism (Lyotard, 1999, p. xxiv).

In the habitual patterns of modernist thinking, postmodernism is often set as a binary opposite to modernism and is viewed in terms of a narrative of progress as an advancement over modernism. Most postmodernists would reject both of these notions. Postmodernism does not generally represent either a negation of all modernist forms of research logic or scientific knowledge production, nor an overcoming of them. Postmodernists generally call into question the values of Western rationality, logic, and science, but they do not argue automatically against the worth of these values; postmodernity is not a complete negation of the past. The view that postmodernism is nihilistic, or that Nietzsche's statement that "God is dead" is a call for atheism is, Heidegger argues, a product of the tacit acceptance of the binary logic that has become naturalized:

> people come to believe that whatever is not positive is negative and thus that it seeks to degrade reason.... We are so filled with "logic" that anything that disturbs the habitual somnolence of prevailing opinion is automatically registered as a despicable contradiction.... (qtd. in Cahoone, 2003, p. 188).

The postmodern critique of rationality is not, then, a call for the irrational or the dismantling of all scientific inquiry; instead, it is a critique of the central position they hold as the only or most valid form of absolute knowledge. "There is, in short, nothing wrong with the hopes of the Enlightenment," writes postmodernist philosopher Richard Rorty, "the hopes which created the Western democracies.... There is only something wrong with the attempt to [demonstrate] the 'objective' superiority of our way of life over all other alternatives" (1991, p. 34).

Postmodernism is in danger, Grewal and Kaplan suggest, of becoming "its own master narrative with its own exclusive, elitist rhetorics and academic gatekeeping" (1999, p. 6). To avoid this, they argue for an application of postmodernity as "an immensely powerful and useful conception that gives us an opportunity to analyze the way that a culture of modernity is produced in diverse locations and how these cultural productions are circulated, distributed, received, and even commodified" (1994, p. 5). Readers are sometimes frustrated with postmodernist discourse for this reason—the failure of its authors to offer alternative grand narratives in place of the modernist metanarratives that are being deconstructed. Yet to offer new metanarratives would be expressly counter to the purpose of postmodernism—to begin a period of critique and re-evaluation, rather than to conclude it.

In line with Nietzsche and Heidegger, most postmodernists "call the heritage of European thought into question *without* proposing the means for a critical 'overcoming'" (Peters & Besley, 2006, p. 41). Thus, postmodernism defies the metanarrative of progress, which suggests that knowledge constantly accumulates, advancing thought, democracy, and civilization. It rejects the linear logic that its very name (as a "post" condition) suggests. The use of the prefix "post-" in "postmodernity," indicates a taking leave of modernity's implied developmental narrative of progress and the notion that the history of thought is a progressive narrative of enlightenment implying a consistent upward, positive development toward greater knowledge, freedom, and truth. Thus, as Lyotard suggests, postmodernism does not signify "the end of modernism, but another relation to modernism" (1999, p. 79).

Scientism and "Research-based" Practices

It is common practice in educational discourse to legitimate claims by using terms such as "research-based" or "evidence-based" to support particular policy directions or pedagogical practices generally without disclosing their ideological basis. The implication is that specific policies or practices are neutral and objective because they are founded in science. The widespread use of the terminology, "Research shows" lends credibility to any claim, even when no specific studies or evidence are cited. "Research-based" or "evidence-based" practices are constantly reinforced through federal, state, and grant funding requirements.

Scientism, the belief that science is the primary source of all reliable knowledge, is a central feature of modernist discourse. The rules of Western logic dictate that any argument needs to be supported by evidence, derived from direct observation or primary sources. The scientific method prescribes a strict, linear process, proceeding from making an educated guess (hypothesis), through data collection or experimentation, to analysis of the original hypothesis. The scientific method is treated as the sole, universal means of validating knowledge. As one elementary school handout states: "The scientific method is a series of steps to help you answer *any* question. It is used by scientists in *every* country of the world" (italics added).

The ascendancy of science in the West originated in the work of positivists in the early 19th century with the work of August Comte, a sociologist and philosopher. Comte's notion of "positivitism" refers to the degree to which any individual phenomena can be exactly measured or determined. Comte asserts that valid knowledge or truth could only be derived through direct observation via scientific methods, using logical and mathematical analyses to describe and explain experience. Comte establishes four basic rules to define what constitutes scientific inquiry:

- All knowledge must be proven through the "sense certainty" of systematic observation. Sense experience alone provides access to the domain of facts.
- Methodological certainty needs to be guaranteed by careful adherence to a rigidly structured set of procedures, referred to as "unity of method." Since science must be grounded in careful, systematic procedures, critical theorist Jurgen Habermas states, it "asserts the priority of method over substance" (1971, p. 75).
- Facts have to be connected to theories, which must be constructed in a form to permit the deduction of law-like hypotheses. As Habermas describes, "no isolated fact, no matter of what sort, can really be incorporated into science before it is at least correctly connected with some other conception through the aid of a rational hypothesis" (1971, p. 75). Positivists accordingly seek to impose underlying causal or theoretical connections onto all facts so that they can transcend "mere description."
- Scientific findings must also be practical and technically usable. Science, positivists argue, should make possible the technical control of natural and social processes. As Comte asserts, "all of our sound theories [are necessarily related] to the continuous improvement of our individual and collective conditions of life—in opposition to the vain gratification of a sterile curiosity" (qtd. in Habermas, p. 76). This requirement means that for information to be considered valid or valuable, it must be made to fit into a universalizable metanarrative or schema.

Uncertainty or questions of morality or ethics are not expected to arise, positivists believe, if these four rules are strictly followed. Scientists thus have no reason to call their methods or logic into question—nor subsequently do many educational researchers—because their system of knowledge is constructed as a closed loop, with a built-in network of reinforcement that accepts only a relatively narrow range of possible categories of argument. If the form of the scientific method is carefully followed, positivists assume that the findings will be objectively derived and thus irrefutable.

Another illusion in the field of science is that new research continually advances knowledge in a smooth, unbroken linear sequence of logically related steps. Philosopher of science Thomas Kuhn rejects the view that later science always builds on the knowledge contained within earlier theories, as well as the developmental view that later theories are closer approximations of truth than prior theories. He argues instead that the process of arriving at new scientific discoveries is actually often convoluted and disruptive. The development of a science is not uniform, Kuhn observes, but has alternating "normal" and "revolutionary" phases. These phases represent sharp breaks between agreed-upon knowledge frameworks.

Science operates, says Kuhn, within an overarching framework of knowledge called a "paradigm." A paradigm embodies all scientific knowledge and practice conducted during a particular period of history. According to Kuhn, the world is experienced and investigated according to the principles of the given historical epoch in which it exists. Paradigms thus represent the social consensus among a community of scientists at a given point in time. They reflect prevailing socio-historical beliefs and constructs, and are neither purely objective nor value-free, as positivists would claim. Scientists generally, however, ignore this social and cultural context or consider it irrelevant. Paradigms are an unquestioned part of the landscape within which scientists operate. Cultural invisibility makes the paradigms appear to be static and universal, as feminist philosopher of science Sandra Harding explains, "The problem with linking objectivity to the neutrality ideal is that it permits no procedures for identifying those social values and interests that belong to the entire scientific community" (1992, p. 316).

The given paradigm of any period of time sets limits on what questions might reasonably be asked and determines the scope of possible research. A paradigm is accompanied by the tendency to choose only those research problems that are assumed to have solutions that fit within the paradigm. Teacher education programs, for instance, have rigid expectations for determining a legitimate or "researchable" question. These researchable questions, says Kuhn,

> are the only problems that the community will admit as scientific or encourage its members to undertake. Other problems... are rejected as metaphysical, as the concern of another discipline, or sometimes as just too problematic to be worth the time. A paradigm can, for that matter, even insulate the community from those socially important problems that are not reducible to the puzzle [researchable] form, because they cannot be stated in terms of the conceptual and instrumental tools the paradigm supplies (1969, p. 37).

Kuhn uses the term "normal science" to describe the typical "puzzle-solving" investigations that occur during the period of dominance of any given paradigm for as long as the existing social consensus on the paradigm holds.

The researchable questions accepted in the field of education require researchers to look for relationships between two or more variables, such as the relationship between ethnicity and amount of praise given by teachers. Even though such studies may have the aim of increasing equity in the classroom, the accepted methodology for conducting this kind of inquiry requires the acceptance of essentialized systems of difference that further the naturalization of racialized differences. The exclusive acceptance of a scientistic paradigm means that research questions and justifications continue to reinforce Western norms.

The conventional educational research methodologies for quantitative, qualitative, and mixed-method studies require the operationalization of all variables, so that they can be measured or manipulated. Categories like motivation, interest, and achievement are often quantified, with levels assigned to each category to show degree of variation. Other variables like gender, ethnicity, and teaching or research methods, are considered categorical variables that are "qualitatively different." As one graduate education research methodology text defines it, categorical variables refer to situations where "a person is either in one category or another, not somewhere in between... all members within each category of this variable are considered the same" (Fraenkel et al., 2012, pp. 78, 79). The research methods textbook is critical of research that collapses variables like interest or anxiety into categories, arguing that the "dividing line between groups (for example, between individuals of high, middle, or low anxiety) is almost always arbitrary (that is, lacking any defensible rationale)" (Fraenkel et al., 2012, p. 80). Yet, in the modernist tradition, the text defines both ethnicity and gender as homogenous, either-or categorical variables, rather than matters of degree or hybrid, shifting constructs. Inherent in the research process is, then, the homogenization of gender, ethnicity, class, and other common research variables that simplify and collapse student identities to fit the scientistic paradigm.

In the scientistic paradigm, there is also a general assumption that each variable is pure and available for study. Investigating various teaching methods, for example, researchers may try to measure the learning outcomes of different instructional strategies, assuming that other factors, like teacher-student relationship or content area, are either static, irrelevant, or controlled. By including a comparison group or standardizing procedures, the paradigm holds that threats to validity can be managed, assuming that any randomly sampled group of ninth graders, for example, can be equally compared to another.

Critical of the emphasis in educational research on causal analysis, educational theorists Frederick Erickson and Kris Gutierrez argue that educational program effects cannot be determined from the study of single variables:

> Educational treatments are situated and dynamically interactive. They are locally
> constructed social ways of life involving continual monitoring and mutual adjust-

ment among persons, not relatively replicable entities like chemical compounds or surgical procedures or hybrid seed corn or manufactured airplane wings. High fidelity implementation is rare in education—for reasons of local exigency—and despite the accountability pressures and the wishes of experimenters to avoid this major threat to internal validity, there are real-world limits on how "faithful" the implementation will be of even the most structured of instructional programs (2002, p. 21).

In quantitative research investigating the quality of daycare centers, for example, researchers defined two independent variables: group size and staff-to-student ratio. Causal analysis that isolated these variables led to the conclusion that smaller class sizes were preferable, but when qualitative researchers followed up this study with observations they found that the larger groups had more than one adult in the room, which led to less adult-to-child interactions:

> staff-to-staff schmoozing was the actual proximal independent variable, not the overall staff-to-student ratio or the size of the groups, in and of themselves... at issue was... the specific interactive use of such potential resources within the conduct of instructional practice (Erickson & Gutierrez, 2002, p. 21).

There remains, though, widespread acceptance of scientism in education and a "prescription of a 'scientific culture' as an effective remedy for the ills of educational research and of 'hard science' causal studies of program effects as a remedy for defects in education practice" (Erickson & Gutierrez, 2002, p. 22). Scientism is evident in the continuing reliance on observable measures and the preference for standardized, quantitative measures, such as test scores, attendance, truancy rates, and income level, to inform policy development. This reliance has led to the dominance of behaviorist models of instruction and remediation. From nationwide K–12 testing regimes to movements in universities that specify quantifiable student learning outcomes, educational programs are constantly under evaluation, often by "objective" third parties through external accreditation or "Program Improvement" site visits by certified evaluators. Scientism prevails in educational research, practice, and policy development due to reliance on measures of observable phenomena and widespread acceptance of "research-based" instructional practices as universally valid pedagogies.

Paradigm Shifts and Ethnosciences

Despite the taken-for-granted modernist notion that scientific truth corresponds to an unchanging, independent reality, scientific paradigms do change over time. The practice of actual science is very different, Erickson and

Gutierrez argue, from its idealized characterization:

> real scientists in their daily work are anything but disinterested and canonically rational. In their daily practice they are passionate and argumentative, profoundly selective in their attention to evidence, and aesthetic in drawing conclusions from it... The actual "culture of science," in other words, is far from the white coat image that appears to the layperson. The accumulation of knowledge in actual science is not at all continuous—it moves by fits and starts (2002, p. 22).

Long periods of status quo are interrupted by the buildup of anomalies or research results that do not fit the existing paradigm. Anomalies are generally ignored at first or explained away, if at all possible. The activity of normal science, Kuhn argues, is

> an attempt to force nature into the preformed and relatively inflexible box that the paradigm supplies. Nor do scientists normally aim to invent new theories, and they are often intolerant of those invented by others.... To desert the paradigm is to cease practicing the science it defines (1969, pp. 24, 34).

Thus, scientists, Erickson and Gutierrez add, "change their minds and paradigms only with great reluctance" (2002, p. 22).

The accumulation of anomalies thus poses a serious problem for the existing paradigm, undermining the practice of normal science or revealing inadequacies in some commonly used theory. If normal science relies upon this paradigm, then scientists will find it difficult to continue with confidence until the anomalies are addressed. A widespread failure in such confidence Kuhn calls a "crisis." In such a situation, "the rules of normal science become increasingly blurred. Though there still is a paradigm, few practitioners may prove to be entirely agreed about what it is. Even formerly standard solutions of solved problems are then called into question" (1969, p. 83).

Ultimately, a paradigm shift is not, Kuhn argues, gradual or orderly; it is a revolution in which conceptual apparatuses, experimental methods, and criteria for accuracy change. Scientific revolutions are not cumulative. The rejection of an existing paradigm leads directly to adoption of a new paradigm, for says Kuhn, "To reject one paradigm without simultaneously substituting another is to reject science itself" (1969, p. 79). Different paradigms are described by Kuhn as incommensurable, meaning that there is no single unified theory of all science. Each time a new paradigm is developed it is not necessarily compatible with prior research; thus, it is often not possible to compare theories between one paradigm and another. Competing accounts of reality frequently cannot be coherently reconciled in one metanarrative. This implies that there is no common measure for assessing different scientific theories in many instances, ruling out comparisons between theories from different paradigms.

Paradigm shifts open up new approaches to understandings that scientists would never have considered valid before. Thus, universal scientific truths cannot be established solely by unchanging objective criteria, but are instead defined by the shifting sociocultural consensus of a scientific community: "There is no standard higher than the assent of the relevant community... paradigm choice can never be unequivocally settled by logic and experiment alone" (1969, p. 94). Truth is therefore culturally mediated and chronologically limited, argues Kuhn, and specific to its own paradigm. Progress in science derives from consensual social agreements among scientists, and scientific truth is determined by social consensus at any specific point in time. The search for knowledge through the scientific method can never rely on full, timeless objectivity.

Science is a product of not only a specific time, but also of specific social and cultural norms. Accordingly, all sciences, Harding argues, including Western science, are "ethnosciences." Ethnosciences describe the sciences of individual cultures and communities, their practices of looking after themselves, their bodies, their botanical knowledge, their interactions with physical realm, as well as their forms of classification. Other cultures' accounts of themselves and their environment are not, in the modernist view, considered in the same category as Western science. From a Western perspective, there is one possible true account of reality, which can only be produced by scientific methods. Cultural invisibility makes the Western paradigm appear as the only valid way of obtaining knowledge, rather than as a specific ethnoscience with embedded socio-historical interests and normative implications. According to Harding, the ability to produce a uniquely universal, unitary science is seen in the West as a sign of modernity:

> Such a science should have uniquely valid standards of rationality, objectivity, method, and what counts as nature's order and as knowers. Such purported features of modern science have been called on to legitimate as *uniquely socially progressive* European models of government, law, education, social policy, and even ethics (1998, p. 165).

European science is not necessarily better than other sciences, Harding points out, but developed in tandem with Western/European colonization and global expansion. In many cases, she suggests, Western science may be less effective than other ethnosciences, for instance in understanding human health and ecology.

Contributions and appropriations from indigenous sciences are marginalized or ignored by Western science. As multicultural educator George

Gheverghese Joseph writes,

> For many Third World societies still in the grip of an intellectual dependence pro-
> moted by European dominance during the past two or three centuries, the indigenous
> scientific base that may have been innovative and self-sufficient during precolonial
> times is neglected or often treated with a contempt that it does not deserve (1997, p.
> 61).

Contributions of colonized peoples are ignored or devalued in the West's
rationale for domination. This is despite the fact that Western science, due to
the West's far-flung colonial expeditions, incorporated many elements of
global ethnosciences into the traditions and practices of Western science,
including navigational, medical, climatological, agricultural, and other
practical knowledge enabling prediction and control of nature. These
generally unrecognized contributions demonstrate the extent to which
Western sciences have been universalized and accepted as an objective
means of ever-accumulating knowledge. "It is deeply misleading," conclude
Erickson and Gutierrez,

> to claim that the expressways to educational progress can be engineered socially
> upon the bedrock of smoothly accumulating and consistent evidence about effec-
> tiveness.... The current federal leap of faith to science as a warrant for certainty in
> social policy reminds us of the jejune contempt held by the Renaissance for the
> Middle Ages, a 'presentism' that was repeated in the Enlightenment. For many at
> the beginning of the 20th century and at its ending as well, that hope in progress as
> the result of continuous development of new knowledge came to appear as a delu-
> sion (2002, p. 23).

The Illusion of Objectivity

Though educators are taught to rely on scientific evidence as an objective,
value-free means of informing instruction and determining "best" practices,
the scientific method was not designed to address many of the questions and
concerns that educators have. Scientific inquiry was designed to help make
predictions and control phenomena in the physical world. This method of
inquiry is well suited to technology development and accounts for major
transformations in society's relationship to and mastery of the natural world.
This aim, however, is not necessarily shared by all the disciplines (education,
psychology, sociology, political science, among others) that have tried to
adopt its methods.

The widespread adoption of scientific methods has occurred in large part
because they seem to assure an objective means of arriving at universal
"truths." Scientific methods are thus legitimized as the highest form of

knowledge in modernist discourse. "But why," asks Rorty,

> should we say that a terminology which might conceivably enable us to do some-
> thing we presently have no idea how to do is the best candidate for the "absolute"
> conception of reality?... Why should we think that the explanations offered for this
> purpose are the "best" explanations?... [T]here is no such thing as a "best explana-
> tion" of anything; there is just the explanation which best suits the purpose of some
> given explainer (Rorty, 1991, pp. 58, 60).

There are events, phenomena, causes, and patterns beyond the reach of
the narrow methods of scientific investigation proposed by Comte and the
positivists. "The practical consequences of a restricted, scientistic consciousness of the sciences can be countered," Habermas writes, "by a critique that
destroys the illusion of objectivism" (1971, p. 316). Habermas challenges the
objectivist presumption of science, or the idea that the world is conceived of
as a universe of facts independent of the knower, whose task is simply to
describe the facts independently "as they are." Knowledge, in other words,
cannot be divorced from the knower. The "sense certainty" claim of positiv-
ism, in particular, ignores the existence of certain phenomena or conditions *a
priori*, that is, prior to the observation or measurement of these scientific
facts.

The distinction between "hard facts and soft values... objectivity and
subjectivity," writes Rorty, "are awkward and clumsy instruments. They are
not suited to dividing up culture; they create more difficulties than they
resolve" (1991, p. 36). Yet the objective/subjective binary is a foundational
construct in the field of education. Teachers continually ask students, for
example, to sort facts from opinions on practice worksheets and analyze texts
in order to locate the factual information. They further require students to cite
their sources or "show their work." The structure of academic expository
writing further enforces a rational, scientific account by requiring students to
provide a thesis statement and support their argument with clear evidence.
Print material, primary historical sources, and scientific accounts are privileged in the classroom, with authority accorded to what are considered
objective rather than subjective accounts. Educators thus reify "hard facts,"
generally privileging them over "soft knowledge" or subjective opinions,
emotions, internal experiences, and beliefs.

The US adoption of the Common Core Standards in the early 21st century represents a further shift toward factual discourse, giving "informational
texts" primacy (additional instructional time and emphasis) over "narrative
texts" (fiction or literature). According to David Coleman and Susan Pimentel, the primary authors of the English Language Arts (ELA) portion of the
Common Core Standards,

The Common Core State Standards require a greater focus on informational text in elementary school and literary nonfiction in ELA classes in grades 6–12.... The next generation of materials requires a significant shift in early literacy materials and instructional time (2011, p. 5).

"Informational texts," are defined in the Common Core as, "literary non-fiction and historical, scientific, and technical texts," such as "biographies and autobiographies; books about history, social studies, science, and the arts; technical texts, including directions, forms, and information displayed in graphs, charts, or maps; and digital sources on a range of topics." These texts are assumed to objective, in binary contrast to literary, narrative, or subjective accounts.

The binary that divides fiction from historical narratives is generally taken for granted, as one reading researcher argues that informational text differs substantially from literary text:

The attention allocation and inferential skills that skilled readers employ during reading are enhanced by exposure to texts that vary in structure, difficulty, and content area. Science texts differ greatly from narratives in their demands on working memory management, comprehension strategies, and the use of background knowledge. Thus, practice with science and narrative texts broadens the cognitive "toolbox" that a reader can bring to any text (van den Broek, 2010, P. 455).

Literary theorist Roland Barthes questions this distinction, however, asking "does this form of narration really differ, in some specific trait, in some indubitably distinctive feature, from imaginary narration as we find in the epic, the novel, the drama?" (1981, p. 1). "Informational texts" are generally composed in the third person singular voice, without emotion, most often in the past tense. These structural features lend authority to informational texts by removing any indication of a narrator. The narration of past events or "what happened," since the "time of the Greeks onwards, has generally been subject to the sanction of historical 'science,'" writes Barthes, "bound to the unbending standard of the 'real', and justified by the principles of 'rational' exposition" (1981, p. 1).

Historian Hayden White further observes that in historical narratives "the events are chronologically recorded as they appear on the horizon of the story. No one speaks. The events seem to tell themselves" (1990, p. 3). Barthes argues that suppressing the "I" in discourse does not make historical narratives distinct from fictional narratives, however, as novelists also often employ the same device. "The utterer nullifies his emotional persona," writes Barthes, but substitutes it for another persona, the 'objective' persona.... On the level of discourse, objectivity—or the deficiency of signs of the utterer—thus appears as a particular form of imaginary projection, the product of what might be called the referential illusion (1981, p. 4).

Historical discourse, Barthes argues, only has the appearance of objectivity. In "the discourse of the real" events have an ordered sequence and conform to a specific chronological narrative structure, with a central subject and a well-marked beginning, middle, and end. The presence of this particular form signals "objectivity," "seriousness," or "realism." The more an account conforms to this expected narrative form, the more "real" or "true" it is considered.

Historical or informational narrative is not, then, simply a vehicle for the transmission of "facts." As Nietzsche argues further, "There are no facts in themselves. It is always necessary to begin by introducing a meaning in order that there can be a fact" (qtd. in Barthes, 1981, p. 7). The narrativization of historical events into stories requires, White argues, tropes or figures of thought; it is only the scientistic prejudice of modernism that obscures the metaphorical, imagined nature of historical discourse. The narrativizing of historical events arises out of the need to have events appear coherent; this produces an image that can only be imaginary or as Barthes writes, "the sign of History from now on is no longer the real, but the intelligible" (1981, p. 9).

A "genuinely historical account ha[s] to display not only a certain form," writes White, "but... a politicosocial order" (1990, p. 11). To be accepted as an accurate (or worthwhile) account, the narrative must fit the current paradigm:

It is because the events described conduce to the establishment of social order or fail to do so that they find a place in the narrative attesting to their reality... When... historiography was transformed into an 'objective' discipline, it was the narrativity of the historical discourse that was celebrated as one of the signs of its maturation as a 'fully' objective discipline—a science of a special sort but a science (White, 1990, pp. 23, 24).

The content of any informational account consists as much of its form as it does of whatever facts could be extracted from reading it. The form thus supersedes the content to give authority and value to the text. Objectivity is a product of form and social consensus rather than its purportedly distinct "factual" content.

Literary or subjective narratives are disparaged in the modernist legacy because they do not place a priority on formal legitimation. Ironically, however, states Lyotard, scientific discourse too must rely on narrative argumentation for legitimation, since scientific arguments and proofs are themselves forms of narrative. It is people, says Lyotard, who determine the legitimacy of truth or justice claims in the domain of narrative knowledge through the operations of debate and ultimate attainment of consensus. Lyotard adds that "knowledge is not the same as science" (1999, p. 18). He argues that there is an alternative form of knowledge, what he terms "narrative knowledge." Neither form of knowledge, he claims, may be judged as more legitimate than the other, because their criteria for legitimation differ.

In upholding the informational text/fictional narrative binary, schools devalue narrative knowledge and privilege informational text as the only source of valid knowledge. Cultural theorist Mikhail Bakhtin, however, demonstrates that the study of the popular literature or the "trivial"—from the viewpoint of high culture—can also be a valid source of historical knowledge. Analyzing the work of Rabelais and others, Bakhtin argues: "Gargantua and Pantagruel [scatological novels of Rabelais] teach us more about peasant culture than the... [almanacs as sources of 'official' history] which must have circulated widely in the French countryside" (qtd. in Aronowitz, 1995, p. 122). Bakhtin explores the capacity of literary texts in particular to present social history, remarking that all events are themselves inevitably fictionalized as historians construct imagined narratives from the raw materials of public records. He thus echoes White and Barthes in refuting the separation between the social sciences and the humanities, claiming instead that "Literature may be an authentic, perhaps the privileged site of social knowledge, precisely because of its polyphonic character, as opposed to the monologisms of the philosophy of language and historical writing that remain unaware of their passive character" (qtd. in Aronowitz, 1995, p. 135).

Postmodernist thinkers generally reject the privileging of empirical texts over literary that results from the illusion of objectivity. Rorty calls for the breaking down of the scientific knowledge/narrative knowledge binary, so that "the people now called 'scientists' would no longer think of themselves as a member of a quasi-priestly order, nor would the public think of themselves as in the care of such an order" (Rorty, 1991, pp. 44–45). Recognizing the illusion of objectivity, in educational research and policy, means shifting away from the time and attention devoted to forms and methodologies that purport to offer a path to reliable, valid findings. Instead of worrying about whether there is evidence to suggest the validity of a hypothesis, Rorty suggests paying attention to the choice between hypotheses. This means there would be less talk about method, "less talk about rigor and more about originality" (Rorty, 1991, p. 44). Shifting away from an emphasis on form over content would also change the relationship of scientific knowledge and narrative knowledge, reducing the valorizing of science over the humanities.

Western Knowledge Hierarchies & Popular Culture

The privileging of the sciences over the humanities and arts in the West is predicated on the artificial division between objective/subjective knowledge, informational texts/narratives, and high culture/popular culture. These binaries are naturalized in school settings, in part, through the division of daily activities along disciplinary lines and the separation of what is seen as academic work (science, math, language arts, history) from enrichment activities (physical education, visual and performing arts). Throughout the K–12 systems and university education, instructional departments are created to supervise and define each discipline, setting the coursework and determining the requirements for obtaining a degree in that field. Philosopher Michel Foucault points out that these disciplinary divisions are arbitrary, historical accidents; they could as easily have been organized differently under altered historical circumstances. Foucault's "archeology of knowledge" shows how these bodies of knowledge are historically contingent, rather than natural, universal truths. He rejects the tranquility with which the division of disciplines or other "ready-made syntheses" are accepted: "We must show that [disciplines] do not come about of themselves, but are always the result of a construction the rules of which must be known, and the justifications of which must be scrutinized" (1972, p. 25).

The way curriculum is classified and framed, educational theorists Christine Sleeter and Jamy Stillman suggest further, creates a hierarchy of knowledge:

> the stronger the classification, the more hierarchical the structure of knowledge, the more status academic knowledge has over everyday knowledge, and the greater degree to which teaching moves sequentially from basic facts toward the deep structure of a given discipline (2005, p. 28).

Interdisciplinary programs, though once favored in education, are rare and often dismissed as less rigorous than the more clearly bounded disciplines.

Schools frequently act as vehicles for creating and maintaining privileged canons or collections of work that define "high culture," deeming some cultural forms as more advanced and worthwhile than other "popular" forms. As Bourdieu notes,

The educational system, whose scale of operations grew in extent and intensity throughout the nineteenth century, no doubt directly helped to devalue popular modes of expression, dismissing them as 'slang' and 'gibberish'... and to impose recognition of the legitimate language (1991, p. 49).

Critical education theorists Henry Giroux and Roger Simon argue likewise that schools are often regarded as the "guardians of Western civilization" where the sphere of popular culture is

viewed as a tasteless and dangerous threat to the notions of civility and order.... The dominant discourse still defines popular culture as whatever remains when high culture is subtracted from the overall totality of cultural practices. It is seen as the trivial and insignificant of everyday life, and usually it is a form of popular taste deemed unworthy of either academic legitimation or high social affirmation (1989, pp. 9–11).

Popular modes of expression—the products and ideas created or consumed by youth, such as video games, sitcoms, comics, music videos, dance, and fashion—are generally not considered worthy of classroom time or study. Although popular culture is occasionally explored in schools as a motivational tool, it is rarely the source of sustained or critical study. Many teachers use popular culture in ways that reinforce existing cultural hierarchies. They do this by using popular cultural media (movies, music) as rewards after the "important work" contained in traditional texts has been done. In many classes, this is found in the form of a movie or film at the end of a curriculum unit. Yet the media text is not treated as a legitimate text to be studied; rather it is a "tool of pacification unworthy of intellectual interrogation" (Duncan-Andrade, 2004, p. 322). Critical educational theorist Jeffrey Duncan-Andrade terms such uses of popular culture and digital media as culturally imperialistic on the part of the educational system:

Rather than providing young people with the tools for a critical media literacy, we have villainized their culture of media literacy and unwittingly set off a war between the legitimate knowledge of schools and the nefarious knowledge of youth culture (2004, p. 322).

The dominant view in education presumes that a higher order of culture and intellectual value resides in printed texts, and that educators could not teach the same higher-order thinking skills across academic content areas using a blend of popular media and traditional print texts. Another flawed presumption is the notion that the use of popular cultural texts might prevent children from developing a "love of reading"—as if that were currently the generalizable outcome of mass schooling. "While popular culture is generally ignored in the schools," Giroux and Simon observe, "it is not an insignificant force in shaping how students view themselves and their own relations to various forms of pedagogy and learning" (1989, p. 11). Many cultural theorists argue that some of the most profound acts of cultural creation and interaction are taking place on the level of commodified, mass popular culture (Bakhtin, 1981, 2002; Duncan-Andrade, 2004; Hall, 2002; Dyson, 2003; Giroux & Simon, 1989; Lipsitz, 1990; Morrell, 2002).

From a historical perspective, the persistent boundary drawn between popular culture and high culture unravels. As cultural theorist George Lipsitz points out, "It is only from the viewpoint of Enlightenment ideals of 'high culture' that something called popular culture can be seen to exist" (1990, p. 13). The works of the British novelist Charles Dickens, for example, are often found on school reading lists and are deemed "classics." However, at the time of their publication they were considered a form of cheap popular entertainment, serialized in widely accessible magazines and newspapers. The cliffhangers that are characteristic at the endings of Dickens' chapters are a product of this serialization. Mirroring contemporary blogging practices, Dickens wrote one weekly or monthly installment at a time, often in response to reader feedback. Considered trivial in the late 1800s, Dickens' writings were later judged as significant literary work and social commentary.

Bakhtin argues further that high culture is not the polar opposite of popular culture. High culture is constituted, in part, he says, by its appropriation of the popular. Since popular culture has generally been an oral tradition, in the past it often spoke only indirectly through its incorporation by high cultural works: symphonies incorporated folk melodies, novels incorporated folk tales, and so on. The genres have continued to blur even further in late 20th and early 21st century culture. Many forms of popular culture—ranging from hip hop through graffiti to 'zines and street fashion—have become drivers of high art as well as economic profit centers for multinational corporations; the popular culture/high culture binary has become less and less clear as boundaries have blurred.

Cultural theorist Stuart Hall builds upon Bakhtin's work to suggest that there is a continuing tension in defining popular culture. Hall offers three definitions of the term. The first definition is what he calls a market or commercial definition. It refers to things that are said to be "popular" simply because masses of people listen to them, buy them, read them, consume them, and seem to enjoy them. A second characterization defines the term as all those things that "the people" do or have done. According to Hall, the structuring principle of "the popular" should be the tension between what belongs to the central domain of dominant culture, and what belongs to the culture of the periphery, the margins, the subordinate. A whole set of institutions and institutional processes are required, he says, to sustain each, and to continually mark the difference between them. The education system is one such institution—distinguishing the "valued" part of the culture, the cultural heritage, the history to be transmitted, from the "valueless" part. Hall's own, or third, definition of popular culture locates class struggle in and over culture, where "popular culture" is in a continuing tension with the dominant culture. This approach examines the relations that structure the field into dominant and subordinate formations and the processes by which some things are actively preferred, so that others can be dethroned— recognizing that almost all cultural forms are contradictory and composed of antagonistic and unstable elements (Hall, 2002).

Popular culture blurs borders, transgressing standard categories and narratives. Bakhtin exposes, for example, how popular forums like the carnival and later the novel provide a counternarrative to the official narratives presented in formal locations such as the church or other authoritarian spaces. Popular culture forms allow for a *heteroglot* dialogue, which he refers to as "heteroglossia." Bakhtin suggests that popular culture gives voice to "unofficial" ways of talking about the world that challenges the monologue of official language users expressing dominant professions, classes, interests, and ideologies. Lipsitz adds,

> The ever changing meanings and deliberate indeterminacies of subcultural slang undercut the authority of the [dominant] word, replacing it with an appreciation of the inevitable metaphoricity of language. Such usage entails a break with the logocentric world of the Enlightenment in which univocal utterances and precise descriptions serve to fix final meanings and identities (1990, p. 15).

Summarizing the importance of popular culture, Lipsitz references jazz saxophonist Rahsaan Roland Kirk: "This ain't no sideshow" (1990, p. 3).

Recognizing the importance of popular culture both as a heteroglot counternarrative and as a way to bring students' funds of knowledge into the classroom, Duncan-Andrade argues for what cultural theorist Lawrence Grossberg calls a "pedagogy of articulation and risk" that values and learns from the popular cultural literacies students bring to the classroom, and seeks to assist them as they expand those literacies and develop new ones. This form of pedagogy is committed to developing students as critical civic participants, and "...neither starts with nor works within a set of texts but, rather, deals with the formations of the popular, the cartographies of taste... and mobility within which students are located (1994, p. 18). A pedagogy of articulation and risk admits the complexity of culture and the role of the educator in navigating that complexity, recognizing that popular culture is a primary site of contesting dominant forms of cultural hegemony. In addition, according to Grossberg, this pedagogy challenges the notion that cultural hegemony is a zero-sum game by insisting, with Hall, that cultural activity and cultural production—particularly the work of popular culture—is "always about shifting the balance of power in the relations of culture" (1996, p. 468).

Case in Point: PSP, Hot Cheetos, and Bobby Jack: Consumption and Students' Narrative Displays

Teachers generally edit out "inappropriate" references or displays of popular culture in the classroom, insisting on only "educational" references and materials. The persistent appearance of popular cultural forms in students' narratives and drawings demonstrates their significance in dictating and shaping student identities and literacies, and their symbolic power in establishing social relationships. Students often weave resources from popular culture into the "official" writing they produce in school, together with other resources they bring from home. Through their schoolwork, students are constantly defining themselves using multiple sign systems and forms of media. At the expense of narrative structure and teacher expectations to "stick to one, important topic," they often load their narratives, for example, with video games, junk food, commercial football teams, celebrities, TV shows, and so on to present themselves in affiliation with high status indicators (Blakely, 2007). In order to display as many products as possible and signal to their audience their connection to these high-value commercial objects, students' narratives often contain rapid shifts between topics or other structural inconsistencies (Bloome, Katz, & Champion, 2003; Dyson, 1997).

Consumer objects have come to constitute a classification system that structures behavior through a linguistic sign function; advertising "codes" products through symbols and then through various forms of conspicuous consumption, commodities transfer their meaning to individual consumers. A potentially infinite play of signs is thus instituted, which orders society while providing individuals with an illusory sense of freedom and self-determination. Consumption is thus not simply what individuals do to find satisfaction and fulfillment, says Baudrillard. Rather, it is a coded system of signs, messages, and images through which people communicate with each other (Baudrillard, 1988, 1994).

Consumer objects are part of a network of what Baudrillard calls "floating signifiers." He contends that "culture is now dominated by simulations—

objects and discourses that have no firm origin, no referent, no ground or foundation" (Poster, 1988, p. 1). In Baudrillard's view, the new condition of society is characterized by a hyperreality of floating signifiers as commodities. He advances the concept of hyperreality to describe how culture, media, language, science, and technology operate as an integrated code based, not on specific referents (concrete objects or events), but on simulations–floating images, models, and signs.

Consumption is not, then, limited to material goods; images, words, sounds, texts, symbols, and identities have all been commodified. Images and symbols have become a primary means of gathering and distributing knowledge and crafting identities. As art education researcher Paul Duncum writes, "never before in human history has imagery been so central to the creation of identity" (2001, p. 102). While in an earlier phase of capitalist development there was, Duncum notes, "a shift from being to having, there is now, in the society of the spectacle, a shift from having to appearing... foreshadowing a stream of postmodern theorizing.... [critical theorist Guy] Debord argued as early as 1967 that 'Everything that was directly lived has moved away into representation" (2001, p. 102).

Narration becomes an arena for conspicuous consumption; students display a coded system of signs to communicate status. Though most writing assignments are considered independent work, where students sit at individual desks, often with file folders upended on desks to prevent eye contact or discussion, students still constantly edit their writing based on peer proximity and their perceptions of the narrative's audience. In one prewriting activity, for example, fifth-grade students in a California classroom were asked to generate a list of their likes and dislikes. The students added items to their list to signal friendships. The configuration of students in the classroom is easily mapped from a reading of their lists. Kelly and Lucia, sitting side by side, each borrow ideas from the other's work.

> Kelly: I like boys; I like candy; I like babies; I like basketball; I like small puppies; I don't like cats; I don't like root beer; I like juice; I like hot cheetos; I don't like sharks; I like my friends; I don't like killer whales.

> Lucia: I like reading; I like boys; I like babies; I like soccer; I like dolphins; I like puppies; I don't like Bulldogs; I like planting plants; I like to play with my friends; I like hot cheetos; I like fruits; I don't like whales; I don't like sharks.

The journal entries of two fifth-grade girls, seated across from each other at a classroom table, further demonstrate how the students use narratives to signal friendships and status through their displays of brand names and products.

Veronica: I like Bobby Jack. He is a funny and cute monkey. He is brown with white teeth. I have two sweatshirts of him and they are so so warm that I could wear them when I'm going to the snow. My mom bought the sweatshirts at the mall. That is why I love Bobby Jack!!

Christina: I like to go to the mall. I love Bobby Jack. Bobby Jack. He hearts me. I heart him. He is funny. Bobby Jack is a monkey on my shirt. Bobby Jack is sometimes way mean on some shirts. His teeth are white. When I saw Bobby Jack, I screamed and felt I was in heaven. He sometimes gets angry in some shirts. I almost forgot. I heart him. He hearts me. I heart him. He hearts me. He is funny that is the only thing that is nice. I wear his shirts every day. I buy the shirts. I am wearing the American Jesus one.

When asked to describe their ideal classroom, students load their narratives with references to high status commercial and media possessions. Heriberto, a fifth grader, describes his ideal classroom: "My ultimate classroom has every video game and you can do whatever you want and when you play video games you play on a 64 inch plasma screen TV." Heriberto's ideas are echoed in multiple narratives, as Kevin writes:

If I had an ultimate classroom it would have computers. It would have a 3,185 inch plasma TV... It would have all the video game systems. It would have a Jacuzzi... It would have six 64 inch plasma TV on the walls to learn. One would have a history channel. It would have a math channel. It would have a movie theater. It would have a big stereo.

Or as Eduardo writes: "My ultimate classroom will be so awesome. First the wall will have Raiders signs all over... Children learn by playing a game or by seeing a plasma screen TV."

TV and video games, in particular, have become key references for students in defining themselves and their social status. One student, for example, drew a GameCube in place of his own face and body for a concrete poetry self-portrait assignment that asked students to use words to draw themselves. Another fourth grader, Evelio, drew the wrestling arena from the TV show "SmackDown" for an assignment to draw the most important places in his life. In his autobiography, Enrique, a fourth grader, writes:

The best day in my life was when my dad bought me a PS2 [PlayStation 2]. The PS2 is very special to me. It has such good graphics and really good sound effects. It has a lot of games you can't play on the Xbox or the GameCube. Sometimes, since I really liked the PS2, I might wrap it up with like 11 blankets to keep them warm at night and to keep it safe in case I sit on it on accident.

The worst day in my life was when I did something bad, so my parents took my PS2 away. I miss the sound effects, good graphics, the pressing of the buttons. Some of the buttons are called X, circle, square, and triangle. Those are the simple buttons. Also, there are hard ones like R1, R2, R3, L1, L2 and L3. Mostly R3 and L3 are the hardest ones, but not for me. I miss my PS2 a lot.

The importance of consumption as a means of communicating status is evident especially in the following case. Two fifth grade boys, Evelio and Jose, are working on lists as a prewriting activity for their autobiographies. Evelio writes the following list, including PlayStation Portable (PSP) twice:

I like PSP; I like to eat hot cheetos; I care about my family; I go for the Raiders; I like to play tetherball; I like to play computer; I like to watch TV; I have a PSP; I like to watch movies; I like to ride bikes; I hate homework; I hate reading class.

Reading Evelio's list over his shoulder, Jose shouts, "What! You don't have a PSP." Evelio hangs his head and says, "I know." He looks up and adds, "My cousin has one." Jose counters, "You only have a Game Boy." Later, Evelio drafts the first page of his autobiography, writing contradictorily:

I have a PSP at home. I have Grand Theft Auto and Tony Hawk Wasteland. I like to share it with my friends. I like to hear music on it. I played it at the video game store. I play for thirty minutes. Then I might buy a new game for my Game Boy Advanced. The PSP is more high tech.

Evelio's passage may appear at first a confusing, poorly executed text. His passage is, however, more comprehensible as an attempt to use narrative as a means of communicating with peers and reconciling a conflict.

Narrative construction is in every case a collaborative activity, shaped by concerns with the text and the social interactions that take place in the telling. The decontextualization of narratives and the dismissal of popular culture common in the classroom reduces the potential to expand students' literacies and alienates students' from the communicative purposes behind these literacy practices. To expand students' literacy requires teachers to both acknowledge how commodities work as "floating signifiers" in communicating and negotiating social status, as well as break down the binaries of high culture/popular culture, scientific/narrative knowledge, and school/home discourse.

3 Multiculturalism and the Domestication of Difference

In educational policy and research, culture is most often ascribed to Others and defined as a static, independent variable; cultural processes are frequently reduced to a single factor (race, gender, class, nation). This conceptualization of culture is a product of modernist binaries (White/Other, male/female, high income/low income) and the colonial notion that other cultures can be described, quantified, and captured. Schools typically organize cultures into distinct, homogenous groups, often depicted only through their visible manifestations (foods, clothing, language, music, holidays, or rituals). Common school assignments fit this conceptualization of culture, with discrete units of study on Native Americans, African Americans, Latinos, or other ethnic groups, country reports, or international festivals where students bring a typical food and dress in traditional costumes. Cultural processes are, likewise, reduced to comparative summaries in "cultural proficiency" manuals that are intended to inform school policy and practice.

In contrast to the static, surface-level view of culture often found in schools, anthropologist Clifford Geertz argues that culture constitutes a symbolic code. Geertz describes culture as the webs of significance that individuals spin around themselves. Culture is constructed and transmitted through numerous symbol systems: language, gestures, fashion, art, consumption patterns, religion, science, and law, among many others. It cannot be reduced to a single variable or two, Rogoff argues; this destroys "the coherence among the constellation of features that make it useful to refer to cultural processes" (2003, p. 12). There is little consensus historically on even the definition of culture. It has been described variously as:

- the total way of life of a people
- the social legacy that individuals acquire from their group
- a way of thinking, feeling, and believing
- a store-house of pooled learning
- a set of standardized orientations to recurrent problems
- a mechanism for the normative regulation of behavior (Geertz, 1973).

Rosaldo argues that this symbol system is always in flux; culture, in his view, is a process rather than a static system. His conceptualization of culture encompasses both states of social order as well as non-order, including uncertainty and improvisation as significant cultural processes. In this processual view, the meanings and practices that are characteristic of a particular culture are complex, heterogeneous, and shift over time, though the sense of distinctness and difference among cultures is continually maintained by persistent boundaries (Rosaldo, 1989).

Few, if any, educational policies reflect a processual view of culture; static, reductive, and bounded notions of culture are predominant. Race, especially, remains an essential, unchanging unit of analysis in education, a certainty employed without question. It is accepted as a naturally occurring category that is used in schools for: classifying students for school assignments; addressing attendance and retention policies; framing educational research agendas; targeting curriculum and instruction; assessing school progress; and measuring the "achievement gap." Race has historically determined both educational access and outcomes. "Race," writes educational researcher Maria Kromidas,

> infuses subjectivities, creates racial subjects, and profoundly affects how humans come to know—or, more precisely, not know—one another... [There is] extraordinary effort in the social production of seemingly naturalized differences in the processes and practices of everyday life... We are inculcated as racial beings and come to know one another as these racial beings (2011, p. 583).

During the era of slavery in the US, for instance, most enslaved African Americans were barred from attending school and becoming literate, since slave-owners viewed literacy as a possible tool of liberation. After the Emancipation Proclamation in 1863, schools in many parts of the country were racially segregated under the doctrine of "separate but equal." Over half a century after the US Supreme Court issued its landmark *Brown v. Board of Education* decision in 1954 to outlaw school segregation, many American public schools remain racially segregated.

There is a pattern of resegregation in increasing numbers of US cities and urban centers in Europe that have large immigrant populations. In Amsterdam, for example, there are substantial pockets of Moroccan-Dutch immigrant families whose children attend largely sub-standard schools. Resegregation in the US is driven not only by residential patterns, but also through school choice policies that allow parents in low-performing "Program Improvement" schools to transfer to more highly-ranked or charter schools. This policy contributes to "white flight," as it privileges well-connected families who have access to the cultural capital—information and transportation—necessary to make transfers possible.

The multicultural policies introduced to integrate schools and increase equity have, for the most part, instead perpetuated the naturalization of racial systems of difference and collapsed differences into White/Other dichotomies. Multiculturalism has domesticated difference. As transnational feminist theorists Minoo Moallem and Iain Boal argue, "Multiculturalism… masks the legacy of racism and its systematic connection to dominant definitions of culture and civilization" (1999, p. 244). In its typical implementation, multiculturalism "erases histories of oppression, dehumanizes ethnic and racial Others while leaving whiteness intact, and essentializes and reifies culture, thereby exaggerating and even creating differences among cultures" (Kromidas, 2011, p. 582). To counter this domestication, multiculturalism needs to be relocated at the meeting point of naturalization, normalization, and nationalization. This requires investigating how racial discourses emerged and how they have been utilized in education to naturalize identities, normalize social hierarchies, and build nation-states.

The Invention of Race

Although contemporary meanings of race are taken for granted, the history of the term reveals shifting uses. It has been synonymous in different eras with "species," "culture," "nation," and "ethnicity." Each of these overlapping and sometimes conflated constructs is an invention created with the purpose of ordering social relations. The ahistorical approach to race in education obscures the colonial power structures and history that, Quijano argues,

> produced the specific social discriminations which later were codified as 'racial,' 'ethnic,' 'anthropological' or 'national,' according to the times, agents, and populations involved. These intersubjective constructions, product of Eurocentered colonial domination were even assumed to be 'objective,' 'scientific,' categories, then of historical significance. That is, as natural phenomena, not referring to the history of power (2007, p. 168).

During the 19th and early 20th centuries, race was seen as a natural phenomenon whose meaning was fixed. It was widely accepted that specific racial categories were natural, scientific in nature, and biological in origin. Anthropologists, surgeons, and statisticians in the 19th century measured the geometry of the human body: the length and shape of the head, protrusion of a jaw line, the length of the forearm, and the flatness of the nose. These measurements were recorded and made to demonstrate some races as more physically characteristic of the ape and thus "scientifically" less evolved. The allure of numbers and measurements, allied with evolutionary theory and the narrative of progress, provided biological evidence for social rankings. Inventories of physical attributes were collected to provide proof of the difference and inferiority of "prostitutes, the Irish, Jews, the unemployed, criminals, and the insane" (McClintock, 1995, p. 50). McClintock refers to this as "scientific racism" (1995, p. 49).

Through the legacy of modernity—elevating science and granting it the power to reveal the truth—racial categories are presumed to be natural, biological facts. The assumed neutrality of science hides both the racism inherent in many of these "objective" measures, as well as the imperial history that underlies the categories and language of race. As Quijano asserts,

> Coloniality of power was conceived together with America and Western Europe, and with the social category of 'race' as the key element of the social classification of colonized and colonizers. Unlike in any other previous experience of colonialism, the old ideas of superiority of the dominant, and the inferiority of the dominated under European colonialism were mutated in a relationship of biologically and structurally superior and inferior (2007, p. 171).

A review of colonial history exposes that race is not a real, material, objective condition. Nor is it purely an illusionary ideological construct. Sociologists Michael Omi and Howard Winant argue that it is a "social fact" with only a blurred objective, physical basis. It exists and has power, but for social and historical reasons rather than biological ones. It is thus, they argue, more important to examine the racial formation process—how race is constructed and how its meaning changes—in order to fully understand its continuing impact (Omi & Winant, 1993).

Racial categories were first developed and codified in the 17th and 18th centuries with the aim of disciplining social boundaries in the new colonies. As Quijano writes,

> New social identities were produced all over the world: 'whites', 'Indians', 'Negroes', 'yellows', 'olives', using physiognomic traits of the peoples as external manifestations of their 'racial' nature. Then, on that basis the new geocultural identi-

ties were produced: European, American, Asiatic, African, and much later, Oceania (2007, p. 171).

Art historian Ilona Katzew observes how these emerging racial categorizations in the New World were documented in a distinct pictorial genre produced in colonial Mexico known as "*casta* painting." During the time of Spanish colonial rule in the Americas, the blurring of social boundaries that resulted from *mestizaje* or race mixing greatly concerned the authorities, and attempts were made to establish a set of racial categories to maintain power relationships among people of Spanish, Indigenous, and African origin (Katzew, 1996).

Casta (caste or race) paintings articulated a social hierarchy through visual symbolism. They contained a series of scenes, each presenting a man and woman of different races with one or two of their progeny. At the beginning are scenes portraying figures of "pure" Spanish race, lavishly attired and engaged in high status occupations. As the family groups in the pictures become more racially mixed, their social status diminishes as portrayed through the lighting, foregrounding, position, posture, clothing, and props. The process of defining the *castas* was guided by one immutable principle of imperialism: the purity of Spanish or White blood was linked to civilization; yet Spaniards themselves were hardly pure, given several hundred years of North African Muslim occupation and rule in the Iberian peninsula. *Casta* paintings charted a path for how to acquire civilized status or return to Spanish or White blood. One could never return to Spanish status, however, with Black mixtures; even one drop of Black blood consigned one permanently to marginal status.

The paintings expose the extent of objectification that occurred for colonized people, as they are presented alongside tropical fruits as objects of exotic display. These images and many like them were shipped back as curiosities for wealthy and royal families, as part of large collections of images and artifacts from the New World that were sent to lure money and interest in colonizing missions. These artifacts became the foundation for personal royal collections that led later to the development of national museums throughout Europe, such as the Museo de América in Madrid and the Museum of Ethnology in Vienna.

The collected *casta* paintings created a catalog of different races, using newly invented terms to classify and order social relations. A broad range of terms were devised to refer to the different *castas* and their increasingly hybrid offspring. The most widely used terms referred to mixtures between the three main groups: *mestizo* (Spanish-Indian), *mulatto* (Spanish-Black), and *zambo* or *zambaigo* (Black-Indian). Many racial terms in use today originated in the *casta* paintings, including *mestizo*, *mulatto*, and *lobo* for someone of Amerindian, Spanish, and African ancestry. Contemporary racial terms, thus, do not refer to a set of natural, biological categories, but were formed in the Americas in response to colonial power relations.

Race was not invented to simply describe "natural" categories of people based on their skin color or shared physical features, but to organize citizenship, labor, class, and gender relations. As McClintock argues, race, gender, and class were all formed in the context of imperial colonial relations, and in intimate relation to one another:

> [R]ace, gender and class are not distinct realms of experience, existing in splendid isolation from each other; nor can they be simply yoked together retrospectively like armatures of Lego. Rather, they come into existence *in and through* relation to each other—if in contradictory and conflictual ways. In this sense, gender, race, and class can be called articulated categories (1995, p. 5).

These articulated categories cannot, then, be isolated; this standard practice in educational policy and research oversimplifies race, class, gender, and nation, ignoring how these categories cross-cut one another. Racial categories are entangled with many forms of social classification, such as labor relations. As Quijano writes, "During European colonial world domination, the distribution of work of the entire world capitalist system, between salaried, independent peasants, independent merchants, and slaves and serfs, was organized basically following the same 'racial' lines of global social classification" (2007, p. 171). Focusing on single-label descriptors (race, gender, class, or nation) alone and without examination of the ways these categories were historically articulated and jointly formed remains standard practice in educational research policy and practice. When schools rely on static racial categories to describe and enroll students, secure funding, and report outcomes they unwittingly perpetuate the systems of difference that multicultural rhetoric promises to eradicate. As Moallem and Boal note,

> America as the land of diversity imagines itself… as tolerant of others without however, questioning the dynamic by which othering proceeds in American society. The recent deployment of the categories documented/undocumented, a variant on the old alien/native division, is an example of this continuous process of hierarchical dichotomizing (1999, p. 254).

A History of Multicultural Education

In contrast to the narrative of progress that assumes ever-more advanced policies, the history of multicultural education shows cyclical patterns of addressing or retreating from critical perspectives on race and schooling.

Educational responses to the question of difference fall generally into three broad perspectives: a deficit-assimilation perspective; a multicultural perspective; and an empowerment/anti-bias perspective (Cohen & Cohen, 1986; Hemphill, 1992).

The origins of multiculturalism date back to an early ethnic studies movement in the 1930s initiated by African American scholars such as Carter G. Woodson, Charles H. Wesley, and W.E.B. DuBois. DuBois opposed accommodation with White America and the prevailing views that embraced assimilation for Blacks as the key to achieving equity. He advocated for Black representation, arguing that

> equality in political, industrial and social life which modern men must have in order to live, is not to be confounded with sameness. On the contrary, in our case, it is rather insistence upon the right of diversity;—upon the right of a human being to be a man even if he does not wear the same cut of vest, the same curl of hair or the same color of skin (1935, p. 110).

DuBois did not accept the premise of the US nation-state as a legitimate object of loyalty for Blacks. Instead he promoted pan-Africanism in defiance of linking African identity to the bounds of the US nation-state. He also critiqued the prevailing ideology of scientific racism and the notion of a biological basis for White superiority. The work of DuBois and other scholars in the 1930s contributed to the emergence of the contemporary discipline of ethnic studies. This emphasis on ethnic pride and empowerment of specific ethnic or racial groups resurfaced in the 1960s, but it did so within the framework of the nation-state to build tolerance of difference and support a cohesive national identity for what came to be known as African Americans. This is the first of a series of examples of domestication in the history of equity initiatives and multicultural reforms, where critiques have been sanitized, leaving in their place apolitical or ahistorical programs of multiculturalism that support the nation-state and its hierarchical systems of difference (Blassingame, 1971; Carmichael & Hamilton, 1967; Robinson et al., 1969).

Different from the ethnic studies movements that preceded it and followed it, the late 1940s saw the emergence of what was called the intergroup education movement. This early anti-bias movement did not focus on ethnic attachment, but instead on intercultural interactions. The movement grew out of massive internal labor migration caused by World War II and the ethnic and racial tensions that developed over competition for jobs in war-related industries. In response to race riots, intergroup education was developed with the goal of reducing prejudice and creating interracial understanding among students from diverse national, religious, and racial groups. Though the focus in intergroup education was on intercultural interactions within a shared, common national culture, there was also intensive research and scholarship, led by educational researcher Hilda Taba (1952) and associates, on authoritarianism and the nature of racism and prejudice. The scholarship resulted in a social pedagogy that focused on understanding the origins of prejudice and developing skills in conflict resolution and social relations. This anti-bias approach was subsequently domesticated in later multicultural education work through a return to ethnic attachment, a retreat from research on the origins of social problems, and a renewed focus on assimilation in schools (Cook, 1947; Taba et al., 1952; Banks, 1993).

The 1954 *Brown* v *Board of Education* decision ushered in a new era of multicultural reform movements and research. Scholars such as Nathan Glazer and Daniel Patrick Moynihan and James Banks argued for multicultural education to replace the assimilationist approach with a model of cultural pluralism. Although multicultural reforms of this era adopted the anti-assimilationist stance of DuBois and colleagues from the 30s, the multicultural reforms implemented in the 50s and beyond "disarticulated elements of black radical demands for the restructuring of school knowledge and rearticulated these elements into more reformist professional discourses around issues of minority failure, cultural characteristics, and language proficiency" (McCarthy, 1993, pp. 228–229).

Multiculturalism has never been a homogenous social movement, nor does it represent a single theoretical approach or educational paradigm. Variously and amorphously defined, and seldom—if ever—institutionalized in a deep or structured way, multicultural education has taken on multiple meanings and approaches. As Buras and Motter suggest, "Multiculturalism has become a slogan under which a great variety of interests and concerns, some oppositional, have been pushed forward" (2006, p. 246).

The term multiculturalism has been criticized from both the political right and left in the US and Europe. From the conservative right, multiculturalism is often construed as an approach that undermines classic national values and identity and detracts from "serious" academic pursuits or the traditional canon. From the progressive left, multiculturalism is critiqued as an apolitical, uncritical, or liberal acceptance of an unequal status quo. As Shohat and Stam point out, the concept of multiculturalism is:

> subject to diverse political forcefields; it has become a contested and in some ways empty signifier onto which diverse groups project their hopes and fears. In its more co-opted version, it easily degenerates into the diversity of college catalogues or the state and corporate-managed United Colors of Benetton pluralism whereby estab-

lished power promotes 'ethnic flavors of the month' for commercial or ideological purposes (2003, p. 6; Hirsch, 1987; Schlesinger, 1992).

At its simplest, multiculturalism implies "accommodation of difference." Its primary aim is to promote mutual respect between individuals belonging to various race, class, gender, and religious groups. Multicultural school reforms have primarily sought better representation of diverse racial groups in instructional content, resources, and materials. One of the most common multicultural approaches is referred to as a celebratory approach, the "Easter bunny/Fourth of July/Cinco de Mayo" approach, or the contributions approach. This multicultural perspective emphasizes and promotes the positive qualities of all cultures. A related method, defined by Banks as the additive approach, brings varied ethnic content and concepts into the curriculum, going beyond celebrations of heroes and holidays. It may, for example, teach about the internment of Japanese Americans during a study of World War II, or include Alice Walker's *The Color Purple* into a unit on the 20th century. In this approach, inclusion is sought for each specific ethnic group, with African Americans advocating for curriculum about African Americans, Mexican Americans advocating curriculum about Mexican Americans, and so forth (Banks, 1994, 2007; Bruch et al., 2004; Gay, 2004; Hemphill, 1992).

In recent years, multiculturalism has broadened to encompass the study of multiple minority groups in the same curriculum, as well as ethnicity, social class, gender, language, national origin, immigration, and less frequently, sexual orientation, age, and disability. As multicultural education theorist Geneva Gay notes, "These changes were signaled by shifts in the language of identity for the movement—from 'minority studies' to 'ethnic studies' to 'multiethnic education,' and then to 'multicultural education'" (2004, p. 202). Additive approaches are also associated with terms such as "cultural understanding," "cultural competence," "cultural proficiency," and "cultural responsiveness."

Multicultural education is too often perceived, Gay argues, as separate content that must be added on to the existing curriculum. She advocates instead that it should be an integral part of everything within education: "Multicultural education is much more than a few lessons about ethnically diverse individuals and events or a component that operates on the periphery of the education enterprise" (2004, p. 33). Gay argues further that educators are primarily using multicultural education approaches only in social studies, language arts, and fine arts, and have generally targeted instruction for minority students. Critics of the additive multicultural perspective argue that it ignores issues of racism and bias, reinforces existing differences, and trivializes cultural practices (Bazron et al., 2005; Cohen & Cohen, 1986;

McCarthy, 1993).

While this additive approach has led to the inclusion of multicultural content in school curriculum, the basic nature and modernist structure of the existing mainstream curriculum remains largely untouched. Textbook publishers responding to the demand for multicultural reforms have, for instance, added photographs in history textbooks of minority leaders or special rainbow colored boxes with historical snapshots, such as Sacagawea's role in the Lewis and Clark mission or African American journalist Ida B. Wells' coverage of lynching in the South in the late 1800s, but the central historical narrative is unchanged. These colored boxes or additional supplements at the end of the chapter are easily identified in a "flip-test" and thus fit publishers' aims for the book to scan well for administrators looking to purchase updated curriculum, but they have little impact on the historical narrative already in place. The additive approach maintains the impression that women, for example, are not an integral part of the history or "progress." It is common, for example, to find a heading for "African Americans" or "Women" in the indexes of school textbooks, with a list of a dozen or so page numbers that refer to specific historical figures or movements. Yet there is no similar listing for "Whites" or "Men." Thus, the textbooks continue to enforce the taken-for-granted centrality of male, white, and middle- or upper-class perspectives.

Banks identifies multiple dimensions to consider in the implementation of multicultural education: (1) *content integration*, the extent to which content from a variety of cultures and groups is integrated into the curriculum; (2) *knowledge construction*, the extent to which teachers and students understand how the perspectives, biases, and frames of reference in particular disciplines help shape knowledge in those disciplines; (3) *prejudice reduction*, the way in which teachers help students develop more democratic attitudes and values; (4) *equity pedagogy*, in which pedagogical strategies are modified to help students of all backgrounds learn effectively; and (5) *empowering school culture and social structure*, where the climate and organization of the school promote an equitable learning environment (Banks, 1991).

Taking a more critical approach to multicultural education, many social justice and critical race theorists have advocated for an empowerment/anti-bias approach that includes influences of racism and discrimination in daily life. Banks identifies two empowerment/anti-bias approaches, which he refers to as the "transformative approach" and the "social action approach." He describes the transformative approach as a practice that enables students to view issues from multiple points of view. For example, a teacher using the transformative approach may teach a unit on the American Revolution from the varied perspective of white revolutionaries, white loyalists, African Americans, Indians, and British. The social action approach incorporates all the components of the transformative approach, but also works to educate students for social criticism and change. Students are taught to identify critical issues, gather and analyze data, and take reflective action to resolve the problem. Proponents claim that the anti-bias approach can help develop critical thinking skills. Opponents argue that these methods are overly deterministic, expressing fear that "over-emphasizing domination can prove debilitating and demoralizing to all students" (Bruch et al., 2004, p. 13; Banks, 2007; Cohen & Cohen, 1986; Hemphill, 1992; Derman-Sparks & Ramsey, 2006).

In the late 1990s, an additional approach called "whiteness studies" was developed in response to the "quiet yet overpowering normativity of whiteness" or "the process by which race and ethnicity were attributed to others while whites were tacitly positioned as an invisible norm" (Shohat & Stam, 2003, p. 3). While whiteness studies promise the denaturalization of whiteness as an unmarked norm, it also tends to recenter whiteness and limit the debate to modernist binaries that "pit a rotating chain of marginalized communities against an unstated white norm or to pit various Third World cultures against a Western norm" (Shohat & Stam, 2003, p. 4).

Outside the research literature, empowerment/anti-bias or whiteness studies lessons are seldom observed in widespread practice in schools. They are sometimes taken up individually by teachers, often without the formal consent of the school administration and increasingly in defiance of scripted curriculum and standards-based instruction. The current trends in the West toward standardizing curriculum and packing school schedules with mandated content leaves less and less flexibility for teachers or students to determine topics of study or critique instructional norms.

High-stakes testing and accountability measures, lack of teacher training on differing cultures, and the increasingly heavy reliance on tightly scripted curriculum have contributed to the shallow implementation of multiculturalism and the persistence of the deficit-assimilation perspective in US schools. Despite movements to reconceptualize assimilation and nationalistic definitions of citizenship in the 1960s and 70s, when metaphors such as the "salad bowl" or "multicultural mosaic" replaced the melting pot, assimilation has resurfaced as the goal of many 21st-century schooling practices. The deficit-assimilation perspective views cultural differences as deficiencies and works to bring subordinate cultures into the dominant culture. According to educational theorist Cameron McCarthy, this deficit model consciously attempts to "cultivate norms of citizenship, to fashion a conformist national identity, and to bind together a population of diverse national origins" (1993, p. 226). Some scholars refer to this as a mainstream-centric model; others define it as subtractive schooling (Banks, 2007; Bazron, Osher, & Fleischman, 2005; Sleeter & Stillman, 2005).

In this melting pot, deficit-assimilation model, immigrant or minority students are positioned as at-risk and in need of special services (counseling, English Language Development (ELD), academic intervention, and parent education). In US schools the,

> integral elements in the Americanization process include (a) the requirement to become English speaking at the expense of one's native language; (b) academic marginalization and the disproportional tracking of immigrant students into remedial, special education, and vocational classes; and (c) the exorbitant pressure to find and take one's pace in the racial hierarchy of this country (Lam, 2006, p. 226).

The model of the native English speaker and standard English language usage continue to be the unquestioned targets of most schooling for immigrant youth. As Rosaldo asks, "Why is it that five-year-old children are at risk if they speak a language other than English? And why is it that at age 21 they are not at risk but are becoming cultured as they struggle to learn another language?" (1994, p. 403). Echoes of the deficit-assimilation model include English-only movements, California's Proposition 227 passed in 1998 to disallow bilingual education in public schools, and Arizona's anti-immigrant legislation of the 1990s and early 2000s.

There has also been a resurgence of an assimilationist movement in Europe in the early 2000s. German Chancellor Angela Merkel, for example, declared in a speech in 2010 that multiculturalism had "utterly failed," and argued for a return to assimilationism:

> In Frankfurt, two out of three children have an immigrant background. We are a country which, at the beginning of the 60s, actually brought guest workers to Germany. Now they live with us and we lied to ourselves awhile, saying that they won't stay and that they will have disappeared again one day. That's not the reality. This multicultural approach, saying that we simply live side by side and are happy about each other, this approach has failed, utterly failed.... This means that the demand for integration [assimilation] is one of our key tasks for the times to come (Merkel, 2010).

In a related pronouncement in 2011, British Prime Minister David Cameron critiqued his country's decades-old policy of multiculturalism, saying it has encouraged segregated communities where Islamic extremism can thrive. Cameron also condemned "hands-off tolerance" that encourages Muslims and other immigrant groups "to live separate lives, apart from each other and the mainstream." He argued that Britain's multiculturalism policy—in place since the 1960s—has failed to promote a sense of common identity based on human rights, democracy, integration, and equality. He added that the government would no longer support Muslim nonprofit groups that have been "showered with public money despite doing little to combat terrorism" (Burns, 2011). Similar assimilationist initiatives have been implemented in France, where Muslim headscarves were banned in schools in 2004, and in Switzerland, where a rightist national referendum imposed a national ban on the construction of minarets, the prayer towers of mosques, in 2009.

The persistence of deficit-assimilationism and additive multicultural models defy a narrative of progress as an organizing principle for the history of multicultural education. Multiculturalism, historically and in present iterations, reflects a domestication of difference. Even when schools have adopted some multicultural education reforms, they generally adhere to modernist principles that reinforce the White/Other binaries and systems of difference that prompted their implementation.

Essentialism, Reification, and Other Pitfalls of Multiculturalism

An ongoing aim of multicultural education research and practice is to present the practices of distinct cultural groups in order to create "culturally competent" curriculum, instruction, assessment, and policy. The normative patterns distilled from this research rely on modernist notions of subjectivity that assume the existence of static cultural groups and stable, fixed identities. This modernist form of multiculturalism reinforces an essentialist analysis, which presumes that there are "essentially Latino," "essentially female," "essentially African American," or "essentially gay" characteristics and features. Inherent in essentialist thinking, argues educational theorist Chet Bowers, is cultural reductionism that leads to "little more than a tourist industry level of understanding cultural differences" (1995, p. 101). Essentialist understandings of others ignore shifting and complex social positions, differences within communities, and the histories and discourses that produce them. Anthropologist James Clifford counters the essentialist depictions of others, arguing that "cultural difference is no longer a stable, exotic otherness; self-other relations are matters of power and rhetoric rather than of essence" (1988, p. 14).

Essentialist multicultural research, curriculum, and school policies frequently over-simplify or reduce cultures, creating neatly packaged, generalizable, unchanging entities to produce "recipe knowledge" for the convenience of educators. As Geertz argues, to claim that culture is the "brute pattern of behavioral events we observe in fact to occur in some identifiable community or other is to reduce it" (1973, p. 11). Reductionism occurs, for example, when educators are presented with "research-based" professional development that makes suggestions for policy and practice based on homogenized notions of communities, with assumed universal norms. Statements such as, "Girls are more likely to be ready for Kindergarten than boys" rely on essentialist notions of what girls and boys are like. These gendered norms are backed up with "scientific" data, such as the following: "Because [boys] are hard-wired to enjoy spatial-mechanical play, boys require more physical space than girls and will bounce off the walls when confined" (Boyd, 2010).

Research in education often takes the form of confirming "scientifically" the norm-based perceptions of educators. Teachers' perceptions, for example, that "female students do better at making friends, working in groups, and helping their peers" are supported with scientific evidence: "Even at this [preschool] age, higher levels of oxytocin (which helps bond mothers to their babies) encourage girls to love and care for their dolls, while boys see them only as inanimate objects to be thrown around" (Boyd, 2010). Popular literature and school intervention policies confirm these essentialist and reductive depictions of boys, asking educators to accommodate the "male learning style" or the "male brain." For instance, neuropsychiatrist and popular author Louann Brizendine observes, "By the time boys are in first grade, they get a brain high when they show their strength and aggression. Using physical force together with insults is even better... These boys are just trying to have their kind of fun (2010, p. 23). Such observations reify male identities, contributing to the normalization of discipline problems and the disproportionate number of boys who have school discipline and behavior problems; boys make up 80% of school discipline problems.

Collapsing cultural traditions into a single label reduces and reifies cultural groups. Reification involves endowing a concept, "culture X," with a life of its own, or as Geertz writes, "to imagine that culture is a self-contained 'super-organic' reality with forces and purposes of its own" (1973, p. 11). When specific remediations are assigned to what are assumed to be homogenous groups of students and families, such as discipline programs for boys, literacy interventions for English Language Learners (ELLs), or family engagement strategies for low-income communities, cultural groups are overdetermined for single categories of identity. The use of a single label, such as male, ELL, African American, or Asian to box together many disparate traditions produces a false reality based on those identifications (Rogoff, 2003). The essentialist, reified binaries enforced in school discourse, Westwood argues, "work on fixity and fixed positions black/white, male/female, gay/straight and the notions of a unitary subject defined by a single identity. But the lived experience of blackness, whiteness, masculinity, and so on belies this fixity" (2000, p. 34).

The reductionism and reification of cultural groups hides the heterogeneity within communities. Single-label descriptors like "Hispanic/Latino," for example, obscure the divergent immigration, labor, and language learning experiences within Latino/a communities that often differ sharply on class, gender, or national lines. Families from northern Mexico, for instance, may have higher social status in immigrant community hierarchies and differential access to resources than indigenous Mayan families from southern Mexico, Guatemala and El Salvador, who are often learning Spanish, English, and literacy skills simultaneously. Students may perceive additional hierarchies within their school-assigned ethnic groups, categorizing their "Latino" peers, for example, by shade of skin color, ascribing the highest status to those who can pass as "White" or those with the lightest skin tones. These hierarchies can exist even within a single family, as one sixth-grader, Eric, describes:

> My mother is brown-skinned and I am of a lighter skin tone. They call me 'White Chocolate' and my brother 'Café con Leche.' They [my friends] say I don't fit with this group and I say, 'No, I'm Latino'... They are just jealous of my skin tone. They want to be that color because that color gets more privileges like to get into college, they like people more (Blakely, 2007, p. 116).

"I am different from my family," he adds, "because they like sushi and I don't. They also like Spanish movies and I don't like them because I don't understand what they're saying" (Eric speaks only English, while his parents and brothers speak Spanish exclusively at home) (Blakely, 2007, p. 116). In the US school system Eric, his brother, and friends are all lumped together in the same essentialized racial/ethnic category and classified reductively as English Language Learners (ELLs) or Latinos. Heterogeneity within communities — including literacy rates, regional affiliations, job positions, ascribed social privilege, and immigration status — is more intense than the differences among the racialized communities that schools refer to in policy and practice.

Multicultural programs generally do not take into account shifting identities, race-bending or how categories of identity cross-cut one another. The promises of multicultural reforms are thus undercut by their reductionism and reification of cultural groups, which universalize essentialist identities and reinforce Western norms and systems of difference. Buras and Motter amplify this argument:

Multiculturalism has succeeded in preserving to the point of petrifaction its central object: culture... When guided by these logics, multiculturalism is aimed at normalizing, framing, and managing difference: It has become a set of propositions about identity, knowledge, power, and change in education, a kind of normal science, which attempts to discipline difference rather than be transformed by it.... (2006, p. 248).

Multicultural reforms that simply add diverse content to traditional syllabi or "culturally competent" aims to school reform projects fail to address the centrality of Western perspectives or the naturalization and normalization of Western knowledge and social hierarchies in school curriculum and practices. Mainstream multicultural discourses, Kromidas concludes,

see difference as a matter of natural repulsion, the source of conflict, division, and inequality in social relations. Living with difference is seen as an unfortunate but inevitable problem to be solved .... [it] posit[s] "sticking to your own kind" as the inherent state of things, the normal way to behave, even, and especially, when encouraging people to be tolerant or color-blind. In the end, [multiculturalism]... reproduce[s] the historically and socially constituted differences of humanity as "real" and existing in "nature" (2011, pp. 582–583).

Case in Point: Race-Bending

"Schools are key sites where U.S. young people and adults, in a striking 'institutional choreography,' actually make each other racial," argues educational researcher Mica Pollock (2005, p. 45). The use of naturalized racial categories to promote equity, Pollock discovers in a study of students at one urban public high school in California, frequently amounts to little more than ethnic cheerleading or race-group competitions. Students complain, for instance, when Samoan students, dancing in grass skirts "got hella time" at the multicultural school assembly while the Black rapper "didn't even get to finish"; the school's sound system broke mid-assembly, but the students read this as a sign that "this school's racist." Students further question curricular choices, such as, why the history teachers "give blacks a whole month—for us it's one day... Cinco de Mayo" or why the study of the Philippines is last in the semester.

Pollock observes how students adopt and rely on the static racial categories of the school even while recognizing that their own identities do not fit easily into this fabricated system of difference. The students at Columbus High School represent the demographic complexity and global criss-crossing of families common in many school districts across the US. They list long strings of ethnic, national, and racial identifiers to describe themelves: "I'm Samoan, Black, Puerto Rican, Filipino, and Indian." Yet, they generally collapse their ethnic identifications to align with one racially defined student group.

The racial groups identified at Columbus High—Samoan, Filipino, African American, Latino, Asian, and White—are themselves a mixture of ethnic and national signifiers. As Pollock notes, "Calling all these groups 'racial' indicated primarily that they were competitive parts in a local, shifting social hierarchy of groups" (2005, p. x). The students, Pollock observes,

> left the full complexities of their identities outside the classroom... Despite the mixed up roots and global routes central to the Columbus youth experience, these young people, in conjunction with the adults around them, worked daily to squash their diversity into six groups they called "racial" (2005, pp. 48, 56).

Though students in Pollock's study constantly collapse their identities to fit into one race group, they also recognize that their racial identity is not absolute or fixed. The students acknowledge, for example, that it is often difficult to "tell what somebody is." They make guesses based on physical features (hair color, the size of the nose, etc.), along with accent and peer associations. Through such guessing games, they indicate that one can "guess wrong."

Students retain race labels as the dominant descriptive tool, characterizing their lunchroom and campus using a racial geography, even while they invent new terms like "niggapino" or "Japapino." Pollock calls this "race bending." By playing guessing games and inventing new terms, the students demonstrate recognition that the practice of racial classification is an invention, not an immutable fact of nature.

The students also engage in race-bending as they shift their self-identification from context to context, depending upon the strategic needs of the situation—to be accepted for enrollment at a particular school site, advocate for particular resources for a given racial/cultural group, identify with a sought-after clique on campus, or achieve numerous other purposes. Students identified by themselves and peers as Filipino, for example, might apply for inter-district transfer as Latino, using a Puerto Rican grandmother as evidence for the switch, in order to take advantage of a desired school's larger attendance quota for that group. This practice is also referred to as "strategic essentialism" or "the politics of recognition" (Spivak, 1988; Taylor, 1992).

Race-bending is also documented among nine-, ten-, and eleven-year-olds in New York City. In the "About Me" section of her MySpace profile, one ten-year-old writes for example, "I am 50% Rican 50% Mexicana and also 50% from Montenegro." This "funny math," Kromidas argues, represents "not only their authentic longings and alternative belongings but a defiance of the impoverished arithmetic of larger ideologies of racial and ethnic difference" (2011, p. 582). In conventional terms, the student would be considered Puerto Rican, but this neglects her close friendships with Patricia, from Mexico, and Ade, from Montenegro. The primacy of these friendships in developing an identity challenges the stable boundaries imposed in the conventional racial discourse that assumes racial identification is fixed.

In general, school experiences require students to describe themselves using single-label descriptors. Thus, students actively reinforce or redraw received lines of racialized difference. To counter the ethnic-cheerleading or racial divisions that sometimes result from multicultural school policies and practices, Pollock proposes that educators foster race-bending discourse in schools. She suggests that teachers highlight the intersections between races when structuring school curriculum, and initiate conversations about "racial categorization itself, bringing to light the youth contestation of 'race groups' occurring already in the margins of our institutions to expose the lines we draw around 'races' as human-made" (2005, p. 62). The race-bending practices happening in schools provide evidence that youth are already aware that racial categorizations are murky despite the way they are depicted, normalized, and unchallenged in school policies and practices.

Hybridity and the Third Space

Though most educational policies and practices rely on discrete categories of cultural identity, cultural theorists across many academic disciplines have moved away from the static trio of race, class, and gender. Difference, says Bhabha, should no longer be hastily interpreted as the reflection of pre-given, essential ethnic or cultural traits. Instead, he argues for the concept of hybridity—cultural mixing and blending—that maintains a sense of fluidity. He avoids essentializing identities, conceptualizing blends of race, class, gender, ability, sexual orientation, generation, geopolitical location, and institutional location. Clifford too describes collective identity as a hybrid, discontinuous, inventive process; culture, he claims, is not a pure product. Buras and Motter further argue that we live in a world of "mixtures, of migrations, of crossing over... [where] there are no insulated cultures or civilizations" (2006, p. 248). Though hybridity theories are largely absent from the field of education, the notion of hybridity or "how cultural forms and practices intermingle and traverse social boundaries," according to Lam "is no longer a sequestered academic discourse of cultural theory but has become a driving engine of the corporate sector, media industries, and grassroots producers and consumers" (2006, p. 217; Bhabha, 1994; Clifford, 1988).

Hybridity challenges modernist and colonial narratives that rely upon such fictions as cultural purity, essential cultural features, or homogenous cultural identities. The term hybridity provides a conceptual tool that goes beyond notions such as multiculturalism, *mestizaje*, syncretism, or other terms of reference for diversity and cultural mixing. Cultural theorist Sabine Mabardi argues for the use of the term hybridity for three reasons. First, it accommodates diverse kinds of intercultural mixtures—not just the racial mixtures to which ideas such as *mestizaje* tend to be limited. Second, it has a broader scope than terms like syncretism, which are usually limited to religious or symbolic fusions. Third, it implies a dimension of forced union, given the word's biological roots (as in hybrid plants or crops), thus accommodating notions of power through colonization or cultural domination. The concept of hybridity acknowledges and articulates the power relations that are inscribed in cultural blends. Cultural mixing rarely implies even exchange; there are almost always asymmetries in the conditions of mixing (Mabardi, 2000).

Hybridity, then, is more than simply a new word to describe culture mixtures. As communication theorist Marwan Kraidy observes, "If hybridity consists of mere observing, cataloging, and celebrating multicultural mixture, the inequality that often characterizes these mixtures is glossed over" (2002, p. 318). Hybridity instead refers to a communicative practice constitutive of, and constituted by, sociopolitical and economic arrangements. Understanding hybridity as a practice, says Kraidy, marks the recognition that transcultural relations are complex, processual, and dynamic. For Bhabha, too, hybridity implies both a condition and a process that can function as a counternarrative to authority. As Mabardi notes, "It subverts the concept of pure origin or identity of the dominant authority through the ambivalence created by denial, unsettling, repetition, and displacement. It is also a threat because it is unpredictable" (2000, p. 6).

Hybridity is not a new phenomenon or state of cultures. There is a long, often unrecognized history of complex interactions between cultures, yet multiple processes have amplified conditions of contemporary hybridity. Anthropologist Nestor García Canclini argues that new technologies of reproduction of the last few decades—photocopiers, video cameras and recorders, digital media, video games, computers, MP3s, DVDs, the Internet, and wireless devices—have permitted individuals to form their own collections and cultural repertoires. These tools have in turn been used to "crack the orders" that were traditionally used to classify and distinguish cultural traditions and products. As a result, there has been an expansion of many hybrid or "impure" genres, such as graffiti art, graphic novels, infotainment, blogs, hip hop, and 'zines (García Canclini, 1995; Said, 1979).

Contemporary, globalized youth, Lam argues, are developing identities that "disrupt a one-to-one correspondence of culture and ethnicity and thrive on hybrid innovation to create new forms of competence and knowledge" (2006, p. 222). Youth in Montreal, Canada, for example, display multiple affiliations through their music. Linguists Mela Sarkar and Lise Winer describe how these youth code-switch or mix Quebec French, European French, standard North American English, African American vernacular English, Haitian Creole, Jamaican Creole, and Spanish in their lyrics to signify multiple affiliations. Code-switching gives the artists more flexibility, drawing from many languages to create densely rhymed lyrics, and it allows them to take on and perform multiple identities, positioning multilingualism as a natural, desirable condition even if the lyrics are not understood by all listeners. The lyrics used by hip hop artists then constitute a discursive space in which they juxtapose multiple identity claims, using languages they may not fully speak or with which they have no direct ethnic or national connection (Sarkar & Winer, 2006).

Hybridized commercial and media narratives both reinforce and conflict with traditional national claims to identity. For example, while anti-immigrant discourse in the political arena has alienated undocumented immigrants and Latina/os, US corporations and media companies have opportunistically reached out to this group. Their customized advertising campaigns often use hybrid language mixtures or Spanglish, even while this language form is ignored or dismissed in other public arenas. A similar commercial effort is under way in Germany, where, despite generations of anti-Turkish, anti-immigrant sentiment, corporations have adopted a hybrid German-Turkish marketing patois. As Lam observes, "Ethno-marketing is targeting German Turks and thereby contributing to a redefinition of their cultural and social space across national boundaries" (2006, p. 214).

Another process that has amplified contemporary hybridity, García Canclini argues, is the reorganization of the public and the private in urban cultures. In recent decades the proportion of the population throughout the world living in urban versus rural locations has rapidly expanded. In Latin America, for example, the rural-urban population balance shifted from 90% rural and 10% urban in 1900 to 70% urban by the end of the 20th century. García Canclini suggests that in urbanized settings, collective identities tied to specific locations are found less and less often. Instead, urban culture has been restructured by giving up face-to-face communication in favor of electronic technologies. Urbanization is thus accompanied by greater personal anonymity in the production and restructuring of communication through electronic media, which modifies connections between the public and the private. "The national as container of social process and power is cracked," argues sociologist Saskia Sassen, "This cracked casing opens up a geography of politics and civics that links subnational places. Cities are foremost in this new geography... The new network technologies, especially the Internet, ironically have strengthened the urban map of these trans-boundary networks" (2002, p. 217).

As a result of ongoing processes of hybridization, all cultures are to a large extent hybrid, border cultures, with most cultural forms developing in dialogue with other cultural forms—a contemporary social manifestation of what Bakhtin calls dialogism. The concept of dialogism and hybridity applies not just to questions of ethnic identity or national origin, but to a broad range of cultural products and categories. In the field of popular music, for example, numerous genres—including rock, jazz, blues, R&B, country, and hip hop—are all hybrids, having evolved through historical interplays of people, musical styles, cultures, and experiences (Bakhtin, 1981).

Hybridity in any form is resistant to binary oppositions; as Bhabha suggests, it is neither self, nor Other. Bhabha contends further that hybridity does not resolve tensions between two cultures, but exists in a continuing state of ambivalence. He argues that there is a "third space" that signifies a new frame of reference existing between cultures. In this third space, the hybrid ways students make meaning and craft identities are not simply mixtures of established cultures and identities, but signs and meanings that are constantly appropriated, translated, rehistoricized, and read anew. Through their engagement with popular media, students often create and reside in this third space.

Lam offers a case study to illustrate how youth negotiate identities from this third space. She tells of a 16-year-old immigrant youth from Hong Kong named Willis who spent four years in sheltered ESL classes, ignoring taunts about his thick accent and lack of progress. Instead of associating with or "mixing well" with either Asian or American students, he finds his strongest identification with the characters in his valued collection of Japanese comics. From this third space, he critiques both American and Hong Kong comics. He appreciates the nuance of Japanese comics and heroes who are less than perfect ordinary people (like one protagonist who struggles in school, but solves complicated criminal cases in his community). He contrasts the Japanese plots to the static American comics, where "arrogant" superheroes defeat an endless string of "bad" guys, "one falls dead and another rushes up, one falls dead and another rushes up" (Lam, 2004, p. 11). Likewise, he critiques the Hong Kong comics for their sloppy renderings and trendy plot lines, believing they are only made for a quick profit. Lam observes:

> In creating a 'third space' for himself in this transnational discourse of popular youth culture, Willis was able to develop a sense of agency in making flexible cross-cultural identifications and in critiquing the socio-cultural practices represented in the different varieties of comics.... Between the impossibility of identifying with the native Hong Kong person he used to be and his refusal to identify with the standardized American person whose English he now speaks, Willis appropriated a textual identity from the Japanese comics, and used it as a third place from which to reflect.... By creating this position for himself, Willis was able to verbalize the arbitrary nature of the linguistic and cultural norms of the two societies (2004, p. 8).

Static identity categories and reliance on grouping students together by national origin, language, or ethnicity ignore the pervasive experience of popular culture and the mixed possibilities for student affiliations. Ethnographer Norma González notes that the sense that culture is bounded and static is increasingly destabilized by the boundary-blurring and border-crossing activities of youth who inhabit a media-saturated universe, multi-task, and shift genres or even identities regularly. "Increasingly, the boundedness of cultures gives way," she writes,

> to the interculturality and hybridity of cultural practices.... Increasingly students draw from an intercultural and hybrid knowledge base, appropriating multiple cultural systems, as youth culture permeates greater and greater spheres (González, 2005, pp. 37–38).

Youth access to new media and technologies has expanded the capacity for cultural consumption on a global scale. Students and teachers not only consume cultural products, but they continually produce culture and add to, blend, or alter cultural practices through their representations. As Duncan-Andrade notes, "Culture is not just a process of consumption (critical or passive); it is also a process of production, of individual and collective interpretation (meaning making) through representations of styles, discursive practices, semiotics, and texts" (2004, p. 314).

Growing up multicultural, says literacy researcher Allan Luke, "is about being between 16 or 18 different worlds... it's about navigating a sea of texts. Each one of these texts is trying to position you, sell you, define you" (qtd. in Besley, 2003, p. 170). Thus, the acquisition of identity cannot be described solely in Western terms, where an adult, autonomous self slowly emerges in a linear way. Instead, Luke argues, growing up involves a "hybridization pastiche process of stitching together an identity like trying on clothes, becoming your own hybrid, blending, shaping, and putting together something that's a range of cultures" (qtd. in Besley, 2003, p. 170). Identity is then a process of articulation, argues Hall, that entails discursive work and the marking of symbolic boundaries. It is neither an essential internal state nor the exclusive result of external discourse as schools often assume, but instead is a process of intertwining categories, norms, and narratives over time (Hall, 1996).

Learning contexts, like student identities, are hybrid productions. Urban classrooms in particular are diverse, not only in terms of racial, ethnic, socioeconomic and linguistic difference, but also in terms of the mediational tools and roles that teachers and students employ. Educational researchers Kris Gutierrez, Patricia Baquedano-López, and Carlos Tejeda propose hybridity

> both as a useful lens, a theoretical tool for understanding the inherent diversity and heterogeneity of activity systems and learning events, as well as a principle for or-ganizing learning.... Utilizing multiple, diverse, and even conflicting mediational tools... promotes the emergence of third spaces, or zones of development, and thus expands learning (Gutierrez et al., 1999, p. 288).

Analyzing classroom interactions, they note, that there is an official in-teractional space that includes teacher-directed activities related to the standard curriculum. The unofficial space refers to "unauthorized side talk" and play that happen between peers. These "inappropriate" interactions are generally silenced, redirected, or disciplined. Teachers can foster learning by breaking down the binaries between official/unofficial interactions, for-mal/informal language registers, and school/home knowledge. They suggest that by intentionally operating in the third space between these discourses, teachers can expand students' engagement. The authors cite one example where a student makes a joke at his own expense during a class reading about the human body; "no wonder they call me bony," the student, Jorge, teases when students are asked to locate their spine. Rather than treat his comment as an unwelcome disruption, the teacher folds the student's comment into the class discussion. His comment then,

> becomes part of the classroom text.... Jorge... reemerges as expert in the official space as he answers the question that the teacher had been so intent on asking.... His answer and the teacher's enthusiastic response co-constructs Jorge's identity as a knowing contributor. He is not simply the comical contributor; he is also a resource in the classroom (Gutierrez et al., 1999, pp. 299, 300).

In an intentionally developed, hybrid third space, student talk, jokes, slang, and emotions are re-scripted and included in the official class discussion, enabling students to bring their funds of knowledge into the curriculum: "affective stances can not only be displayed, they are also welcome additions to classroom ethos and official knowledge" (Gutierrez et al., 1999, p. 295). Operating in the third space then helps teachers build student vocabulary and also enables students to use the full potential of their linguistic resources. In this third space, "no single language... is privileged, and the larger linguistic repertoires of participants become tools for participating and making meaning in this new collaborative activity. In fact, these hybrid language practices... [can increase] the possibility of dialogue — and thus, interpretation" (Gutierrez et al., 1999, p. 293). Use of the third space includes: using conflict as a starting place for negotiating and reorganizing lessons; drawing parallels between home and academic discourse; accepting slang, humor, informal language, and mixed languages (like Spanglish) in class discussions. Rather than viewing difference — as schools often do — as a problem to overcome, hybridity and third spaces can become cultural resources to promote and expand learning.

4 Globalization, Transnationality, and Citizen-Consumers

Classrooms are increasingly occupied by students who move within and between communities and nations. "Even when young people are not themselves traveling across national borders, or leaving their own bedrooms, they can find themselves, implicated within transnational networks" (Maira & Soep, 2005, p. xix). The movement of people across borders, the globalization of marketplaces and media, and the multi-faceted, shifting identities of students challenge educational theories that rely on a bounded conception of culture through which people's traditions and identities are tied to the regions and nations where they reside. Cultures in schools have long been reified as homogenous and what Dirlik calls "spatially mappable entities" (1999, p. 17).

The increasing number of students who are embedded in social networks of two or more nations challenges fixed and homogeneous notions of race, geographic space, and social identity. There is a need, writes globalization theorist Arjun Appadurai, to reconceptualize the "landscape of group identity" to reflect current conditions in which "groups are no longer tightly territorialized, spatially bounded, historically unselfconscious, or culturally homogenous" (1996, p. 191). A relatively new discipline, transnational studies, confronts the reductive manner of describing communities as pure, stable, separable entities. Transnational theories challenge the "linear temporality of historiographic periodization," "the inscription of neatly separate community narratives," and other features of modernist discourse that underlie many educational practices and school curricula (Shohat & Stam, 2003, p. 2).

The idea of transnationality emerged in the work of social scientists, feminists, and immigration researchers in the 1990s who were trying to explore the cultural and economic ties between multiple nation-states, and the links between the nation-state and global capital. Transnationality is defined by one author as "the processes by which immigrants forge and sustain multi-stranded social relations that link together their societies of origin and settlement" (Basch et. al, 2008, p. 263). Transnational theories, argues Lam, offer educators a way to:

> shift from a unilinear view of acculturation that focuses on adaptation to the structural and cultural conditions of the host society to a more multidimensional view of transculturation that looks at the multilayered modes of belonging and participation within, across, and at the intersections of societies (2006, p. 227).

This scholarship provides a vocabulary for examining how identities emerge from the knowledge produced by nationalism, multiculturalism, school disciplinary power, media, and the marketplace (Khagram & Levitt, 2008).

Time–Space Compression and Global Networks

Most references to globalization within the field of education are found in reform rhetoric urging educators to raise standards to prepare students to compete in rapidly changing global markets. In this rhetoric and in popular discourse, globalization is commonly imagined as the Americanization of the world, symbolized by the presence of Coke cans or laptops in faraway locales. Educational discourse largely refers to globalization as an objective reality of changing market forces and new communication forms and technologies. "Such objectification," Lam observes, "turns global processes into something we have to respond to or fit our lives into—something that has power over the way we live, learn, and work" (2006, p. 222). References to globalization in education reform rhetoric often make globalizing forces appear as the natural, inevitable evolution of nations and economies that teachers and students must respond to and fit into their classrooms and lives. Yet viewing globalization as a set of naturally evolving economic processes reifies it and ignores localized complexities, as well as the long history of cross-cultural links.

The term globalization first appeared in popular and scholarly discourse in the late 1980s to describe multidimensional processes and networks of electronic, economic, political, cultural, and ecological border crossings and multinational links. These processes involved transnational capital, mobile labor markets, popular culture imports, global warming, species extinction, information flows, Internet use, air travel, and related phenomena. Widespread attention to globalization was ushered in by the presence of: multinational corporations (Microsoft, Sony, News Corporation); nongovernmental organizations (Greenpeace, Amnesty International); and intergovernmental organizations and agreements (United Nations, World Bank, International Monetary Fund, World Trade Organization, North American Free Trade Agreement) (Baumann, 1998; Besley, 2003; Castells, 1996 & 1997; Harvey, 2000).

Globalization, though, does not mean simply the presence of international organizations and links. Globalization has transformed both the economic sector and social relationships, altering the material foundations and processes of society. Globalization has, for instance, transformed notions of space and time, leading to the phenomenon of time-space compression. Time compression, postmodern theorist David Harvey argues, is exemplified by the volatility and ephemerality of fashions, products, production techniques, labor processes, ideas and ideologies, values, and established practices. This "speeding up of time" has provoked a broad range of reactions in the economy, including flexible hiring practices, advanced pay check cashing, and hedging bets in futures markets. Time compression has also yielded a transition to flexible accumulation of capital accomplished through rapid deployment of new organizational forms and technologies in production, subcontracting, outsourcing, just-in-time delivery—all accelerating turnover time. Parallel accelerations in exchange and consumption have resulted via electronic banking, plastic money, and rapid international flows of capital. Mobilization of fashion in mass—as opposed to elite—markets, says Harvey, has accelerated globalized consumption over a wide range of lifestyles. Time compression has led to a shift away from consumption of goods to consumption of services, which often have a shorter "lifetime" and thus can be marketed more often.

Youth have been particularly affected by globalizing forces of time compression, as they rapidly construct, revise, and consume new identities based upon information that becomes available to them—and that they create and disseminate—through multiple electronic devices and social media networks. Educators have limited resources to integrate 21st-century youth identities and experiences into the 20th-century curricula and instructional processes that remain in place in most schools. Textbooks, still reliant on print media, also remain tied to multi-year replacement cycles. Thus, school systems cannot take advantage of advances in electronic publishing and electronic e-readers, which have rapidly come to dominate the world of publishing in the early 21st century. The lack of access to technology in schooling amplifies this disconnect between 20th-century schooling practices and 21st-century globalized realities and the manifestations of time compression.

In addition to the compression of time, there has also been a decrease in the significance of physical distance. Satellite communications, airfreight, containerization, mass media consumption, and the internet have all contributed to space compression. Location or physical distance is less relevant than the economic conditions of a place. Manufacturers quickly move from one location in Mexico to another in South Asia, for example, in order to take advantage of more favorable market conditions for labor costs or tax structures. Specific locations have also been altered to make them more attractive to mobile capital, as in corporatizing of local governance in Bangalore, India to attract technology and customer service industries. The less significant the spatial barriers, notes Harvey, the greater the incentive for places to be differentiated in ways attractive to capital. Heightened competition has led to emphasis on relative locational advantage; paradoxically then small differences in location take on heightened significance. For example, Shenzhen, China, located directly across the border from Hong Kong, serves as the location for thousands of factories producing everything from shoes to electronics, while Hong Kong (still a "Special Administrative Area" of China) specializes in value-added financial, insurance, and related services to facilitate the process of trade with China.

Schools, however, remain tied to static systems. They have yet to respond, for example, to the mobility of families' labor migrations. Attendance policies tend to punish students who move seasonally or reside in multiple places, only sometimes allowing limited independent studies to accommodate these migrations. Though technologies exist that would allow students to participate from a distance, few efforts have been made to enroll them in multiple districts, share data across school sites or national borders, enable students to video conference into classrooms, or participate via distance learning programs.

Despite the assumption in education that schools serve static neighborhoods, the organization of information, capital, labor, and family in a globalized era no longer relies wholly on geographical location. It has been transformed through the structure of globalization. This structure, sociologist Manuel Castells argues, is a network of interconnected nodes. A node can be a stock exchange, a council of ministers, a collection of coca fields, a money-laundering institution, or a grouping of school districts. Networks are open structures, able to expand without geographical or chronological limit. In network logic, the geographical distance between two points is irrelevant because if both points are nodes on the same network, then they are the same functional distance from each other. Thus, inclusion in or exclusion from a network—and the relationships between networks—determines access. Microfinance institutions, for example, with networks in indigenous communities in Central America may mean that one village connected to "fair trade" distribution outlets has more immediate access to raw materials and capital in developed nations than in a neighboring city. Though geographically closer, it may not be in the network.

The globalized economy is organized through transnational networks of capital, management, and information, where access to technological know-how is the basis of productivity and competitiveness. Lotteries to get into desirable charter schools, for example, appear to be an equitable means of enrolling students because they are random, but the knowledge of how to apply for the lottery is held by particular, privileged parent networks, where information is unevenly disseminated, shaped by class and race barriers. Thus, some parents who live in close proximity to a desirable charter school may still have no access to the network that holds information about enrollment or program offerings.

The pervasiveness of networking forms of management and production, suggests Castells, mean that capitalist modes of production now shape social relationships globally. Capital exists in what Castells calls "the space of flows, while labor exists in 'the space of places'" (1996, p. 378). Workers and work do not disappear in the global network of capital flows, but the social relationships between capital and labor are transformed. Globalization has thus transformed not only labor and capital, but also social relationships and identities. Relationships are formed in reaction to the forces of globalization and whether one is positioned within the network. According to sociologist Alain Touraine,

> In a post-industrial society, in which cultural services have replaced material goods at the core of its production, it is the defense of the subject, in its personality and its culture, against the logic of apparatuses and markets, that replaces the idea of class struggle (1994, p. 168).

The fear of homogenization or cultural absorption by polities of a larger scale is only one piece of globalization processes, which, according to Appadurai, can no longer be explained by center-periphery models even those that account for multiple centers and peripheries. Communities in the global economy exist with "no sense of place," contributing to their hyper-real or imaginary quality. The larger polities, such as the US, no longer dominate the transactions in a one-sided manner, rather they function to construct and export/import "imaginary landscapes," primarily through media products. Instead of using static, national identities to define communities, Appadurai offers an alternative model of cultural transactions that defines five scapes or categories of cultural interactions, movements, and flows: Ethnoscapes—movement of people (tourists, immigrants, refugees, etc.); Technoscapes—movement of technologies (mechanical and informational); Financescapes—rapid flow of global capital (currency, stocks, commodities); Mediascapes—distribution of information through various media (film, newspapers, magazines, TV); and Ideoscapes—movement (and reinterpretation) of ideologies (terms like *democracy, freedom, rights,* and *citizenship*) (Appadurai, 1996).

Myths of Globalization

Globalization is widely viewed as a one-way, Western-driven economic force that homogenizes local culture in the image of the West. Though often regarded as a new phenomena, globalization has long, often unrecognized histories. The common belief that globalization is a recent phenomena limited to the economic sector is challenged by historian Walter Mignolo. Over the past 500 years, Mignolo identifies four major overlapping and co-existing forces of globalization: Christianity, the Civilizing Mission, Development, and the Global Market (Mignolo, 2000; Quijano, 2000).

The first two forces of globalization, Christianity and the Civilizing Mission, spread European values and ways of knowing in the "new" world. From the perspective of European observers, the geographical boundaries of the world that was known to them represented the limits of humanity. What lay beyond the frontier was "vacant land" from the point of view of economy and government and "empty space" in terms of theory and intellectual development. Through defeat of the Moors, expulsion of Jews, and the "discovery" of America, the hegemony of Christianity was legitimated by its promise to help "civilize" and "save" distant places and peoples. Missionary zeal to save souls eventually gave way to the ideology of modernization and development. European views of Others in the lands they colonized or sought to dominate thus shifted from savages and cannibals in the 1600s to primitives, exotics, and Orientals in the late 1800s. A repurposed metanarrative of progress emerged in the post-World War II era, establishing development and modernization as goals for former colonies that emerged as new nation-states. Through maintaining a discourse of the Other, European powers continue to legitimize the colonizing and globalizing of indigenous communities, positioning them as the beneficiaries of modernization. Global markets now enable colonialism to operate without a colonizing nation, through transnational corporations and market penetration.

The constant positioning of the West as the center and the rest of the world as peripheral perpetuates the belief that globalizing forces have been exclusively initiated in the West. Though the West, and the US in particular, have dominated a world system of images, globalization does not just spread from the West to the East, nor does it only result in "Americanization." As Appadurai argues,

> It is worth noticing that for the people of Irian Jaya, Indonesianization may be more worrisome than Americanization, as Japanization may be for Koreans, Indianization for Sri Lankans, Vietnamization for Cambodians, Russianization for the people of Soviet Armenia and the Baltic Republics (1996, p. 40).

There are also multiple examples of population movements that predate Western industrialization. As Luke and Luke note,

> In the case of Thailand, Central Siam in the nineteenth century was accustomed to a polyethnic population long before the term 'multiculturalism' was invented... and the massive numbers of Chinese who migrated to Siam, beginning in the eighteenth century via the junk trade... has been key to Thailand's post-World War II economic expansion (2000, p. 284).

Another common assumption is that globalization is an inevitable force of cultural homogenization. In its focus on Westernization or Americanization, most dialogue about globalization in education and the media assumes that globalization means the end of local cultures. Images of teens across the globe clad in hip hop attire, listening to English language pop songs, and consuming American fast food products reinforce the widespread myth that globalization leads to cultural homogenization. As Luke and Luke observe in their studies of globalization in Asia:

> On the Myanmar-Thai border, kids wear Chicago Bulls hats back to front, pirated copies of Hong Kong videos and CDs are on offer, and Thai-made Toyota pickup trucks rule the road.... Yet there is more than meets the Western eye to globalization in Asia. It is analytically tempting and rhetorically powerful to describe the practices and consequences of globalization principally around the metaphor of the Golden Arches.... Yet such a position risks flattening out, one-dimensionalizing, the complex processes of globalization. These processes are not simply uncritical reproductions of Western cultures. Rather, their formation flows out of (1) a hybridization and reappropriation of Western cultures; and (2) long-standing incorporations and appropriations of other Asian and regional cultures (2000, pp. 282–283).

Though globalization involves such instruments of homogenization as advertising techniques, language hegemonies, popular music, fast food, or clothing styles, they are often absorbed into local cultural economies to remerge as cultural hybrids. The meanings of imported products and texts are constantly in translation and adopted according to the histories of individual communities. Thus, the English-lyric hip hop songs that youth play across the globe may refer more to the solidarity they feel to their peers and local identity politics, than to an affinity for America or the West. As cultural theorist H. Samy Alim suggests, "In the same way that local Hip Hop artists build community and construct social organization through rhyming practices… Hip Hop communities worldwide interact with each other… in ways that organize their participation in a mass-mediated cultural movement" (2009, p. 1; Alim, et. al, 2009; Besley, 2003; Maira & Soep, 2005).

Globalization is often credited with the loss, in particular, of linguistic diversity. Yet there is evidence that the technologies introduced through globalization can also help maintain local languages and cultural practices. The globalization of information flows, for example, has enhanced the accessibility of networking for the impoverished communities of Chiapas in southern Mexico. During the Zapatista rebellion of the 1990s, indigenous people adopted modern technologies, including written Spanish and the internet, to articulate the discriminatory assimilation policies of the Mexican government and to build international support for bilingual education reform and political resistance. Similar patterns of using globalizing technologies can be seen in the building of global solidarity among scattered cultural groups such as the Hmong (Miao) of Southeast Asia and Southern China and their diasporic counterparts in Minnesota and California, or the Basques of the Pyrenees in Spain and France and members of that community who have migrated to Nevada, Idaho, and California (Alonso & Arzoz, 2003; Reinke, 2004; Schein, 1998).

Globalizing forces can have mixed effects for local communities. The introduction of Wal-Mart in Mexico, for example, simultaneously disrupts rural and agricultural economies and environmental sustainability by eliminating local agricultural distribution networks and farmer's markets in favor of mass-produced goods, while also offering low cost products and technologies that give low-income communities access to globalized markets and information flows. Throughout its history, globalization has been fraught with paradoxes and contradictions. Globalizing forces both widen and narrow income gaps between nations, diminish or intensify political domination, and lead to both homogeneity and hybridized cultural identities.

Globalization, argue Luke and Luke, is neither a story of "rapacious Western multinationals nor hapless Eastern victims" (2000, p. 286). Though it is often assumed that globalization is a negative, homogenizing force on local cultures, they argue that the people of East Asia do not feel particularly "contaminated" or "disrupted." They claim that even the concept of subaltern (any social group excluded from hegemonic power structures) cannot be applied without regard to its Western focus or the Western tendency to produce and theorize the Other. "[Subaltern] is certainly not a concept of identity that many East Asian cultures readily adopt or identify with" (Luke & Luke, 2000, p. 286).

Diasporas, Borderlands, and Elastic Communities

Despite the context of globalization, an assimilation model remains predominant in US and other Western-influenced schools that assume migration is a one-time event rather than an ongoing, dialogical process. School policies are generally based on a traditional, straight-line, three-generation immigrant assimilation pattern in which each succeeding generation adopts more and more of the dominant culture. Attendance regulations, semester schedules, and English-only mandates tie students' culture to their current place of residence and view national identity as singular and fixed. The standard definition of community in education refers to "a discriminable population with a single bounded space—a territory or place" (Rouse, 1996, p. 248). Anthropologist Roger Rouse adds: "It also assumes that members will treat the place of the community as the principal environment to which they adjust their actions, and correspondingly, that they will monitor local events much more closely than developments farther afield" (1996, p. 249). A bounded notion of community denies the rising number of students who straddle two or more communities or nations and maintain social relationships across large distances (Gordon, 1964; Waters & Jimenez, 2005).

"The saliency of nation-ness is not diminished," argues Westwood, "and yet the understandings of nations in a globalized world have shifted" (2000, p. 19). Though nations remain a potent force in defining communities, they are no longer linked to fixed territories. This deterritorialization describes the loss of what was previously seen as a natural relation of culture to specific territories or geographical locations. Deterritorialization also indicates that certain cultural meanings and processes transcend specific territorial boundaries in a world where images and meanings are in motion.

Student experiences defy both traditional conceptions of bounded communities and the notion of stable identities that can be contained by single-descriptors. The drawings and narratives of elementary school students from one California urban school provide an example of how significant physical and symbolic borders can be in ordering students' lives. As part of a self-portrait/autobiography project, a group of fifth-grade students, who were living between a city in the US and various urban and indigenous communities in El Salvador, Guatemala, and Mexico, were asked to create a map of important places in their lives. They were instructed to illustrate at least three places, ranging from general landscapes to a specific corner of a bedroom, using community maps, road atlases, and world maps for reference. The student-created maps included the places they frequented, parks and schools, and many high-status locations, ranging from the local mall to chain restaurants, bowling alleys, toy stores, and fairgrounds. Almost all of the maps also included traced outlines of multiple nation-states. The students' maps were not reproductions of given geographies, but rather represented family histories and complex cartographies of belonging (Blakely, 2007).

The ways students connected nations in their drawings signaled their distinct transnational relationships. One student, for example, drew a unidirectional arrow, documenting her family's one-way trip from Mexico to the US. Another student drew a solid thick line, like a road or thoroughfare to connect the tip of Guatemala to the edge of the US. Her drawing documented her family's constant movement between the two countries, spending two seasons in each place every year. Still others drew multiple isolated countries, disconnected and floating on the page. One student disregarded the teacher's directions to draw at least three important places and instead drew a single diagonal line across his page. He topped the long line with barbed wire and wrote "border" in crayon across the fence. On the opposite side of the page he drew a giant Mexican flag. When the teacher asked him how this fence-line could be his "map of most important places," he responded, "because that is where we cross. That is where my uncle died." The border is primary for many students located between cultures, as echoed in the words of feminist cultural theorist and poet Gloria Anzaldúa: "This is my home, this thin edge of barbwire" (1999, pp. 24–25).

Students live in communities separated and policed on geopolitical terms, but also joined by legal and illegal practices of crossing and communication (Clifford, 1997). Anzaldúa terms this spatial and cultural juncture the borderlands: "a vague and undetermined place created by the emotional residue of an unnatural boundary. It is in a constant state of transition" (1999, p. 25). Similarly, historian Madeline Hsu uses the term "elastic community" to describe, for instance, the historical migration practices of laborers from Taishan County in Guangdong, southern China to the US: "Continually in transit, they belonged neither here nor there; they were not really American and not really Chinese" (2000, p. 3).

There is growing evidence of "flexible citizenship," argues anthropologist Aihwa Ong. Mobile Asian managers, technocrats, and professionals seeking to circumvent and benefit from different nation-state regimes select different sites for investment, work, and family. As Ong describes it:

> Flexible citizenship refers to the cultural logics of capitalist accumulation, travel, and displacement that induce subjects to respond fluidly and opportunistically changing political-economic conditions. In their quest to accumulate capital and

social prestige in the global arena, subjects emphasize, and are regulated by, practices favoring flexibility, mobility, and repositioning in relation to markets, govern-
ments, and cultural regimes. These logics and practices are produced within
particular structures of meaning about family, gender, nationality, class mobility,
and social power (1999, p. 6).

A broad collection of terms are used in cultural theory to describe experiences that resist conventional depictions of culture as static and territori-
ally-bound. As Clifford observes, "An unruly crowd of descriptive/
interpretative terms now jostle and converse in an effort to characterize the
contact zones of nations, cultures, regions: terms such as 'border,' 'travel,'
'creolization,' 'transculturation,' 'hybridity,' and 'diaspora' (as well as the
looser 'diasporic')" (1997, p. 245). The term diaspora refers specifically to
displaced people who maintain, revive, or invent a connection to a prior
home. This connection is strong and resists erasure through the normalizing
processes of forgetting, assimilating, and distancing. Diasporas have the
following features, argues Clifford: a history of dispersal, nostalgia or
longing for the homeland, alienation in the host country, desire for eventual
return, ongoing pride or support of the homeland, and a collective identity
defined by this relationship. Diasporas encompass a wide range of populations and historical situations, ranging from the classic understanding of the
Jewish and African/Atlantic diasporas to contemporary, evolving diasporic
networks that see continual movement back and forth. Historically, diasporas
signaled a community separated by large distances with only a remote
possibility of return. The "old" diasporas, literary theorist Gayatri Chakra-
vorty Spivak argues, were caused by religious oppression, war, slavery,
indenturing, trade and conquest, and intra-European migration. The "new"
diasporas are offshoots of contemporary globalization that include the
migration of skilled labor to developed nations, the migration within nations
from rural to urban areas, and political asylums (Spivak, 1988).

In both old and new diasporas, it is common for immigrants to recreate
national communities when settling across borders, often forming pipelines
from one nation to another. Among the many examples of this are the
communities between San Francisco, California and Hong Kong, or Brook-
lyn, New York and Haiti. Urban clusters of immigrants are often formed,
such as Little Saigon in Orange County, California, Little Haiti in Miami,
Florida, or France's I'Ile St-Denis—a suburb of Paris where immigrants from
North African colonies cluster in what are now often referred to as Muslim
ghettos or *banlieues*. Moving across borders can even strengthen or consoli-
date national ties with new claims to identity, such as the Puerto Ricans in
New York City (many of whom are second or third generation American

citizens) who host Puerto Rican festivals and parades, display the Puerto Rican flag on windows, tattoos, T-shirts, and describe themselves as "Nuyoricans."

This establishment of national groups in new locations, referred to as reterritorialization, often occurs immediately after deterritorialization, and the two phenomena are sometimes seamlessly linked. An example of reterritorialization from the Central and Latin American diasporas can be seen in the rapid growth of Spanish language media and entertainment in the US. The *telenovelas* (Spanish language TV soap operas) produced by Mexican companies in Miami, Florida both deterritorialize and reterritorialize identities. The globalization of media paradoxically functions to reinforce national identities. For example, Westwood argues, *telenovelas* "generate a national space shared in time and place by viewers," which becomes "a common currency" and creates "a sense of belonging essential to the production of national identities" (2000, p. 28).

Anthropologist Louisa Schein provides an example of how the realities within diasporic communities—in this case the Hmong culture—defy prevailing territorialized, essentialist conceptions of communities. The Hmong are an ethnic group from the mountainous regions of China, Vietnam, Laos, and Thailand. As a result of their recruitment to fight for the US during the Vietnam War, many Hmong fled their homeland and resettled as refugees in the US and other Western countries in the mid-1970s. Despite a rhetoric of unity that surrounds the community spread across multiple sites in the US, Australia, Vietnam, Canada, France, Argentina, Thailand, and Laos, there is disagreement even over their name. "Miao" is the official designation of this minority nationality within China, where some have achieved positions of respect in Chinese society. However, many coethnics abroad reject the term imposed by China as derogatory and refer to themselves instead as "Hmong." As Schein concludes,

> The divisions and political struggles around the ethnonyms Miao and Hmong highlight the obstacles to internal unity and the extent to which solidarity is a fragile edifice constructed upon the ground of tenuous identifications. Much cultural production and identity formation is entailed in the forging of transnationality (1998, p. 186).

Case in Point: US-Mexico Transnational Migrant Circuits

In his studies of the Aguilillan population from Michoacán in Redwood City, California, Rouse documents how the constant migration between a California suburb and a rural Mexican town have created "one community in two nations." He terms this a "transnational migrant circuit," which defines the continuous circulation of people, money, and goods between separate places as a community. The constant border crossing experiences defy the deficit-assimilation model still prevalent in education, which assumes that crossing the border is a one-way trip to a better life and a stable, irrevocable choice to accept a new identity, language, and community.

The residents of this transnational migrant circuit equip themselves and their children to operate effectively on both sides of the border through dual citizenship, bilinguality, and schooling. As Rouse argues,

> Today, Aguilillans find that their most important kin and friends are as likely to be living hundreds or thousands of miles away as immediately around them. More significantly, they are often able to maintain these spatially extended relationships as actively and effectively as the ties that link them to their neighbors (1996, p. 253–254).

In Aguililla, Mexico teens wear the latest clothing purchased in Redwood City, "RWC" is spray-painted on blank walls, and donkeys roam the streets next to SUVs with California plates. Many Aguilillans know more about Redwood City than their state capital, Morelia. Likewise, in California mariachi bands play *ranchera* music from home in Redwood City's "Little Aguililla" restaurants. Rouse concludes that the two locations, Aguililla and Redwood City, now constitute a single community. Rouse illustrates many outcomes of this flow of people, capital, images, and products.

> In a small village in the heart of Mexico, a young woman at her father's wake wears a black T-shirt sent to her by her brother in the US. The shirt bears a legend that some of the mourners understand but she does not. It reads, "Let's Have Fun Tonight!" (Rouse, 1996, p. 247).

Aguilillans maintain two distinct ways of life and expect that these contradictions will continue for their children. This cultural bifocality plays out, for example, in two distinct class identities. In the US the Aguilillan migrants are working-class, whereas in Aguililla they are part of an entrepreneurial class.

> Aguilillans see their current life and future possibilities as involving simultaneous engagements in places associated with markedly different forms of experience. Moreover, the way in which at least some people are preparing their children to operate within a dichotomized setting spanning national borders suggests that current contradictions will not be resolved through a simple process of generational succession (Rouse, 1996, p. 255).

Transnational migrant circuits, suggests Rouse, disrupt the traditional linear understanding of economic and cultural assimilation processes. The conventional perspective on migration as a movement from one set of social relationships to another does not recognize the contradictions that arise when people combine practices from their homeland with those of their new residence.

Although it is generally presumed that the US is a receiving country and Mexico is a sending country for migrant families, transnational educational researchers Victor Zuñiga and Edmund Hamann report on the experiences of large numbers of transnational students who have moved in the reverse direction, returning to Mexico after having lived and gone to school in the US for several years. For these transnational students, becoming fluent in the language of their host country and learning its norms is insufficient, for they need to (re)learn the language and cultural norms of their sending country as well.

The researchers gathered data from Mexican classmates, asking for their opinions of their newly-returned classmates. The opinions were positive overall, generally referring to the English-speaking ability of the transnationals, although there were some negative comments about the quality of the US education system, "especially mathematics."

Zuñiga and Hamann also interviewed Mexican teachers, discovering that transnational students were usually invisible to them. Even when transnational students were recognized by teachers, they reported that the transnational students were behind their native Mexican peers. According to one teacher,

> There are a lot of *those* children who can express their ideas well in Spanish, but when we ask them to write something, you can see they cannot write; they do not know how to write it. Look at their notes! Look at their homework, it is impossible to understand! ... There are a lot of mistakes. They change the words; they cannot distinguish a 'b' from a 'd' (Zuñiga & Hamann, 2009, p. 345, italics added).

Another teacher declared, "They mixed both languages; they speak Spanglish," and a third teacher said, "They speak unacceptable Spanish." Several teachers also complained about the transnational students' lack of knowledge about history and geography.

When teachers realized that there were transnational students in their classrooms, they expressed interest in supporting them, but they had no idea how to support them. They often generated paternalistic responses or expressed their own need to learn English in order to be able to teach the transnational students, showing little or no understanding of the possibility of developing a second language learner pedagogy for the transnational students. This mirrors the responses heard from teachers in traditional receiving countries who describe "those" students as at-risk.

The majority of the transnational students in Mexico (78% of Zuñiga and Hamann's study) expressed a desire to return to school in the US in the future. In general, they reported favorably on their US schooling experience. Those who had the highest self-perceptions of their own English proficiency, as well as those who self-identified as American or Mexican American (as opposed to Mexican) also expressed stronger desires to return to the US. Zuñiga and Hamann's work suggests that the prospect of enduring geographic mobility affects the complicated work of identity formation and affiliation for transnational students. Central to this negotiation are Mexican schools, which like US schools, are rarely designed to consider the needs, understandings, or interests of a transnational, mobile population.

Flexible Citizenship

Historically, citizenship required an exclusive allegiance to a state, though there was considerable variation as to how states defined citizenship and how they articulated citizen's rights and responsibilities. Citizenship is no longer a unitary category or a mere legal status. "The aggressive nationalism and territorial competition among European states in the eighteenth, nineteenth, and well into the twentieth centuries" made dual or multiple nationalities an unthinkable or unfavorable concept, "incompatible with individual loyalties and destabilizing of the international order" (Sassen, 2002, p. 7). Transformations in labor, capital, and technology at the end of the 20th century, however, changed the parameters of citizenship and nationality and made it possible to conceive of dual or multiple nationalities as the norm.

The terms *citizen* and *nationality* continue to refer to the legal status of an individual. They are not, however, simply formal descriptions of state membership, but rather represent a normative project implicated in the formation of individual rights, identities, and aspirations. From ancient times to present, citizenship has entailed a discursive struggle over the meaning of community membership. The articulation of citizenship is dependent not only on state-sponsored definitions of who legally qualifies as a citizen, but also on the norms of the community, which regulate social membership. Formal equality as citizens does not indicate inclusion or full participation in public life. Many groups defined by race, gender, class, or other identities are excluded from many of the rights and privileges of the state, while some undocumented immigrants are able to navigate state systems and engage in the same routine practices of formally defined citizens.

Border crossings have created a series of new forms of informal citizenship. Undocumented immigrants from Guatemala and El Salvador, living illegally in the US, are one example of a community that is "unauthorized yet recognized." Their daily practices—employment, schooling, family life—represent partial if not full participation in the US akin to "effective" rather than "formal citizenship." Undocumented immigrants are negotiating tensions not only between citizenship norms in their place of residence and their place of origin, but also between changing gender and social relationships. Immigrant women, for example, may move into the public sphere as a result of the availability of regular wage work, namely housecleaning and childcare. They may also have unique access to public services in their role as mothers or caretakers may shift their "culturally specified subordinate role to men in the household. Immigrant women gain greater personal autonomy and independence while immigrant men lose ground compared to what was their condition in cultures of origin" (Sassen, 2002, p. 15). These cultural tensions can surface in many ways in the classroom and can conflict with school expectations around, for example, parent involvement. Notices sent home to recruit "Room Moms," for example, may discourage the involvement of families where the father has taken on domestic responsibilities in absence of full-time employment or access to higher-wage work.

Citizenship is not an either/or matter, but exists along a continuum from full citizenship to second-class citizenship, which is defined distinctly by different classes. In a low-income neighborhood, Rosaldo observes that first class citizenship is defined in a vernacular way by access to goods and services, jobs, health care, housing, and education. In contrast, in higher-income communities, first class citizenship is a matter of well-being, thriving, dignity, safety, respect, and acknowledgment. "The process of learning vernacular definitions of full to second class citizenship involves the art of listening attentively to how concerned parties conceive, say, equity and well-being" (Rosaldo, 1994, p. 402). In addition to understanding local perceptions of equity, Rosaldo argues, static, legal notions of citizenship need to be replaced with the idea of "cultural citizenship" or understanding citizenship as participatory membership in a group. Rosaldo advocates for the notion of a polyglot citizen or individuals who have multiple national and community memberships and the ability to mix and blend them. There are, he suggests, contradictory processes of absorption and rejection simultaneously at work: "The undocumented both comply and deviate, bobbing and weaving between assimilation and resistance. They neither remain what they once were nor become fully absorbed into the culturally transparent Anglo-American middle class" (1989, p. 211).

Assimilating into the nation-state while still maintaining connections to a prior homeland are not, transnational theorists argue, necessarily contradictory social processes, but can occur simultaneously. Transnational researchers Peggy Levitt and Nina Glick Schiller describe how individuals often incorporate daily activities, routines, and institutions located in both a destination country and a homeland, or even a scattered global network of relatives and associates. They term this condition "simultaneity," arguing that "migrant incorporation into a new land and transnational connections to a homeland or to dispersed networks of family, compatriots, or persons who share a religious or ethnic identity can occur at the same time and reinforce one another" (2008, p. 284).

Transnational subjects occupy many social fields at once. Bourdieu describes social fields as the networks between individuals or institutions—domains with fluid boundaries where social relationships are structured by power. Levitt and Schiller expand on this notion by defining a social field as a set of interlocking networks of social relationships, where resources are unevenly exchanged, organized, and transformed. They use this concept to describe an array of transnational experiences: "Social fields contain institutions, organizations, and experiences, within their various levels, that generate categories of identity that are ascribed to or chosen by individuals or groups" (2008, p. 287).

Schein, for example, investigates how members of diasporic communities adapt, perform and assimilate American, masculine identities through their participation in the social field of a local Boy Scout troop. The Hmong participation in the Boy Scouts documents how institutions can simultaneously promote assimilation—the making of "American boys"—while also Othering the Hmong boys and reinforcing their identities of difference. The Hmong boys, Schein suggests, "already well trained in filial duty through their 'Asian' heritage, emerge as especially inspiring, effectively outscouting White Scouts in their respect for elders and offering a new spin on the notion of Asians as 'model'" (1998, p. 184). This display of Southeast Asian refugees joining the American Boy Scouts to teach Americans better American values is one example of the ways the "transnational jostles up against the nation and the state" (Schein, 1998, p. 185) in the creation of youth identities.

Individuals may be embedded in a particular social field, but choose not to act or identify with labels or cultural politics associated with that field. Levitt and Schiller distinguish between ways of being and ways of belonging. "Ways of being" refers to the actual social relations and practices that individuals engage in, rather than to the identities associated with their actions. "Ways of belonging," in contrast, refers to practices that signal or enact an identity, which demonstrates conscious connection to a particular group. Students' displays of clothing (T-shirts with national soccer team logos), locker decorations (flag stickers or national slogans), and regional music selections, all demonstrate ways of belonging to nation-states or related identities. As educational researcher Thea Renda Abu El-Haj documents, students display national affiliations by decorating their schoolwork, clothing, backpacks, key chains, and jewelry with national symbols. She argues that the nationalist longing for an independent state amplifies national displays for Palestinian students in one US urban high school. When asked to create a tile for an after school mosaic project that represented themselves, the students drew the Palestinian flag, the Dome of the Rock (the golden-domed Islamic shrine, housing the rock from which Muslims believe the Prophet Muhammad ascended to heaven), the black and white checked *keffiyeh* headscarves that signal the resistance movement, or they wrote Palestine across their tile in Arabic calligraphy, assembling a mosaic that was "bursting with symbols of Palestine" (Abu El-Haj, 2007, p. 8).

"Being American," thus, involves everyday practices and commonsense beliefs generated in many social fields. Students may claim, "I am from Palestine," though they were born in the US and have spent their entire life living in the US. Abu El-Haj documents how US high school students forge identities that are "culturally produced at the nexus of multiple, intermingling systems" (2007, p. 6). Students may simultaneously acknowledge that they are "American Palestinian" while rejecting that they are both American and Palestinian, claiming "I don't think of myself as both. I only think of myself as Arab... I just want to be a Palestinian... I was born here, but my home, it's not here" (Abu El-Haj, 2007, p. 6). Schools have historically functioned as gateways, where rights of citizenship are granted or limited. Schools are key places, argues Abu El-Haj, where students grapple with complex identities and affiliations and construct national and citizenship identities. The identities youth craft often

> involve a fractured rather than a hybrid or even hyphenated sense of identity....
> [T]he capacity to participate fully and contribute meaningfully depends on helping
> [students] develop a sense of belonging in this era of transnational migration, as
> youth are positioned and position themselves in relation to multiple imagined com-
> munities (Abu El-Haj, 2007, pp. 6, 2).

Students in many classrooms frequently demonstrate the importance of national affiliations as a way of positioning themselves on a social hierarchy, as well as the simultaneity possible in those affiliations. They add national flags, country outlines, and the names of nations to the margins of their paper not only to signal affiliations to a prior home, but also affiliations with classroom peers. When asked to color paper cutout organs to create a scale model of the human body, for example, one fifth-grade student in California used red, green, and white to create the Mexican flag across his paper cutout stomach. The national flag drawn on his work did not, however, signal his place of origin, family, national pride, or longing for a prior home; he was from Guatemala. Like many other students in the same class who decorated their schoolwork with the Mexican flag, he attached it to link himself to his group of friends and their cultural status. His community ranked those who came from places closer to the US border higher than the Mayan-speaking families from the indigenous communities of Central America. As Levitt and Schiller put it, "Because these individuals have some sort of connection to a way of belonging, through memory, nostalgia, or imagination, they can enter the social field when and if they choose to do so" (2008, p. 287).

In another instance, fourth-grade boys in the same Northern California school were told to list ten ways to describe themselves. One student named Saul wrote, "1) I'm from San Rafael." Roger, the student next to him read over his shoulder and said aloud, "Oh, I'm from San Francisco." He copied this onto his page. The student across the table wrote, "I'm from El Salvador." When Saul saw this entry, he erased "I'm from San Rafael" and wrote over it, "I'm from El Salvador," while Roger instead added, "2) I'm from El Salvador." The narratives of transnational students contain complexities and contradictions that teachers or students may try to edit without recognition of the simultaneity inherent in their experience. The typical fill-in-the-blank activities and writing rubrics in many mandated public school curricula, for example, require students to stick to "one main topic" and provide supporting evidence for each point, often eliminating possibilities for students to express and explore simultaneity. Students are generally taught to edit out or chronologize the contradictions in their narratives rather than explore the possibilities of simultaneous ways of being and belonging.

The bounded notion of citizenship and identity in discussions of learning, literacy, and achievement, ignores the border crossing of many families and the flexible forms of citizenship many students adopt. There are many complex ways teachers and students use and respond to the ideoscape of citizenship. Teachers often use the term "citizenship," for instance, as a character-building norm, alongside respect and honesty, to refer to desired classroom behaviors. This meaning of citizenship, however, is complicated by many immigrant student and family perspectives, where citizenship refers to an unattainable legal status. Thus, teacher admonitions to "be a good citizen" may not have their intended effect.

Globalized Marketplaces and Youth Identities

Consumption and the role of affinity groups has replaced or augmented the nation-state as the main way individuals construct and maintain identities. Youth identities are formed at "the intersections between popular culture practices, national ideologies, and global markets" (Maria & Soep, 2005, p. xv). In a globalized era where relations of social belonging are steeped in consumption, youth cross national, ethnic, and linguistic borders, developing hybrid identities. Youth are drawn into local communities, national ideologies, and global markets, yet they tend to occupy an ambiguous space within and between them. They are not only the recipients and frequent targets of globalizing forces; youth also actively participate in creating and reshaping global products locally. Through using technologies, producing and reshaping popular culture media, crafting multilingual and multimedia texts, and developing cross-ethnic solidarities and transnational networks, youth are themselves forces of globalization. Media, images, and products promoted by multinational corporations shape the possibilities for young people to create new forms of identity and knowledge, though as consumers they deconstruct and actively reshape corporate-sponsored materials (Alim, et. al., 2009; Besley, 2003; Lam, 2006; Sarkar & Winer, 2006).

Though institutions and nationalisms remain integral to identity development and citizenship status, the processes by which youth form identities and achieve citizenship are not limited to schools, state institutions, religious groups, or other organizations. As García Canclini writes,

> For men and women, especially youth, the questions specific to citizenship, such as how we inform ourselves and who represents our interests, are answered more often than not through private consumption of commodities and media offerings than through the abstract rules of democracy or through participation in discredited legal organizations (2001, p. 5).

The brands of clothes or shoes that students wear, the content of their iPod playlists, and the icons or images displayed on their phone or computer screen backgrounds may provide more telling signals of their identity, peer affiliations, and cultural status than traditional designations of social position via religious affiliations, family employment, or state citizenship.

One of the primary ways that youth signal their identities and affinities is through consumption of products and media. Baudrillard argues that "people define themselves in relation to objects.... [and] actualize themselves in consumption" (1988, pp. 16, 12). Consumption does not refer here to simply purchasing a product, but to the entire range of symbolic uses of products, services, technologies and people. Consumption, according to Baudrillard, is a coded system of signs through which people communicate with each other.

Marx defined a commodity as "an object outside us, a thing that by its properties satisfies human wants of some sort or another.... To become a commodity a product must be transferred to another, whom it will serve as a use-value, by means of exchange" (Marx, 1971, p. 48). The difference between a commodity and a product is that a commodity must be exchanged and have attached "social use values" connected to a specific historical epoch. Objects can move in and out of the commodity state with movements that can be "slow or fast, reversible or terminal, normative or deviant" (Appadurai, 1986, p. 13). Thus, a commodity is not one type of object rather than another, but one phase in its life. Some things are frequently found in the commodity phase and they become the quintessential commodities of a society, whereas other things may move into a commodity phase most intensely at certain periods, such as women who may be highly commoditized during marriage negotiations.

The value of commodities is inseparable from the context of their exchange; goods and services are often bartered or priced across divergent cultural frameworks and in ways that are dependent on needs specific to time and circumstance. There are many stereotypical instances in history of value divergence in "intercultural exchanges," where Africans, Asians, or Amerindians traded away land and resources for European trinkets. In other cases, the West, with its taste for the things of the past and of the Other, turns objects produced for aesthetic or ceremonial reasons in small-scale societies into "tourist art" in the marketplaces of larger economies seeking authentic or unique items for display. The value of objects is often intensified in their decontextualization, for example, by displaying utilitarian objects like Indian baskets or African spears in affluent homes or museum collections. Consumer culture plays a significant role in creating a "world without boundaries"; it allows consumers to travel through purchases.

Youth now face a highly commodified world, where most things in their society meet the criteria of a commodity. Not only are goods and services the objects of consumption, but the body and culture have also become commodities. The commodification of the body, for instance, means that it is not only used to sell things in advertisements, but it is also an object that can be pampered, adorned, and improved by a broad range of therapies, regimens, diets, clothing, jewelry, tattoos, or piercings. Youth from early ages are trained in the habits and disciplines of consumerism, as advertising techniques propel the mixing of style and identity to develop niche markets and create demand. Fashion, celebrity images, TV and film merchandising, sports paraphernalia, music, video games, smartphone apps, social media, and the associated advertising, all provide youth with the material to craft hybridized personal identities. These identities may feel unique given the broad range of choices in the marketplace, but they also reflect specific limits set by the kinds of products available and the practices and values of consumerism. As Besley argues:

> Kids assemble their identities in the global marketplace on the basis of what their local culture predisposes them to make. They make individual choices that are reinforced by market logic that creates them as niche markets that... has the effect of manufacturing, legitimating, and then exploiting their identities/subjectivities (2003, p. 168).

Buying and wearing the rapid-turnover, high-fashion clothes from the malls, boutiques, and marketplaces of the globalized world, for example, enables young consumers to send messages about their status and rank, suggesting the illusion of total access and choice. Yet, as Baudrillard and Bourdieu show, the establishments that control the fashion industry effectively limit social mobility and mark social rank by "placing consumers in a game whose ever-shifting rules are determined by 'taste-makers' and their affiliated experts who dwell at the top of society" (Appadurai, 1986, p. 32).

Culture itself has become an object of intense commodification. Cultural commodification occurs when the red, black and green colors of the African Liberation Army are marketed globally on apparel and shoes without any reference to the histories of those symbols or the meanings behind them (red to represent bloodshed; black for the African people; and green for the stolen land). The colors become a fashion statement rather than a message of resistance. As another example, English-speakers ink Chinese characters on their bodies that they cannot read. They may believe their tattoos signal association with exotic places, worldliness, or enlightened, spiritual knowledge, though the characters themselves are often distorted or mistranslated. Numerous other examples of globalized cultural commodification can be cited, including the personas, images, or cultural productions of deceased cultural and political innovators such as Bob Marley, César Chávez, Michael Jackson, Tupac Shakur, Che Guevara, or Nelson Mandela.

Consumption practices are entangled with national, racial, ethnic, and gender identity formations. As Grewal argues, "'American' subjects were created not only through discourses of citizenship and civil society but also through lifestyle consumption, such as through 'buying American' and thus a contingent participation in discourses of identity linked to consumption" (Grewal, 2005, p. 95). The increasing numbers of youth who reside in diasporas are particularly susceptible to cultural commodification. The promise of affiliating with traditional culture, for example, drives many migrants to purchase commodities direct from the homeland. Through consumption in the global marketplace, then, youth interact with multiple nationalisms, racisms, gender formations, and social hierarchies. These both dictate youth identities and offer spaces for youth to create and display hybridized cultural combinations that define their transnational identities and communities.

The static depiction of culture has led to school policies that reduce and reify culture; single-label descriptors for identity (race, class, gender, and nation) obscure the complexity and transnationality of students' experience. Little attention is paid to the various social fields students navigate. The focus of teacher preparation remains on the preparation of lessons and "best practices" to help assimilate students."[W]hat would happen if we took the collective social nature of our existence so seriously that we put it first; so that crafting identities in practice becomes the fundamental project subjects engage in?" asks cognitive psychologist Jean Lave: "Crafting identities is a *social* process," she continues,

> and becoming more knowledgeably skilled is an aspect of participation in social practice. By such reasoning, who you are becoming shapes crucially and fundamentally what you "know." "What you know" may be better thought of as doing rather than having something—"knowing" rather than acquiring or accumulating knowledge or information (Lave, 1996, p. 157).

The effectiveness of teachers, thus, may have more to do with their capacity to foster identity markers that signal belonging in the school community than with their fidelity to a scripted curriculum or "best practices."

A sample of a fourth grade student's "map of important places" for an autobiography project. The map illustrates the global origins of the student's family and their current place of residence in California.

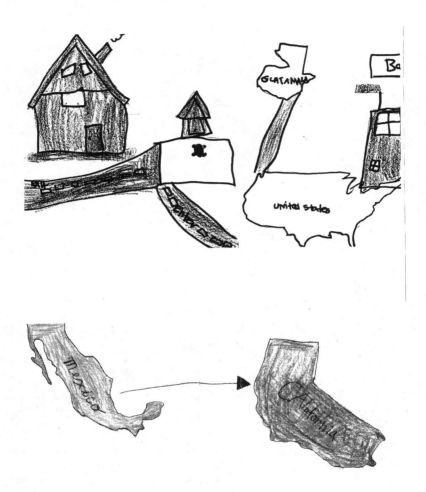

Top: A sample of a fourth grade student's "map of important places" for an autobiography project. The map depicts a path of continuous travel between the student's homes in Guatemala and the US. *Bottom:* Another sample of a fourth grade student's "map of important places" shows a one-way trip from Mexico to California.

A sample of a fourth grade student's "map of important places" for an autobiography project. The student drew the barbed wire at the US-Mexico border as his most important place because, in his words, "that is where we cross. That is where my uncle died."

5 Social Cognition

Cognition is generally defined in educational discourse as the facility of the individual learner to perceive, process, and apply information in an abstract fashion. Prevailing views of intelligence privilege quick recall, rapid calculation, decontextualized knowledge, and form over content. The predominant conception of cognition is dependent on many taken-for-granted, modernist assumptions about the nature of knowledge, particularly the primacy of the individual. Countering the assumption in education that cognitive skills are universal and measurable across individuals, sociocultural and situated learning theorists define cognition instead as a function of communities, where learning is inseparable from identity development, context, and social relationships (Lave & Wenger, 1991; Scribner and Cole, 1981).

In the testing regimes that now dominate school systems globally, the primary concern is with individual differences, notions of better and worse, and making comparisons across normal groups of students. Common achievement measures and standardized tests are designed to reflect normal curves, which locate a small group of learners in an advanced category and the majority of learners in an average middle range, called basic or proficient. Educators are asked to prescribe paths to advanced proficiency and identify predictive data to describe the kinds of individuals who should achieve success. The "below basic" students who do not move as swiftly from some imagined common starting point are labeled as "at-risk" or subnormal. Teacher and school accountability systems, like the Common Core Smarter Balanced Assessments, are built on a contradictory logic that requires an ever-increasing percentage of diverse groups of students to attain proficiency on tests biased in favor of a culturally-mediated, narrow range of presumably universal cognitive skills.

The Measurement of Intelligence & Test Bias

Educational researchers in the West rely on the notion that it is possible to accurately measure the general mental abilities of an individual, sometimes called "g" or "IQ." Standardized tests are commonly used in schools to make inferences about individual students' mental capacities and their potential for success. The primary tests of intelligence and performance in schools claim to measure global cognitive skills, but these tests are designed to evaluate only the kinds of cognitive skills valued in the West–logical-mathematical, linguistic, analytic problem solving skills and speed. There are, though, distinct sets of cognitive goals that students bring with them when they enter the classroom, "often diverging sharply," cross-cultural psychologist John Berry argues, "from the Western 'quick, analytic, abstract' cluster so much inculcated by the school system" (Berry et al., 1992, p. 110; Altshuler & Schmautz, 2006; Madaus & Clarke, 2001; Onwuegbuzie & Daley, 2001).

The meaning of intelligence varies across cultures. In the US, rapid problem solving is regarded favorably, whereas Ugandan villagers associate intelligence with adjectives such as "slow" and "careful." Still other cultural communities define intelligence in terms of capability as well as social responsibility, viewing dignity of others and the ability to contribute to the family's welfare as signs of maturity. As anthropologist John Ogbu recounts,

> The cognitive problems posed by the technoeconomic environment of Western middle-class culture require and promote a distinct set of cognitive abilities and strategies involving grasping relations and symbolic thinking... But they are not universally valued, nor equally functional; other cultures require and stimulate the development and use of other cognitive skills for coping with their environments. In other words, members of other cultures possess different intelligences (1994, p. 367).

Western schooling leads to particular forms of cognitive development, namely the abilities to: perceive and analyze two-dimensional patterns and graphic conventions; solve formal operational problems that require hypothesis testing; remember lists of often disconnected items; and classify objects into taxonomic categories (i.e. animals, foods, tools). The cognitive skills of groups without formal schooling differ in their tendency to rely on immediate experience rather than abstract, learned knowledge, to make judgments. Groups without formal schooling tend to classify items into functional categories (such as putting a hoe with a potato since they are used together), rather than classify them into taxonomic categories (separating food from tools) (Rogoff, 2003).

Students' familiarity with Western culture–its patterns of categorization, language norms, and analytical processes–correlates with academic success and higher measures of general intelligence. The number of years of formal schooling that students have had is the single best predictor of test scores; this means that standardized test scores serve more as measures of accumulated schooling and acculturation to the dominant culture of schooling than as measures of general intelligence, "g," or student achievement.

The validity and reliability of testing in a homogenous population— "when there is one language, equal exposure to media, equal access to education, one ethnic identity" (Berry et al., 1992, p. 111)—relies on the test's ability to measure the phenomena that it purports to measure in a consistent manner across settings and over time. This task alone is elusive in most cases and further compounded by the fact that most school settings are testing heterogeneous populations. Standardized tests are designed, for instance, to measure underlying cognitive skills, such as a student's ability to "compare and contrast." The following prompt is offered to test this "basic" language skill: "Compare and contrast baseball and tennis." Though educators may assume that this is a neutral query, it requires cultural background information and vocabulary that not all students share. Students may not have similar experience with these sports; some may have never seen a tennis match or baseball game played. Thus, this test item does not simply measure "compare and contrast" skills, but instead measures a specific kind of cultural knowledge and level of experience. Test bias is therefore a constant factor in communities with differential amounts of cultural capital or exposure to dominant norms and practices.

To attempt to transfer cognitive tests across heterogeneous groups requires, Berry argues, addressing the following questions: 1) Does the behavior sampled have at least approximately the same meaning across groups?; 2) Does the ability or trait measured play "approximately the same role in the organization of behavior of members of the new culture as in the original culture?; and 3) Does the score in a quantitative sense have the same meaning across cultures?" (1992, p. 111). Testing regimes cannot be fairly administered if they do not account for local meanings of "cognitive competence."

The use of a standardized test in a cultural group other than the one for which it was originally designed has often led to disproportionate numbers of low scores in minority groups. Euphemisms such as "achievement gap" or "at risk" are then invented to describe such differences in test performance. Many assessment packages claim to offer "culturally-fair" tests, but as Berry argues, "culture-fair tests of cognitive abilities (that is, tests in which each person independent of cultural background has an equal chance of knowing the correct answers) are a fiction" (1992, p. 111).

Cultural Transmission, Tools, and Schemas

Despite the propensity in Western thought to define cognitive skills as universal and separable from context, studies in the development and evolution of human cognitive ability show that culture is integral to cognition. Anthropologist and primate cognition researcher Michael Tomasello argues that culture is the only explanation for how humans acquired cognitive skills distinct from great apes in only six million years, a relatively short evolutionary period:

> The fact is, there simply has not been enough time for normal processes of biological evolution involving genetic variation and natural selection to have created, one by one, each of the cognitive skills necessary for modern humans to invent and maintain complex tool-use industries and technologies, complex forms of symbolic communication and representation, and complex social organizations and institutions (1999, p. 2).

Normal evolutionary processes, Tomasello observes, require much longer periods of time for change to occur. He suggests that the solution to this puzzle is cultural transmission—the ability to pass knowledge to others. Cultural transmission works many orders of magnitude faster than those of evolution. Geertz echoes this view:

> The Pleistocene period [Ice Age]... seems to have been a period in which a cultural environment increasingly supplemented the natural environment in the selection process so as to further accelerate the rate of hominid evolution to an unprecedented speed.... The fact that... distinctive features of humanity [culture and mind] emerged together in complex interaction with one another rather than serially as for so long supposed is of exceptional importance in the interpretation of human mentality; because it suggests that man's nervous system does not merely enable him to acquire culture, it positively demands that he do so if it is going to function at all (1973, pp. 67–68).

The accumulation of cultural traditions and artifacts, modified over time, exploit already existing knowledge and skills. This process of cumulative cultural evolution requires both creative invention as well as social transmission of these innovations to others that works, says Tomasello, as a ratchet to build-upon prior knowledge. Culture, therefore, not only allows individuals to "stand on the shoulder of giants," but it also enables new forms of learning and sociogenesis—the ability to create something collaboratively that could not have been created on its own.

Tomasello identifies several subtypes of cultural transmission processes or forms of learning, including imitative, instructed, and collaborative. All three rely on the ability of individuals to understand conspecifics—those of the same species—as being like themselves, with intentional and mental lives like their own, so that they can learn not only from but through others. The ability of individuals to perceive others as intentional agents (the "theory of mind") and the ability to focus on the same issues or phenomena as other individuals ("joint attention") enables humans to take multiple perspectives and to comprehend symbolic representations developed by others from different perspectives. To illustrate the importance of these elements in cognitive development, Tomasello points to research with autistic children, noting that it is their inability to engage in joint attention that limits their capacity for cultural learning and impedes their ability to acquire language. Likewise, the rare cases of a "wild child," who has lived without any cultural input and never fully acquires language thereafter, demonstrate the impact of cultural transmission on cognition.

Learning is facilitated and shaped by the cultural tools and technologies a community employs. Mental functioning, according to developmental psychologist Lev Vygotsky, emerges as a result of mastering varieties of tools and signs, especially the varieties of language in a range of cultural and institutional contexts. Cultural tools and signs include maps, rules, lists, language, mathematical formulas, and computers. Vygotsky argues that the incorporation of tools and signs does not simply facilitate a form of action that otherwise could not exist, but alters the mental structures that may develop:

> By being included in the process of behavior, the psychological tool [or sign] alters the entire flow and structure of mental functions. It does this by determining the structure of a new instrumental act, just as a technical tool alters the process of a natural adaptation by determining the form of labor operations (Vygotsky, 1981, p. 137).

A major cultural tool that underlies social relations and cognitive functions is the schema. Schemas are abstract representations of regular patterns that store general knowledge about objects, events, and systems in a network structure. Schemas constitute a set of expectations about the substance and order of events. In addition to storing general knowledge about objects, events or situations, schemas help individuals to make inferences that go beyond literal experiences and know what to expect in novel situations. Linguistic anthropologist G. Elizabeth Rice writes,

> A schema can be thought of as an abstract pattern onto which information can be organized; as a set of rules or strategies for imposing order on experience. A schema

is best seen as being at the same time both structure and process—a set of rules. In perception, schemas have an assimilation function: they work to recognize and process input. In memory, they provide organization for the storage of memories, and they may reorganize these memories in the face of new information or changing goals. In recall, schemas provide the rules of arranging memories, and for determining the "what must have been" for any gaps they detect (1980, p. 153).

Schemas are organizers of experience—rich structures that guide not only the expression of information, but also its comprehension. Schemas, argues Bowers, are like cultural maps:

> Over time humans collectively create conceptual schemas that influence what information they will be aware of, as well as the interpretation of what the information means—which often involves connecting it to larger cultural themes and anxieties. These cultural maps, in turn, are acquired by new members as they learn to think and communicate in the cultural languages of their group (Bowers, 1995, p. 129).

Schemas influence what is attended to and remembered and what is not. Memories, for example, are rehearsed and reshaped through the use of schemas; individuals remember only those things that are consistent with their current framework.

Culture acts through schemas to shape cognitive functions, including the memory, comprehension, and analysis of experience. Rice reports on the influential effects of cultural expectations on the comprehension process in her study on the recall of stories. She conducted two experiments to test the recall of stories that were either familiarly structured, fitting neatly into the "American story schema" with episodes arranged in a problem/resolution format, or unfamiliarly structured "culturally foreign" Eskimo stories, or stories that had been systematically mis-structured. Rice documents how individuals comprehend and recall unfamiliarly structured stories in ways that more closely match their own schemas or story expectations. They fill in missing information with their "default values," remaking others' narratives to fit their own schemas or rejecting the unfamiliar forms as incoherent or invalid.

Rice notes that in recalling the stories, participants made modifications to the stories to make them match familiar cultural norms: "The (American) culturally assumed default value for conclusions is a happy ending... people assumed happy endings even if the story had to be modified to provide one" (1980, p. 155). She finds, additionally, that this effect increased over time. After one week, many participants remembered the protagonist as "living happily," though there is no mention of this in the original story. Rice concludes that errors made in the recall of stories are not due to simple forgetting, but instead indicated a rationalization on the part of listeners, who try to render the material acceptable and reduce any confusing elements. Individuals then comprehend and recall unfamiliarly structured events and discourses in ways that reshape them to more closely match their normalized expectations.

Individuals are generally unaware of the schemas and cultural tools they employ; these symbolic tools are part of their culturally invisible perceptions. Some cultural schemas, however, have been publicly named, recorded, disseminated, and promoted for their symbolic power, referred to as "codified cultural schemas." Codifying involves the distillation of an informal set of practices into an explicit body of rules and organizing principles. Through this process the practices are often reified and viewed ahistorically. These codified cultural schemas all have clearly articulated sets of rules and syntax that privilege certain forms of knowledge and expression (Hemphill, 1999).

One example of a codified cultural schema is the Western scientific method. The Western scientific method is reified and passed down to students as the only method for conducting research. The schema of the scientific method is codified in textbooks and lessons, where students are provided with organizational charts that lay out the step-by-step process required to test a given hypothesis. Students are taught the scientific method in K–12 science classrooms throughout the world; there are posters of Thomas Edison and Isaac Newton on the walls of science labs globally. In the modernist privileging of form over content, students are assigned experiments designed to reproduce and reinforce the process. The experiments do not originate from a legitimate sense of inquiry, nor do they result in the experience of discovery, which is the stated objective of scientific exploration.

The history of the scientific method and its development as a way of generating new knowledge rarely accompanies K–12 science lessons, and alternative epistemologies are seldom, if ever, legitimized. This scientific method is, however, seldom critiqued. The Western scientific method emerged in 15th and 16th century Europe. European Renaissance artist-engineers like Leonardo da Vinci experimented constantly and codified their findings from experience. The elements of this codified cultural schema over time came to include a formalization of deductive and inductive reasoning, experimentation, and mathematics. The logic of deductive reasoning assumes that a valid conclusion can be drawn from any valid premise, moving from the general to the particular. Inductive reasoning shifts from particular examples to broader generalizations. Induction presumes that if enough information is collected without any preconceived notion about its significance, then inherent, generalizable relationships will emerge. The scientific method moves back and forth between deductive and inductive reasoning. First, investigators work inductively, moving from observations to the formation of hypotheses, then deductively to empirically test the validity and compatibility of the hypothesis with accepted knowledge.

Science is now, across the globe, a privileged form of knowledge that is accorded greater validity or legitimacy than other kinds of knowledge. The success and undisputed power of the scientific method has enabled tremendous technological development for many centuries, but like many codified cultural schemas, it is viewed ahistorically and uncritically as a pre-ordained cognitive universal that is naturally occurring and valid in all cultures. The preeminence of the scientific method limits the kinds of phenomena that are accepted as evidence to those that are observable and measurable. This leads to conceptualizing knowledge and learning in only one, narrowly focused way.

Codified cultural schemas are not only found in privileged, modernist knowledge forms, but in popular culture as well. The Blues—an American popular music genre with non-European, African roots—is a codified cultural schema that has existed for over a century. Like the scientific method, the Blues represents a substantive cognitive, political, and aesthetic framework that underlies a broad field of thought and action. As historian Samuel Floyd observes, "the Blues appears to be basic to most forms of Black music, and it seems to be the most prominent factor in maintaining continuity between most of them" (1995, p. 79). Growing out of a blend of field hollers, minstrelsy, and church music, the Blues gradually took a consistent 12-measure form that came to flavor American popular music, including rock, jazz, R&B, and country. The musical characteristics of what are now called the Blues came together in a consistent form around 1900. The enduring African features of the Blues schema include: a repeated 12-measure form; the use of "blue notes"—flatting the 3rd, 5th, and 7th notes of a major scale; bending pitches and sliding between notes; the use of call and response, often between accompanying instruments and a vocalist; and an AAB lyric pattern and rhyme scheme—one line of lyrics is sung, then repeated, then a new third line concludes the verse (Jones, 1963).

The Blues, however, is more than a listing of stylistic forms. For some, the blues is a specific musical style; for others, it is an emotion evoked by music with "blues-like" features; for still others, it is a form of social commentary. Critic and historian Albert Murray describes the Blues as an African American cultural schema that conveys not simply musical messages, but also complex aesthetic, cultural, and political messages. He suggests that the Blues reflects a value system that includes: affirmation in the face of adversity; improvisation, creativity, innovation, adaptability, and continuity in situations of disruption and discontinuity; grace under pressure; and an unsentimental but heroic and romantic struggle in the face of bad odds. In addition, he argues that a blues statement employs its own language and syntax, including such language forms as: vamps, riffs, breaks, fills, call and response, chase, bar trading, and polyrhythms. Thus, the Blues conveys messages not just through its lyrical content, but through its form and practice. The Blues also has the capacity, writes feminist critical theorist Angela Davis, to convey complex meanings and counternarratives on sexual politics, ideology, resistance, emotion and other psychosocial realities (Murray, 1996; Davis, 1998).

Despite the now-global pervasiveness of the Blues and its musical spinoffs such as hip hop, R&B, and rock, it is almost entirely ignored as a substantive cognitive process in schooling, although it overshadows the scientific method in its capacity to shape wide areas of cultural life and represent the identities of many globalized youth. This is, in part, due to the fact that music education in the US is considered enrichment, generally offered only in elective courses that are considered "less than" reading, science, or math courses. An ahistorical approach to music education, with its focus on skill-building and instrumentation, reinforces this view and the lack of recognition of music and other art forms as legitimate dimensions of knowledge and cognitive development on par with science or other "hard" disciplines.

Understanding how non-Western codified cultural schemas operate on the same cognitive and cultural basis as the scientific method counters the cultural invisibility that often promotes Western, modernist norms in education to the diminishment and exclusion of non-dominant paradigms. Another example of a non-Western codified cultural schema is the Chinese system of Confucian social and moral thought. Confucianism was developed from the teachings of the philosopher Confucius (551–478 BC) and numerous other subsequent thinkers and commentators. Though sometimes considered a religion, Confucianism is primarily a system of structuring social relations that has had a lasting influence on the culture and history of East Asia for many centuries, spreading beyond China to include Taiwan, Singapore, Hong Kong, Korea, Vietnam, and Japan. Confucian ethics, historian Tu Wei Ming suggests, serves as a "common discourse" among modern East Asian economic powers. Confucianism, he writes, is characterized by faith in

> the betterment of the human condition through individual effort; commitment to family as the basic unit of society and to family ethics as the foundation of social stability; trust in the intrinsic value of moral education; belief in self-reliance, the

work ethic, and mutual aid; and a sense of an organic unity with an ever-extending network of relationships (1996, pp. 33–34).

There are several key ideas in Confucian thought: *Ren* (humanity) refers to the Confucian version of the ethic of reciprocity or the "Golden Rule"; *Li* (ritual) refers to knowing and performing the appropriate acts in a particular setting (school, home, work); and *Xiao* (filial piety) refers to the respect that must be shown to both the living and the dead. Relationships (*Guan Xi*) are central to Confucianism, and specific duties arise from one's particular situation in relation to others. The individual stands simultaneously in several different relationships with different people: as a junior in relation to parents, elders, or teachers and as a senior in relation to younger siblings, students, or others. While juniors owe their seniors reverence, seniors also have duties of benevolence and concern toward their juniors. This theme of mutuality is prevalent in many East Asian cultures. For example, in Japan there is the essential *sempai–kohai* seniority-based status relationship system that is found in schooling, the workplace, and the martial arts.

Confucianism was—and still is—not a rule of law, but a codified ordering of social relationships. Confucian orthodoxy made politics and morality traditionally synonymous with education. The mass population of China, while not formally educated throughout history, was still provided with the basic Confucian philosophy of the "five relationships" (father/son, ruler/subject, old/young, husband/wife, and friend/friend) that gave each person clear rules of acceptable conduct, legitimated the power of the state, and reinforced patriarchal social relations. Specific duties are prescribed to each of the participants in these sets of relationships. These duties are also extended to the dead, which leads to the veneration of ancestors.

Confucianism was rejected for several decades by the People's Republic of China after the communist revolution in 1949. Confucian ideology was overthrown by the revolution and characterized by Mao Zedong and others as backward, anti-progressive, feudal, and responsible for many of the ills of the old Chinese society. Beginning in the early 21st century, however, China began to develop its "socialist market economy with Chinese characteristics," pursuing rapid market expansion and economic development. Communist party leaders observed a loss of a sense of ideological direction in the country, leading them to resurrect the image of Confucius. The ancient scholar became the worldwide symbol for a Chinese government propaganda campaign. The government had set up more than 320 "Confucius Institutes" in 96 countries by the end of 2013. These institutes were established to teach Chinese and promote the spread of Chinese culture and knowledge. In early 2011, a bronze statue of Confucius, 9.5 meters tall, was unveiled near

Tiananmen Square in Beijing, one of the country's most important symbolic spaces. The central place of Confucianism in Chinese and East Asian cultural values was thus once again formally re-codified by the Chinese government.

The codification of Confucianism has direct impact on the structure of education in China. Even the most disengaged students, who cluster in the back, unable to hear the lesson, do not dare to defy the Confucian authority of teachers. They remain seated, do not speak out of turn, and when called upon, rise to recite the lesson. In the most poorly equipped classrooms with well over 50 students, there are rarely classroom management issues. As soon as the teachers enter the room, students rise to greet them with a chorus of "*Lao Shi, hao!*" ("Good day, teacher"). Examining the origins and history of codified cultural schemas, then, illustrates the impact of cultural norms not only on cognition, but also on the construction of identities and social relationships in and beyond the classroom.

Case in Point: The Codification of Storytelling in Elementary Classrooms

One of the most prevalent, widely disseminated codified cultural schemas in Western classrooms is the expository/narrative writing binary. Expository writing (informational texts) is codified as a linear presentation of information that "sticks to one topic" facilitated by transition words (first, then, next...). Narratives (personal stories or fiction) are also codified in a linear way; they are expected to have a clear beginning, middle, and end. The typical "classic high point narrative" story plot includes a main character, a problem to solve, a climax, and a resolution. This story schema is generally assumed to be the universal structure for telling a story, rather than a product of a specific culture and history. It is publicly named and promoted in many mandated, state-adopted curricula across the US and other English-speaking countries. Teacher instructional manuals, such as the elementary *Step Up to Writing* curriculum, provide scripts for direct instruction, framed paragraphs, practice guides, models, worksheet templates, and rubrics "to give [students] concrete information about what constitutes a proficient paper" (Auman, 2008, pp. 1–2). In this curricula, the classic high point narrative structure is codified in a set of explicit instructions and rules and presented as the only narrative possibility that students can pursue in class. As the *Step Up to Writing* manual states, the aim is to "help students establish a sense of order and control over the information they include in a paper" (Auman, 2008, p. 12).

"Formal schooling," suggests Rice, "or the written response mode exaggerates the tendency to impose order on unfamiliar material" (1980, p. 168).

The *Step Up to Writing* manual, as an example of this, encourages teachers to provide students with three illustration boxes, labeled "beginning," "middle," and "end" in order to alleviate the "common complaint" that students "forget that a story needs an ending." The codification of this narrative form is often extended in the classroom, where teachers develop analogies to help students remember and reproduce classic high point narratives. Teachers in one California elementary school design and display posters and worksheets, using images of umbrellas, traffic signals, and hands, among others, to analogously reinforce this presumed universal narrative structure.

The focus on process and form over content—one of the main tenets of modernism—often means the dismantling of the creative or communicative purpose of narratives in favor of "well-structured" texts. As literacy researcher Sarah Michaels argues,

> Much of what goes on in urban, public school settings promotes the *dismantling* or breaking down of narrative performance and artistry—in favor of alternative forms of meaning making deemed more scientific, rigorous, reliable, intelligent, or important... The narrative discourse that *is* tolerated is often shaped by teachers and instructional activities into a simplified, homogenized form (1981, p. 303).

An observation of a narrative writing lesson in one third grade class demonstrates how a singular emphasis on the form—as opposed to the content—of stories can normalize, narrow, and manage the complexity of narratives, altering and even discouraging students' classroom participation. Throughout the 45-minute independent writing time in her class, Ms. L., a veteran teacher, makes a series of announcements that relate exclusively to the mechanics and structure of the students' writing. Ms. L. instructs her class to: edit for capitals and periods; skip lines on their "sloppy copy"; stay within the four margins of their papers; and use transition words on their outline, such as *first, then, next, one, another.* When reviewing their work in individual conferences, Ms. L. sends students away from her desk who do not meet her expectations to skip lines, edit for capitals, indent their first sentence, write their final copy in cursive, or students who leave "too much space" on the page.

In a rare comment on content, Ms. L. tells one student, Jerome, that his writing is "unclear" and "off-topic." "What does exercise have to do with video games?" she asks. Jerome responds, "Video games use up my time." Ms. L. shakes her head, complains about his spelling, and sends him back to his desk for not following directions, observing: "You can't have conference time until you've looked up all the words you don't know how to spell in your desk dictionary." Jerome's writing does not conform to the expectations of his teacher, and in her focus on the textual mechanics of his work, Ms. L. does not inquire about any of the conceptual links he has made. (In a brief interview after class, Jerome explains that he wanted to write about how it has been hard to keep his new year's resolution to exercise more because he feels "addicted to video games.") The teacher's focus on the structure of the narrative precludes her from facilitating the production of Jerome's narrative. He returns to his desk after his writing conference, puts his head down, and begins to doodle on the side of his paper. Ms. L., staring at Jerome, reminds students not working hard that their names will be put on a list.

In addition to contributing to a loss of communicative purpose, singular emphasis on the structure of narratives can also lead to inappropriate disciplining of students and homogenization of narrative forms. For his attempt to write about a complex, conflicted experience—feeling addicted to video games—Jerome is dismissed and disciplined because he did not focus on mechanics and stick to one main topic. In contrast, the following narrative by Jerome's peer, Eric, is highly valued in Ms. L's class. Eric chose a prompt from the approved topic list on the chalkboard:

How to Brush Your Teeth

I know a few steps that I do when I brush my teeth. First, I get my toothbrush. I have to put toothpaste on the toothbrush. Second, I start brushing my teeth. After 30 seconds I spit out the toothpaste. Third, I rinse my (added with caret mark: "big") mouth. When I put water in my mouth I swish the water around. Those are the steps I use to brush my teeth (Blakely, 2007, p. 92).

Ms. L hangs Eric's narrative on the "best work" bulletin board in the classroom hallway, praising Eric for his "excellent organization, use of transition words, adjectives, and neat cursive writing." In contrast, Jerome's choice to write on a topic of his own choosing leads to failure. His attempt to use narrative as a means of grappling with a difficult issue in his life is dismissed and devalued, while Eric is praised for following instructions. The message to students is that their experience is irrelevant in the classroom; success is more likely when students accept the banal topics considered suitable for skill-building. The classic high point narrative, while privileged in most formal school settings, Rogoff argues, "[is] not more or less effective for communicating or organizing thought than the styles used by other groups," but it is seen as more effective when schools promote it while excluding other narrative structures (2003, p. 303).

The influence of the classic high point narrative is not limited to written discourse. When a student's written or spoken discourse style is "at variance with the teacher's own style and expectations," writes Michaels, "interaction between teacher and child is often asynchronous and marked by interruptions and misinterpretation of semantic intent" (1981, p. 424). She describes a case that echoes Jerome's. A first grade African-American student, Deena, tries to share a story with her class during their morning "sharing time." After a few minutes, the teacher ends Deena's turn, annoyed that she could not follow the "sharing time" rule to tell about "one important thing." As Deena puts it: "She [Mrs. Jones] was always stoppin' me, sayin' 'that's not important enough' and I hadn't hardly started talking!" Mrs. Jones assumes Deena's narrative skills are below par because they do not fit her own culturally invisible schematic expectations, namely that a "good" story is about a single topic with a precise beginning, middle, and end.

Often-invisible cultural expectations and schemas impact student evaluations. Multicultural researcher Lisa Delpit records the reactions of two groups of listeners to an African American girl's story. All the White listeners respond negatively, remarking that the girl's narrative was a "terrible story," "incoherent," "mixed up," "hard to follow," or "not a story at all, in the sense of describing something that happened." One White listener feels that the child "might have trouble reading if she doesn't understand what constitutes a story." Others suggest that the student had "family problems" or "emotional problems." In contrast, all the African-American listeners think that the same narrative was the best story they heard, "full of detail and description." They anticipate that the same student does well in school because she is "highly verbal." The African-American respondents, however, recognize her shifts and associations and are "not thrown by them" (Delpit, 1995; Heath, 1982).

The schemas of curriculum, instruction, and assessment of schools cause many students' stories to be appraised poorly, invalidated, or to remain untold. The privileging and normalizing of the modernist, classic high point narrative form as a codified cultural schema has further implications. Its emphasis on maintaining a single topic eclipses interconnectedness, complexity, and contradictions that may develop in more associative, theme-based forms of storytelling. It requires that all experiences fit into a cohesive structure, simplifying and sometimes overly reducing experiences in its mandate for linear, sequential action to solve a problem. The schema also privileges individuals over communities as actors, since classic high point stories generally single out individual heroes and preclude the possibility of multiple characters of equal importance. Finally, the schema requires that all experiences need clear resolutions. The content of the form or "what counts" as a legitimate story has particular consequences for the kinds of knowledge, learning, and identities that are possible in school communities.

"Cognitive Styles" Research

Culture is not only a conduit for cognitive skill acquisition, but may shape the particular kinds of cognitive skills that develop. The first formal, cross-cultural studies of cognition appeared around the turn of the 20th century when psychology and anthropology were developing as distinct disciplines. One early social scientist, Lucien Lévy-Bruhl, asserted that there were two basic mindsets: the "primitive" and the "Western." Utilizing colonial logic, he suggested that the primitive mind was limited in that it could not differentiate the supernatural from reality, nor could it address contradictions. The Western mind, said Lévy-Bruhl, flexibly employed both hypothetical speculation and logic to overcome these shortcomings.

Anthropologist Franz Boas, in contrast, argued in *The Mind of Primitive Man* for "psychic unity," the belief that all humans have the same intellectual capacity, and that all cultures are based on the same mental principles and capacities. Boas' early accounts noted that the intellectual capacity of primitive minds was neither deficient nor "less than" the capacity of civilized minds. His arguments, though, were still based on the colonial logic of his time, as he considered the "lack" of cultural tools available to "primitives" to limit their development. Boas' writings initiated debates over universal and culturally-specific intellectual capacities, and the study of how cultural and environmental contexts shape differential thinking processes of individuals and groups.

In the early 1930s, brain researcher and psychologist Alexander Luria and his colleagues investigated how the context of formal schooling affects cognition and the construction of knowledge. Luria conducted a series of studies in what is now Uzbekistan, employing what he believed was a universal thought form: syllogistic reasoning. A key element of the Greek philosopher Aristotle's deductive logic, syllogistic reasoning is a chain of associations that takes the following form: "If A = B, and if B = C, then A = C." A common example of a syllogism is the following: "If all men are mortal," and "Socrates is a man," then "Socrates is mortal." Working with preliterate villagers with no formal education, Luria and his colleagues tried to test for this reasoning ability, recording the following exchange:

RESEARCHER: In the Far North, where there is snow, all bears are white. Novaya Zemlya is in the Far North and there is always snow there. So what color are the bears there?

VILLAGER: *There are different sorts of bears.*

RESEARCHER: (Repeats the syllogism.)

VILLAGER: I don't know; I've seen a black bear, I've never seen any others... Each locality has its own animals: if it's white, they will be white; if it's yellow, they will be yellow.

RESEARCHER: But what kinds of bears are there in Novaya Zemlya?

VILLAGER: We always speak only of what we see; we don't talk about what we haven't seen.

RESEARCHER: But what do my words imply. (Repeats the syllogism.)

VILLAGER: Well, it's like this: our tsar isn't like yours, and yours isn't like ours. Your words can be answered only by someone who was there, and if a person wasn't there he can't say anything on the basis of your words.

RESEARCHER: But on the basis of my words—in the North, where there is always snow, the bears are white, can you gather what kind of bears there are in Novaya Zemlya?

VILLAGER: If a man was sixty or eight and had seen a white bear and had told about it, he could be believed, but I've never seen one and hence I can't say. That's my last word. Those who saw can tell, and those who didn't see can't say anything!

(At this point a younger villager volunteers, "From your words it means that bears there are white.")

RESEARCHER: Well, which of you is right?

VILLAGER: What the cock knows how to do, he does. What I know, I say, and nothing beyond that! (1976, pp. 108–109).

Most villagers completely denied the possibility of drawing conclusions from propositions about things of which they had no direct personal experience, and they were suspicious of any logical operations of a purely theoretical nature. They recognized the possibility of drawing generalizable conclusions from their own practical experience, but they did not engage in the process of syllogistic reasoning posed to them because it required abstraction beyond direct experience. However, when the researchers studied villagers who had some formal education, the picture changed sharply, according to Luria:

They responded to these logical syllogisms much as we would. They immediately drew the correct, and to us obvious, conclusion from each of the syllogisms presented, regardless of the factual correctness of the premises or their application to a subject's immediate experience (1979, p. 80).

Luria's work shows how cognitive functions, like syllogistic reasoning, are not universal, but instead are culturally mediated. As Luria puts it, "The processes of abstraction and generalization are not invariant at all stages of socioeconomic and cultural development. Rather, such processes are themselves products of cultural environment" (1979, p. 74). This dispels the Piagetian notion that cognition proceeds on a universal linear path that culminates in abstract thought. Cultural environment, especially the context of formal schooling, inextricably impacts the kinds of cognitive skills that are developed, valued, and passed down.

Thought is neither logical nor an objective mirroring of reality, but relies on cultural norms and imaginative mechanisms. Over time, communities develop categorical perspectives on all types of objects, events, and relations that are then embodied in their systems of symbolic communication. Categories are embedded with cultural norms that individuals use to make inferences: "Categorization is the main way we make sense of experience," contends cognitive linguist George Lakoff (1987, p. xi). The creation and maintenance of categories is one of the major tasks of schooling; students are directed daily in numerous ways to identify and sort items based on their common attributes into distinct groupings. Most educational tasks require "mastering the hidden task requirement of placing information into mutually exclusive categories" (Wertsch & Kanner, 1992, p. 341). A category, in educational discourse, generally refers to a collection of items that share the same essentialized properties and are equal in membership. This classical interpretation of categories is based on the taken-for-granted notion that categories are containers with distinct boundaries. Though generally considered a neutral activity, classification tasks naturalize the essentialized binaries inherent in modernist epistemologies.

There is a body of educational research that has tried to create categories of learners by classifying how different, presumably homogenous, cultural environments lead to specific patterns of thinking and learning. Researchers have tried to name distinct "cognitive styles," arguing that learners can be characterized in terms of consistent patterns of difference in cognitive functioning. These invented "cognitive styles" or "learning styles" are conceptualized as a self-consistent mode of dealing with the environment or means of organizing, classifying, and assimilating information which is unique to each community. The stated aim of this research is to help educators differentiate their instruction to meet the needs of individual learners and close achievement gaps. The simplest and most common approach ties learning preferences to three common sensory modalities: visual, kinesthetic, and auditory. There are numerous other approaches with ever more complex breakdowns. For example, the Myers-Briggs Type Indicator (MBTI) lists four dimensions, of which one can have 16 combinations: Extraversion vs. Introversion; Sensing vs. Intuition; Thinking vs. Feeling; and Judging vs. Perceptive (Myers & Myers, 1980, 1995).

Cognitive psychologists Manuel Ramirez and Alfredo Castañeda, building on psychologist Herman A. Witkin's work, try to document the impact of culture and socialization patterns on cognitive development and learning for two specific groups of students. Using a modernist binary, they conclude that White middle-class families encourage their children to be competitive and learn from their mistakes, while rural, immigrant Mexican-American parents try to protect their children and guide them closely to prevent discouraging mistakes. They argue that these distinct socialization patterns result in different expectations, incentive-motivational styles, relational styles, and cognitive styles. Specifically, Ramirez and Castañeda claim that a plurality of immigrant Mexican-American students are "field sensitive" (also known as field dependent) learners who rely on external visual cues and are more oriented toward social engagement. In contrast, the authors claim that White middle-class students tend to be "field independent" learners, relying on internal bodily cues for perceptual and orientational abilities. The authors conclude that since Western schooling traditionally emphasizes autonomous functioning and individual performance, this privileges field independent learners over field sensitive learners. They recommend that educators modify their classroom environments to offer field sensitive students collaborative work arrangements, while letting field independent learners work autonomously (Ramirez & Castañeda, 1974; Witkin, 1967, 1977).

Most cognitive styles research provides such ready-to-use summations that suggest different types of rewards for different students or different classroom configurations for different learning styles. Yet descriptions of cognitive or learning styles are simply constructs—that is to say, imperfect attempts by researchers to describe patterns that they believe their research suggests. This research assumes that individuals present a consistent mode of organizing, classifying, and assimilating information in all situations and at all times. Many reform discourses that promote "cultural proficiency" or "cultural competency" as a method for addressing the achievement gap assume that culture is static and "seen to be known or ultimately knowable, in the sense of being 'defined, delineated, captured, understood, explained, and diagnosed' at a level of determination never accorded to the knower" (Ellsworth, 1989, p. 321). Popular teacher trainers, traveling across the US to support initiatives to close the achievement gap, for example, often present frameworks for developing culturally competent or culturally proficient plans for supporting diverse learning styles. They claim that an "essential element of a culturally proficient learning community" is to "recognize and meet the needs of multiple cultural, linguistic, learning, and communication styles" (Lindsey et al., 2009, p. 9).

These frameworks assume students from specific cultural communities present homogenous, stable and consistent styles of learning in all settings, at all times. Cognitive styles research and cultural proficiency discourses reduce and reify cultures when they fail to represent the hybrid ways in which students make meaning. They do not account for the cultural variations that exist within groups or from moment to moment. These summaries also leave intact narrow notions of intelligence that privilege rapid calculation, linguistic capacity, and abstract thinking.

Contemporary cognitive psychologist Howard Gardner tries to broaden Western notions of intelligence. He applies the notion that culture influences the mental functions and talents that emerge in individuals, developing a theory of multiple intelligences. From his observations and brain research, Gardner has identified and named eight kinds of intelligence—musical, bodily-kinesthetic, logical-mathematical, linguistic, spatial, interpersonal, intrapersonal, and naturalistic. Gardner argues that all individuals possess many kinds of intelligence, but they present a different profile of skills based on "innate endowment" or a "particular history of training" (Walters & Gardner, 1986, p. 165).

> Placing logic and language on a pedestal reflects the values of our Western culture and the great premium placed on the familiar tests of intelligence. A more Olympian view sees all seven [eight kinds of intelligence as of 1999] as equally valid (Gardner, 1993, p. 35).

Multiple intelligence theories (MI) has broadened many educators' conceptions of intelligence and some schools have applied Gardner's theory to help make the case for supporting additional music, visual and performing arts programs, but they remain low on the priority list in the US. Arts programs are dismantled with every budget cut, considered less essential and less rigorous than "academic" subjects.

The more typical application of multiple intelligence theory in schools, though, is to expect teachers to adjust their instructional strategies to correspond with the presumed strengths and weaknesses of each student. Differentiation is often represented as a core instructional strategy, but it is rarely fully implemented at the classroom level. As Gardner notes, implementation has been "very superficial... people label a kid being linguistic or bodily kinesthetic but then teach just the way they did before" (qtd. in Cuban, 2004,

p. 142). Policy researcher Larry Cuban adds,

> MI and other reforms aimed at helping individual children achieve full potential of their diverse abilities often take little notice of institutional norms and structures. In doing so, such reformers unintentionally bolster the already strong societal values of individual success and competition embedded in those very school structures, routines, and teacher cultures. Like many other school reforms, MI in accepting rather than challenging existing school structures, fortifies the school's institutional task of sorting out, through competition, which students are the winners and which are the losers (2004, p. 146).

Decontextualization of Knowledge and Situated Learning

Situated learning theorists argue that cognition and learning are highly context dependent. They call into question both the decontextualization of knowledge and schooling tasks that assume students will transfer the skills they have from one context to another. Lack of performance of a particular skill cannot, situated learning theorists claim, be generalized either to an expectation of nonperformance on other tasks or to the absence of the necessary underlying cognitive abilities. Education is premised on the assumption that the skills learned in one setting (the classroom) will automatically transfer to another (the workplace or community). Although learning transfer is assumed to be the central mechanism of schooling, Lave suggests that almost a century of research in cognitive psychology has produced limited evidence of transfer. She argues further that academic researchers, reflecting their own proclivities, assume that knowledge can be decontextualized and readily measured: "Functional psychological theory treats school as the decontextualized (and hence privileged and powerful) site of learning that is intended for distant and future use" (1988, p. 40).

Research on learning transfer has typically involved laboratory experiments where participants are given tasks of formal problem solving. In one experiment, researchers tried to study the role of analogy in transfer between problems that researchers thought had similar structures. Subjects were first given a problem called "Missionaries & Cannibals." The task—a mathematical one—was to move missionaries across a river in pairs so that cannibals do not outnumber missionaries on either bank. After trying to solve the task, subjects were instructed in various solutions, including flow charts on how to solve the problem. They were then given a new problem, one that (according to researchers) was similar in its underlying reasoning skills, but different in its surface context: "The Jealous Husbands," in which permutations of infidelity were explored. There was little skill transfer from Problem 1 to Problem 2 when subjects were not told that the problems were similar;

people saw little apparent similarity. When subjects were told the problems were similar, a bit more, but still limited, skill transfer occurred. Ultimately, significant skill transfer only occurred when subjects were: told the problems were similar; shown how to transfer the skills from Problem 1 to Problem 2; and directed to use the skills from Problem 1 on Problem 2. None of numerous similar experiments has led to strong evidence of learning transfer without guided support (Lave, 1988).

Thus, what may appear to educators to be "underlying, transferable, basic or global skills" (such as grammar structures or math operations) often do not appear that way to learners. The learners focus on the context of the instruction rather than the presumed underlying skills. Common assignments may include, for example, reading articles about unrelated topics to practice summarization. In the same lesson, students may read about volcanoes, the history of badminton, and ocean tides. The context of the summarization practice is deemed irrelevant by teachers or curriculum developers, yet for many students context is primary. They are distracted and confused by the disconnected specifics of each article. Likewise in math instruction, students are expected to practice general computing skills by solving specific word problems that use fabricated contexts. For the majority of students, however, word problems present a barrier to learning math because students have difficulty ignoring the context and struggle to identify what the curriculum developers presume is the underlying math problem. Students focus on the setting and the details of the word problem, though these details are often made intentionally irrelevant. Students are expected to filter out this context to identify the computational problem to solve.

These common, decontextualized school assignments are based on the assumption that there is a binary division between general and specific forms of knowledge. The separation of general from specific forms of knowledge is a manufactured and misleading binary. As Lave and Wenger point out,

> even so-called general knowledge only has power in specific circumstances... abstract representations are meaningless unless they can be made specific to the situation at hand.... The organization of schooling... is predicated on the claim that knowledge can be decontextualized and yet schools themselves as social institutions and places of learning constitute very specific contexts (Lave & Wenger, 1991, pp. 33, 40).

Rejecting the modernist privileging of abstract, decontextualized knowledge, situated learning theorists believe that cognitive behavior is "context-bound." They focus instead on the community and view learning as an integrated feature of social practice. Lave suggests that since individuals engage with each other as a condition of their existence, traditional behavioral psychological theories that conceive of learning as an individual and specialized universal mental process confuse and diminish the act of learning.

The notion that learning is a function of communities, rather than individuals, was first espoused by Vygotsky. Working in Russia in the 1920s, Vygotsky developed a "sociocultural approach" that was not introduced in the West until the 1980s after *glasnost* and the opening of the Soviet Union. Vygotsky argues that the origin of mental functions is social:

> Any function in the child's cultural development appears twice, or on two planes. First it appears on the social plane, and then on the psychological plane... Social relations or relations among people genetically underlie all higher functions and their relationships (1981, p. 163).

A child develops concepts and skills first in interactions with others (what Vygotsky terms the *inter*mental plane) and later internalizes these new mental functions (on the *intra*mental plane), transforming them in the process.

In multiple studies of cognitive development, Vygotsky demonstrates that intermental functioning between people is a precursor to intramental functioning within the individual. He claims that all intramental functions can be traced to social interactions, "Even when we turn to mental [internal] processes, their nature remains quasi-social. In their own private sphere, human beings retain the functions of social interaction" (Vygotsky, 1981, p. 164). For example, Vygotsky shows how remembering, presumably an individual mental function, is a social process. When, for example, a parent helps a child find a lost object by asking a series of questions about its possible location, it is impossible to pinpoint who did the remembering. Rather, the remembering is a social process, referred to as distributed cognition.

There are differential learning benefits to various types of social interaction, Vygotsky argues, whether peer to peer or teacher-student interactions. Teacher-student interactions may be the most effective when learners need to acquire new forms of knowledge and learn existing social rules. By contrast, the joint discovery processes of peer interaction provide learners with the chance to elaborate their understanding, as they have to negotiate, persuade, and coordinate their goals with peers. Peer interactions help learners "articulate their reasoning, reformulate their understanding, and generate new strategies that they might not create on their own" (Tomasello, 1999, p. 343).

Subscribing to Vygotsky's notion that social interaction is integral to learning, Lave and Wenger investigate how individuals have historically mastered new skills through apprenticeship models. The apprenticeship metaphor, says Lave and Wenger, has useful lessons for schooling, including the value of working in relevant settings, the need for strong goals in educational tasks, the absence of tests, and the opportunity for learners to craft their own curriculum, recruiting teaching or guidance for themselves. Lave and Wenger report that "where the circulation of knowledge among peers and near-peers is possible, it spreads exceedingly rapidly and effectively" (1991, p. 93).

To explain how learning happens as a part of social relations, Lave and Wenger offer the concept of legitimate peripheral participation. The theoretical term describes how new learners participate as novices in the actual practices of an expert member of a group, but only to a limited degree and with limited responsibility for the product. As an example, Lave and Wenger describe how young Mayan women, working alongside their expert relatives, learn to become midwives. Without formal instruction, by observing and gradually taking on the tasks of a midwife, the learners become proficient. Likewise, Lave and Wenger describe how new members to AA meetings, by listening and gradual inclusion in the group, transform their addictive behaviors and discourse. Additional examples of communities of practice that offer legitimate peripheral participation may include a team of construction workers, a research group, a musical group, or a sports team, among many possibilities.

The term "peripheral" in the phrase "legitimate peripheral participation" suggests a position that is both empowering, as learners move towards more intensive participation in a community, and disempowering, as learners are kept—often legitimately—from participating fully. On a sports team, for example, beginners might be initially benched as they practice alongside more highly skilled players, only getting a chance to play in a game when the team has a large score advantage. All the players on the team are considered "legitimate" members, dressed in uniforms and listed on team rosters. The players also have a responsibility to each other; the goals of the team are more important than individual performance.

The kind of coaching, team-building, and player apprenticeships that are common among winning teams run counter to the organization of most classrooms, where individual performance is measured and valued, and there are few opportunities for mixed-age apprenticeships or legitimate ways of participating on the periphery. Many schools, for instance, level their reading classes, placing high- and low-level readers in separate groups to differentiate instruction. This seemingly neutral organization reinforces inequities and diminishes opportunities for learning. For many students in leveled settings, the only possible identity to adopt is an identity of failure, as becoming a member of their community means taking on the role of "struggling reader" or "below-grade level student." "The issue of conferring legitimacy," Lave and Wenger argue, "is more important than the issue of providing teaching" (Lave & Wenger, 1991, p. 92). Educators who examine the forms of membership that their classroom community offers will, Lave and Wenger suggest, have a larger impact on student learning than educators who focus only on traditional instructional strategies or curriculum approaches. The main task of teachers, they suggest, is to enable students to "develop identities of mastery" (p. 41).

The development of identities of mastery is often restricted in school environments where students have little to no legitimate access to high-level curriculum or capacity to participate in high-achieving student communities. Tracking or sequestering English Language Learners in specialized classes, for instance, restricts students' broader school participation and prevents legitimate peripheral participation in mainstream classes. In one case in a suburban high school, Latino immigrant students are isolated all day long in a sheltered English class held in a portable classroom far across the football field from the main school building. Students in the class are thus limited from the kind of legitimate peripheral participation that fosters language learning by the very structure and context of the newcomer English Language Learner (ELL) curriculum. This practice is common in programs for English Language Learners and it frequently prevents students from: gaining legitimate peripheral access to the community of practice of the school; finding apprenticeships with fluent speakers; and developing identities of mastery (Olsen, 1997; Valdés, 2001).

In a further example, science education researchers Julie Bianchini and Lynette Cavazos apply the notion of legitimate peripheral participation to the specific issue of induction of new teachers at a school site. They argue that tools learned in teacher education or formal induction programs, while useful, are inadequate; decontextualized lessons from teacher preparation programs do not appear to transfer readily to diverse classrooms. When beginning teachers arrive at their schools, they need opportunities to participate on the periphery, moving towards full participation as they learn to negotiate the particularities of their students, their school culture, and the community in which their school exists. Examples of tools new teachers need to acquire include: knowledge of the range of student information available (their language proficiency, special needs, years attending the school or district, etc.) and how to gain access to these data; knowledge of curricular resources for students of varying language abilities and academic needs and how to locate and implement them; and knowledge of the resources and opportunities available to communicate and interact with students' families. Without such site-specific assistance provided through a supportive community of practice, Bianchini and Cavazos argue,

> Beginning teachers run the risk of either "dumbing down" the curriculum to avoid making waves with students or teaching... at a high level incomprehensible to all but a few students.... Beginning teachers can best acquire such site-specific tools by participation in department level or school wide teacher learning communities (2007, p. 608).

Creating effective communities of practice among teachers, argues educational sociologist Judith Warren Little, can lead to improvements in teaching and learning as teachers collectively question ineffective teaching routines, examine new conceptions of teaching and learning, discover ways to acknowledge and respond to difference and conflict, and engage actively in supporting professional growth (Warren Little, 2002).

Learning is accelerated, Lave argues, when educators consider and develop student identities and organize classrooms as a community of practice. To shift outcomes of a high school chemistry class aimed at low-achieving students, for instance, one instructor set up her classroom as a community of practice by shifting away from teacher-led decontextualized, abstract chemistry activities. She focused instead on shaping the identities of students as chemists. This involved transforming the collective identities of the students and transforming the chemistry lab, so that its social organization was shaped by the students, with laboratory and class work collaboratively developed. To help them develop identities of mastery the teacher made students dependent on each other in various ways for lesson content. She broke down the division between teaching and learning, as all learners became tutors, engaging with chemistry first for purposes of helping others. This process deepened student engagement with chemistry as an object of study. Lave summarizes the teacher's approach:

> Instead of "teaching chemistry" she engaged in a different kind of "learning practice," making it possible for chemistry to become part of the hard work of learners who were becoming gendered, racialized, classed adults-in this case adults with an impressive interest in chemistry (1996, p. 161).

The teacher initially evaluated the class by observing how much talk there was about chemistry among students in the cafeteria at lunchtime rather than by how well students performed on normative measures. The program ultimately ballooned in numbers and students made record-level national test scores.

Life in schools is constituted by a variety of cultural forms that can either nourish or suffocate the development of identities of achievement, argues cognitive psychologist Peter Murrell: "The task in creating an achiever learning community," he writes, "is arranging activity for the productive and purposeful collaboration of learners as engaged participants" (2007, p. 107). There is a lack of collective identity in most urban schools in the US, Murrell argues, with no shared purpose, instructional focus, and limited capacity to build community. "The absence of these," he argues, "are particularly detrimental to the educational fortunes of African American children and other children of color in urban school contexts laboring within pedagogies of poverty" (2007, p. 116).

Murrell suggests that school life should be refigured so that youth can access academic knowledge as easily as they do in informal settings with family or friends. It is particularly incumbent upon teachers, he suggests, to develop social practices in schooling that lead to more productive participation and engagement in the social life of instructional activity on the part of urban youth by creating legitimate and positive identity opportunities. He argues for a primary focus on what he calls "higher order instructional aims": "Comportment [behaviors] cannot be your only or even your primary aim as the urban teacher seeking to organize the social life of the instructional activity settings in the classroom. It should be secondary to what I call higher order instructional aims" (2007, p. 171). In urban settings, this may require analysis of confrontations or problems concerning racialized practices in schools, as well as the talents, roles, and behaviors valued by the surrounding community. One of the major identity-producing effects of schooling, Lave observes, is racialization. Learning the salient social divisions and identities of their social world is the main task students engage in both inside and outside the classroom. "This is an all-consuming job for children nearing adulthood, reason enough to explain why most curricular 'innovations' or teaching methods designed to improve teaching in classrooms have little effect and short lives." (1996, p. 160).

Learning, situated learning theorists demonstrate, involves developing and "becoming" an identity within the context of a community of practice. Identity development and knowledge acquisition are inherently and inseparably linked: "'Knowing' is a relation among communities of practice, participation in practice, and the generation of identities" (Lave, 1996, p. 157). Understanding that the link between cognition and identity is inseparable means that identity—and the formation of identities of achievement or mastery—can no longer remain on the sidelines of pedagogical discourses.

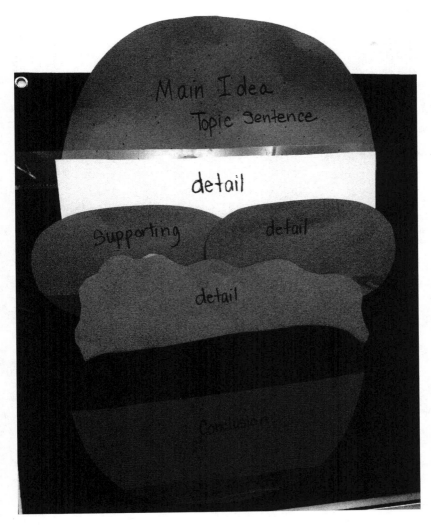

An elementary school classroom poster uses the image of a hamburger to reinforce the codification of the Western expository writing schema.

6 Commodification of Language and Literacy

In schools, language skills and literacy are commodities, objects with a presumed market value that teachers aim to transfer to students. The main task assigned teachers is to provide students with the objective, measurable skills they need to speak, read, and write. Through testing and tracking of individual student progress, teachers quantify language development and literacy. This quantification leads to the taken-for-granted notion that some people "possess" more or less language or literacy than others.

The commodification of language and literacy in schools includes both the quantification of student skills and the reification of language and literacy as objective processes. Language is typically defined in education as a neutral, rule-governed system of symbols that transmits meaning from one person to another. In this modernist framework, language is imagined as being composed of separable components:

- *phonology*—the way speech-sounds are produced and perceived;
- *morphology*—the composition of language from the smallest units of meaning (words and their parts);
- *semantics*—the relationships between words and their referents;
- *syntax*—the organization, rules, and structure for combining phrases and forming sentences; and
- *pragmatics*—the skills and competencies related to using language in a social context.

Educators instruct and evaluate students based on these standard categories, often diagnosing discrete disorders of form, content, or use.

Literacy is similarly broken down into measurable components, such as phonemic awareness, fluency, decoding, and comprehension. Instructional schedules are generally divided along these lines, with separate periods for each. Universal screening measures reinforce this division, providing assessment data on an array of presumably isolable skills.

Both school curriculum and assessments commodify language and literacy and create an artificial separation of the social context of language from its idealized form. Language and literacy skills are decontextualized and then assessed on an abstract, quantifiable continuum. Metrics like the Fry readability graph, for example, provide common standards for measuring the difficulty level of texts, computing the average number of sentences and syllables per hundred words. Students are then assessed on these leveled texts to determine their lexical score or grade level for group placement, report cards, or intervention program criteria. The Dynamic Indicators of Basic Early Literacy Skills (DIBELS) provides K–6 US educators, for instance, with a fluency score for each student based on a one-minute reading sample that measures the number of words a student can read of a leveled text. These universal assessments presume that students' skills remain stable regardless of the subject or context (Fry, 1977; Good et al., 2001).

It is common in the West for educators to assume that cognitive skills are stable and consistent across settings and from one subject to another or from one day to another. Teachers often assess students' literacy skills, for example, by asking students to read aloud from a leveled passage. Students are then informed of their "lexile" or "grade-level score" and directed to particular texts, which may be color-coded or sorted by level in their school libraries. These literacy tests ignore contextual factors and assume that students have the same reading level at all times, regardless of: conditions (noise level, formal or casual setting, number of nearby peers, time of day); student interest in the material; genre of the text (expository or fiction); or media type (book, magazine, comic book, or online article).

When educators assume stable performance and decontextualize students' literacy skills, they often underestimate student potential. Students assessed as "below basic" on standardized reading tests may, for instance, be able to decode advanced texts of different genres—fan fiction or highly technical video game instructions. Literacy measures that label these students as "below grade level" can lead unnecessarily to identities of failure and further limit their access to grade-level texts and curriculum resources.

Standardized measurement systems for language and literacy normalize the idea that context is irrelevant—that students' reading is not affected by passage of time, topic selection, test-taking environment, teacher-student relationship, or other affective conditions. The tacit focus in the West on the individual further normalizes a division of language from its social context. The decontextualization of literacy practices reduces language processes to a form/context binary, where abstract rules are privileged over the social use of language. As a result of this hierarchy, classroom instruction is focused on vocabulary, spelling, and grammar, with an emphasis on written rather than oral language.

Modernist Theories of Language Acquisition

The learning/acquisition and form/context binaries circulating in educational discourse originated in the historical division of linguistics from other disciplines. In the early 1900s, language theorist Ferdinand de Saussure sought to create linguistics as a separate field of study that focused on the structural features of language, as Bourdieu writes,

> Structural linguistics, born from the… [alienation] of language from its social conditions of production, reproduction, and utilization, could not become the dominant field among the social sciences without exerting an ideological effect by giving an appearance of scientificity to the naturalization of symbolic objects, those products of history (qtd. in Saussure, 2011, p. xxiv).

The conceptualization of language and the stages of language acquisition provided to teachers in training are accepted as an objective, scientific account. This account follows a modernist, developmental progression that reifies the following normative stages:

- 0 to 9 month olds – babble, often mimicking the intonations of narratives and the turn-taking of conversational speech;
- 9 to 18 month olds – begin to use single word utterances, often combined with gestures;
- 17 to 20 month olds – create two-word utterances or word combinations that typically emerge in the same pattern regardless of language;
- 2 to 5 year olds – learn to speak in full sentences, often with invented expressions;
- 6 to 12 year olds – develop capacity to understand and produce complex grammatical conventions.

This age-graded developmental picture of language acquisition is universalized in education. Though disseminated in an ahistorical, atheoretical manner, the model is based on behaviorist theories developed in part by researcher B.F. Skinner. He explains language development as a process of shaping, reinforcement, and imitation (classical and operant conditioning). A behaviorist conception of language acquisition underlies widespread features of conventional schooling, including the endorsement of repetition in language and literacy instruction and the use of rewards and negative consequences (loss of privileges, time-outs, detentions, suspensions) to motivate learning (Skinner, 1957).

The development of children's everyday speech, however, demonstrates that imitation and habit-formation are not the only processes involved in language acquisition. There is evidence that children are not just proceeding in a linear sequence, acquiring language by imitating the speech they hear around them. Children recognize patterns in the speech they hear, which they adopt in often uneven, nonlinear ways. For example, once children recognize that adding *–ed* at the end of a verb shows past tense, they will frequently overgeneralize and apply this pattern everywhere. It is typical for children to use "*goed*" or "*teached*" even after they have already used the irregular form of the verb "*went*" or "*taught.*" This kind of error suggests that language acquisition is not limited to conditioning or ever-progressive development. These overgeneralizations demonstrate the insufficiency of the behaviorist approach schools generally use to support their instructional practices (Gee, 1993).

Countering the behaviorist model, linguist Noam Chomsky argues that children can develop language without any overt instruction. In a competing modernist metanarrative, Chomsky claims that language is innate, a genetically determined capacity. He proposes a hypothesized universal aspect of the brain, called the "Language Acquisition Device (LAD)," that enables a child to produce an infinite number of expressions from exposure to a finite set of examples in the first few years of life. Chomsky asserts that the LAD comes equipped with a "system of principles, conditions, and rules that are elements or properties of all human languages" (Chomsky, 1975, p. 29). This "universal grammar" is a deep structure, he believes, underlying all languages. The surrounding linguistic environment, according to Chomsky, only impacts the parameters of this deep structure; the permanent, underlying universal grammar is adapted to fit the particularities of each language.

Applying Chomsky's theory of the LAD, second language acquisition researchers Heidi Dulay and Marina Burt suggest that this device is reactivated in the learning of a second language. Second language learners, they argue, are not passive nor simply imitating the speech they hear. "Contrary to popular intuition," they write, "we found an acquisition sequence that was approximately the same for both Spanish and Chinese children [learning English]" (1974, p. 254). They hypothesize that all children actively create a transitional internal grammar or hybrid "interlanguage."

Following Chomsky, Dulay and Burt also hypothesize that all children learning a language engage in a "creative construction process"—a process

> in which children gradually reconstruct rules for the speech hear, guided by universal innate mechanisms which cause them to use certain strategies to organize that linguistic input... The child's construction of linguistic rules is said to be creative because no native speaker of the target language, whether peer, parent, or teacher, models many of the kinds of sentences produced regularly by children who are still learning the basic syntactic structures of a language (1974, p. 255).

From this evidence, they suggest that acquiring a language is different from learning another new skill because language input triggers innate mechanisms that activate the specific linguistic capacities to transfer and make generalizations.

Drawing a distinct binary between learning and acquisition, second language acquisition researcher Stephen Krashen argues that the innate mechanisms involved in language acquisition are only triggered by "comprehensible input" (language that can be readily understood) in natural settings. Acquisition and learning, he claims, have different outcomes; acquisition supports spontaneous communication and performance, while learning supports meta-level language monitoring. Based on these perceived differences in outcomes, Krashen proposes a "natural approach" pedagogy for second language instruction based on a normative developmental sequence for language acquisition, including a "silent period." Adhering to this modernist developmental approach, many ESL programs emphasize listening and reading comprehension prior to speech production. Some adult ESL programs, for example, spend much of their time on decontextualized listening exercises even if students have an immediate need to practice language for job interviews or to seek social service information (Krashen, 1982).

Rejecting both the modernist metanarratives of behaviorism and Chomsky's structural linguistic approach, sociolinguists argue, in contrast, that language acquisition is a product of specific cultural conditions and social relationships. Vygotsky argues, in particular, that language acquisition is dependent on social interactions, specifically scaffolded opportunities for negotiation of meaning, requests for clarification, and comprehension checks. Early linguistic development is predicated on social interactions that make meaning visible and support children's roles in social and linguistic interaction.

In the sociolinguistic view, language acquisition requires the capacity to categorize, identify patterns, create generalized schemas, and develop other cultural learning skills. The cultural learning skills required for language acquisition, Tomasello writes, include the ability to:

> identify with other persons; perceive other persons as intentional agents like the self; engage with other persons in joint attentional activities;... understand the communicative intentions that other persons express in gestures, linguistic symbols, and linguistic constructions; [and] learn through role-reversal imitation to produce for others those same gestures, symbols, and construction (1999, p.161).

Social context is inseparably a part of second language acquisition as well, argues second language acquisition (SLA) researcher Bonny Norton,

> SLA theory needs to develop a conception of identity that is understood with reference to larger... social structures which are reproduced in day-to-day social interaction.... It is through language that a person negotiates a sense of self... and it is through language that a person gains access to—or is denied access to—powerful social networks that give learners the opportunity to speak (2000, p. 5).

Second language learners, she observes, need opportunities to communicate at length and on a regular basis with native speakers of the target language. Yet, access to this kind of legitimate peripheral participation remains a key barrier for many English language learners, who have limited opportunities to practice speaking English outside the ESL classroom and limited access to English-speaking social networks.

Instead of viewing language and literacy as purely objective abstract systems, sociolinguists redefine language as a system for perspective-taking and subsequently define literacy as acquisition of a secondary discourse. Literacy, from a sociolinguistic view, is not then an activity limited to decoding print, but learning to understand the tacit rules about who is a member and who is not and how they should behave to be accepted as members. When schools confuse literacy solely with its props (books, word lists, essays, spelling tests), instruction is limited to breaking down reading and writing into "analytic bits... getting learners to learn it in such a way that they can 'talk' about, 'describe', 'explain' it" (Gee, 1990, p.147). This meta-level knowledge is helpful for examining and critiquing, but it does not provide learners with the social practice needed to fully acquire literacy as a secondary discourse and be accepted as "literate" or an "insider."

From a sociolinguistic perspective, language acquisition is a context-dependent social process that involves identity construction. "Language is always spoken (and written)... out of a particular *social identity* (or *social role*), an identity that is a composite of words, actions, and (implied) beliefs, values, and attitudes" (Gee, 1990, p.140). Gee refers to these composites of "saying (writing)-doing-being-valuing-believing" as discourses:

> A *Discourse* is a socially accepted association among ways of using language, of thinking, feeling, believing, valuing, and of acting that can be used to identify oneself as a member of a socially meaningful group or "social network," or to signal (that one is playing) a socially meaningful "role" (1990, pp. 144, 143).

By speaking and acting in prescribed, legitimate ways, individuals signal their membership in communities, institutions, and nation-states.

Dialects, Creoles, & Language Varieties

Students who have not fully acquired academic language are often described, through schools' deficit-based discourse, as "at-risk" or "functionally literate." This ranking of students' literacy is based on a colonial logic, which assumes that certain language varieties are inferior to, less complex than, or less developed than standard academic language. Countering the colonial narrative of progress, linguist Edward Sapir argued as early as 1921 that there were no "primitive" languages or people in existence without a fully developed language:

> [The] South African Bushman speaks in the forms of a rich symbolic system that is in essence perfectly comparable to the speech of the cultivated Frenchman… the sort of linguistic development that parallels the historic growth of culture and which, in its later stages, we associate with literature is, at best, but a superficial thing… Many primitive languages have a formal richness… that eclipses anything known to the language of modern civilization… popular statements as to the extreme poverty of expression to which primitive language are doomed are simply myths (2004, p. 17).

Despite the extensive linguistic research that demonstrates the equivalence of all languages as a medium of expression and communication, a hierarchy persists within schools that privileges specific language varieties. This is a common practice globally, where standard language varieties (English, Chinese, Spanish, French, or Portuguese, depending on global location) are exclusively accepted. Signs in the hallways of Central China Normal University in Wuhan, China, for example, admonish "Speak only *pu tong hua*" (standard Chinese or Mandarin); local dialects are not permitted in the classroom. This standardization process serves social, national, and commercial interests, and is spread through institutions, media, and the educational system. "Ultimately," Gee writes, "schools are the guardians of standard language, the place where it is originally transmitted and thereafter maintained" (1993, p. 335).

The middle-class language norms valued in the US school system include "precision in spelling, practice in handling abstract symbols, the ability to state explicitly the meaning of words, and a richer knowledge of the Latinate vocabulary" (Labov, 1972, p. 213). Though they are signals of "being literate," these middle-class norms, sociolinguist William Labov says, are not "better" for communicating, narrating experience, or reasoning. Middle-class speakers, for example, tend to modify or qualify their arguments with a proliferation of passive expressions, modals and auxiliaries, repetitive comments, and filler phrases (*such a thing as, some things like that, could actually be considered, particularly*). These filler phrases do not help clarify or support the speaker's reasoning; they only indicate the speaker's status. "The initial impression of him as a good speaker," Labov argues, "is simply our long-conditioned reaction to middle-class verbosity. We know that people who use these stylistic devices are educated and we are inclined to credit them with saying something intelligent" (1972, p. 220).

The prestige of a language or language variety is not, linguists argue, related to any inherent linguistic factors such as clarity of argument or pronunciation; rather it is dependent on social status. The same accent may be prestigious in one location or era while stigmatized in another. Leaving off the "r" sound, for example, in words like "car" or "guard" had high status in all social classes in New York before World War II. After the 1960s, though, this style of speech became associated with a more casual style and lower social standing.

Language change also occurs through cultural encounters. Trade, slavery, colonization, or waves of immigration have led to the development of new languages from mixtures or hybrid blends of multiple languages. Workers isolated on Hawaiian sugar cane plantations in the 19th century, for example, invented a jargon to communicate with each other, borrowing and mixing words from their various native languages with English. Jargons eventually conventionalize with agreed-upon pronunciations, simplified grammar, and other socially sanctioned norms. These conventionalized hybrid languages are known as pidgins.

In places where children grow up with a pidgin as their primary discourse, they turn it into a language with its own grammatical conventions. This is known in the field of linguistics as a "Creole." The children of African slaves in the US, for instance, did not have full access to the English of their masters, nor communicative opportunities to learn the African languages of their parents. In order to communicate with their peers, they developed a Creole from the mixture of languages around them. In the South Pacific, Africa, and the Caribbean these hybrid languages have expanded through multiple generations to become the official national language; for example, in Haiti one of the recognized national languages is Haitian Creole. Despite the equal complexity of a Creole to any other native language, Creoles are often looked down on by its own speakers and the wider society... Because of the low prestige of the Creole and the high prestige of the accompanying superstrate language (for example, standard English in the US, Portuguese in the Cape Verde Islands), the Creole will through time, become more and more affected by the superstrate language (Gee, 1993, p. 366).

Through a process referred to as decreolization, the Creole may change so significantly that it becomes considered a "dialect" of the dominant language, rather than a separate language of its own. African American English (AAE), also known as Black Vernacular English or Ebonics, for example, originated as a Creole in the language spoken among enslaved African Americans, but it has been decreolized to the point that it is now described by some as a dialect of English or degraded as a slang (Dillard, 1972; Baugh, 1995).

AAE is a cohesive language system rather than, as many educators assume, "poor English" or a street slang full of grammatical errors. It is more than just a distinctive vocabulary used to signal membership in a certain group; AAE is a language system with its own grammatical rules. For example, in AAE (like many languages across the globe—Russian, Hungarian, Arabic), the copula ("to be") is left out in the present tense, so that "She is hungry" becomes "She hungry" (Labov, 1972). Though many English speakers assume that sentences like, "*He always be fighting*" is a mistake or "poor English," this sentence is grammatical; it follows the rule in AAE to use a "bare" be in any expression of an event of extended duration.

Many students enter school with a Creole or primary discourse composed of a hybrid mixture of languages that teachers find unacceptable. They often redirect, correct, or discipline children to use the standard language. Teachers commonly complain, for example, that students do not speak "properly." One teacher in a California PreK–8 Spanish-English biliteracy program describes the constant effort and surveillance involved to ensure that her students do not speak Spanglish or mix languages:

We show them we are switching languages by gesturing [turning an imagined knob at the temple]. We speak only one language for the whole lesson or the whole day and then switch. Students are not supposed to use the other language, but we hear them do it all the time. We have to correct them or they will use words like 'apushar'. We have to constantly remind them that the proper way to say it in Spanish is 'empujar'. We have to teach them academic language (author observation).

"Words distorted by English," writes Anzaldúa, "are known as anglicisms or pochismos" (1999, p. 78). Anglicisms, like *bola* for ball, *carpeta* from carpet, *watchar* for watch, *parkiar* for park, are, Anzaldúa argues, not incorrect as teachers may assume, but are instead products of cultural realities and evolutions that reflect speakers' identity. Thus, trying to eradicate them from the classroom becomes an exclusionary act, promoting student alienation from the academic world: "In childhood we are told that our language is wrong. Repeated attacks on our native tongue diminish our sense of self..." (Anzaldúa, 1999, pp. 80–81).

Language mixtures, Anzaldúa continues, are "not approved by any society" (1999, p. 20). She calls her own language—a mixture of English, Castilian Spanish, Northern Mexican dialects, Tex-Mex, and Nahuatl—the language of the borderlands. Speaking a language of the borderlands, Anzaldúa argues, means that you are a "pocho" or cultural traitor everywhere you go. Her teachers and mother, for example, want her to speak English "without an accent;" other Latinos and Latinas accuse her of speaking the "oppressor's language":

> Chicano Spanish is considered by the purist and by most Latinos to be deficient, a mutilation of Spanish. But Chicano Spanish is not incorrect, it is a living language. For a people who are neither Spanish nor live in a country in which Spanish is the first language; for a people who live in a country in which English is the reigning tongue but who are not Anglo; for a people who cannot entirely identify with either standard (formal, Castilian) Spanish nor standard English, what recourse is left but to create their own language? A language which they can connect to their identity, one capable of communicating the realities and values true to themselves—a language with terms that are neither *español ni ingles*, but both. We speak a patois, a forked tongue, a variation of two languages... For some of us, language is a homeland (1999, p. 77).

Schools construct and maintain language hierarchies that privilege high culture, print-based literacy, and academic language. The promotion of standard languages and the ongoing quantification of students' language varieties is part of the commodification of language and literacy. Students who speak, for example, Spanglish or African American English, are often defined as "at-risk," segregated, or tracked into remedial classes, where they receive only partial access to the curriculum. From a linguistic viewpoint, there is nothing deficient in AAE or any other nonstandard language variety: "All linguists agree that nonstandard dialects are highly structured systems. They do not see these dialects as accumulations of errors caused by the failure of the speaker to master standard English" (Labov, 1972, p. 237). "The notion of verbal deprivation is part of the modern mythology of educational psychology, writes Labov, "typical of the unfounded notions which tend to expand rapidly in our educational system" (1972, pp. 201–202).

Case in Point: Language in the Inner City

In 1972, Labov investigated whether dialect differences were the cause of reading failure for Black youth in New York City. In his landmark study, *Language in the Inner City*, he concludes that the major reading problems for Black youth, often two or more years behind on standardized reading measures, are not a result of "structural interference"—their verbal skill or language capacity—or the "deficiencies" of their home environment or early literacy exposure. Rather, he attributes the failure to "political and cultural conflicts in the classroom," for which dialect differences are important only because they are "symbols of this conflict" (Labov, 1972, p. xiv). His research counters deficit theories, still predominant in many educational settings in the 21st century, that "see the language of Black children as inadequate for learning and logical thinking" (Labov, 1972, p. xvi).

Labov argues that the problem is "reciprocal ignorance, where teacher and student are ignorant of each other's system, and therefore of the rules needed to translate from one system to another" (1972, p. 4). AAE speakers, for example, are told repeatedly from the early grades to their senior year of high school that the ending *–ed* is required for past tense verbs. Yet students continue to write sentences like, "*I have live here twelve years.*" The teachers attribute these mistakes to

> laziness, sloppiness or the child's natural disposition to be wrong. For these teach-
> ers, there is no substantial difference in the teaching of reading and the teaching of
> geography. The child is simply ignorant of geography; he does not have a well-
> formed system of nonstandard geography to be analyzed and corrected. From this
> point of view, teaching English is a question of imposing rules upon chaotic and
> shapeless speech, filling a vacuum by supplying rules where no rules existed before
> (Labov, 1972, pp. 4–5).

In contrast to the deficit-based thinking that locates reading failure in individual student capacity, Labov argues that the reading error may be only a difference in pronunciation or reflect a student who does not know that the *–ed* ending has any meaning. To help the student, Labov suggests, the teacher must first distinguish between the two cases and address problems as differences in pronunciation rather than as mistakes in reading, which can be discouraging or confusing to students who have understood the meaning of the text.

The time and attention teachers spend correcting students' reading, Labov observes, is often ineffective to help children who speak nonstandard language varieties. AAE speakers who read, for example, "He passed by both of them" as "*hi paes ba bof e dem*" may not even hear the difference when their teacher repeats or models the sentence. "If the teacher has no under-standing of the child's grammar and set of homonyms," Labov concludes,

> she may be arguing with him at cross purposes. Over and over again, the teacher may insist that *cold* and *coal* are different, without realizing that the child perceives this as only a difference in meaning, not in sound. She will not be able to understand why he makes so many odd mistakes in reading, and he will experience only a vague confusion, somehow connected with the ends of words. Eventually, he may stop trying to analyze the shapes of letters that follow the vowel and guess wildly at each word after he deciphers the first few letters. Or he may lose confidence in the alpha-betic principle as a whole and try to recognize each word as a whole (Labov, 1972, p. 35).

The problem with standard literacy rankings, Labov argues, lies in teacher expectations, where the progress in the early grades can be drastically impacted by a single random labeling. This "self-fulfilling prophecy" is evident in the alienation of students with nonstandard language varieties from school and their disproportionate rates of academic failure. "[W]hen failure reaches such massive proportions," Labov writes,

> it seems... necessary to look at the social and cultural obstacles to learning and the inability of the school to adjust to the social situation... [Interventions are] designed to repair the child, rather than the school; to the extent that... [they are] based on this inverted logic... [they are] bound to fail (1972, p. 232).

The deficit theories that underlie school language and literacy assessments are "particularly dangerous," Labov contends, because they divert "attention away from real defects in our educational system to imaginary defects of the child...." (1972, p. 202).

Conceptual Metaphors

When schools enforce standard language use they not only diminish stu-dents' funds of knowledge, they also normalize conceptual frameworks that reinforce Western cultural norms. Embedded in standard language are imaginative mechanisms that shape thought and action. The primary imagi-native mechanism at work is the conceptual metaphor. In education, discus-sion of metaphors is generally limited to English language arts or literature classes, where figurative language is identified and analyzed ("the curtain of night"; "a sea of troubles"). Metaphors are, however, not just literary expressions. Rather, they are pervasive in everyday language, shaping reasoning and behavior. There is "an almost inexhaustible list of metaphors," writes linguist Benjamin Lee Whorf, "that we hardly recognize as such, since they are virtually the only linguistic media available" (qtd. in Duranti, 2001,

p. 370; Lakoff & Johnson, 1980, 1999; Kovecses, 2002).

Metaphors are widely used conceptual tools, mapping complex, abstract systems onto physical, concrete entities. The physical experience of "up-down" is mapped, for example, onto the abstract concept of emotional states. The metaphor "Happy is up" makes expressions like *"I'm feeling low" or "Lighten up"* coherent. In dominant discourse, up is associated with positive attributes, while downward orientations reflect negative attributes. These mappings are not random, but rather reflect a coherent conceptual system based on cultural norms and language hegemonies.

There are many metaphorical systems that make everyday speech coherent. "Big is better," for example, is a common metaphor that underlies everyday expressions (*"She feels small"*; *"He has grown a lot professionally."*) The "big is better" metaphor shapes attitudes and actions, creating particular kinds of consumer cultures, identities, and policies. Though there is a systematicity to these conceptual metaphors, subcultures may assign different priorities and privileges to various spatial orientations, such as environmental groups or health advocates who counter the dominance of "super-sizing" messages in advertising campaigns. Speakers often do not recognize the metaphors that structure their everyday speech, making them complicit in the hegemonic systems that normalize their behaviors.

Though they are rarely visible, metaphorical systems influence relationships and actions, as Lakoff argues: "differences in conceptual systems affect behavior in a significant way. It is vitally important to understand just how our behavior is dependent on how we think" (1987, p. 337). In the West for example, arguments are understood in terms of war or physical battle (*"He shot down all of my ideas"; "She attacked the weakest point in his argument"; "I've never won an argument with her"*). This is not a universal view of arguments; some cultures map arguments with dancing, entailing different approaches and expectations for collaboration.

Orientational and other metaphor systems limit what individuals notice and provide part of the inferential structure that they reason with. The abstract concept of time, for example, is perceived in the West on a linear continuum, where the past is thought to be behind and the future, forward. This is not a universal or objective way of perceiving time, but a culturally-mediated orientational metaphor; for speakers of Tuvan in Russia the future is behind them, "not yet seen." The concept of time, in the West, is structured by many metaphors, including the idea that time is money—a commodity that is both valuable and limited. "This isn't a necessary way for human beings to conceptualize time; it is tied to our culture" (Lakoff & Johnson, 1980, p. 9). Expressions about giving, running out of, or spending time in everyday speech create a metaphorical system that structures not only language but also thoughts, attitudes, and behaviors. The commodification of time in many Western languages, along with the work/leisure binary, legitimizes, for instance, many colonial projects to instill the Protestant work ethic and enforce productivity and development norms. The Western practice of dividing time between work and leisure has led to representations of colonized people as lazy, indolent, or unfocused. As postcolonial theorist Linda Tuhiwai Smith points out,

> The connection between time and work became more important after the arrival of missionaries and the development of more systematic colonization. The belief that 'natives' did not value work or have a sense of time provided ideological justification for exclusionary practices which reached across education, land development, and employment (1999, p. 54).

Metaphors operate hegemonically, making speakers complicit in their everyday speech with dominant cultural norms that remain largely invisible.

To counter the cultural invisibility inherent in educational discourse, it is necessary then to examine the metaphors that underlie the reasoning in educational policy decisions, curriculum adoptions, and student program development. Common metaphorical constructions in education include:

- *Thinking is Object Manipulation/Understanding is Grasping/Analyzing Ideas is Taking Apart Objects:* This set of metaphors reinforces the modernist notion that meaning can be independent from context and speaker, leading to the predominance of decontextualized activities in classrooms.
- *Mind is a Container/Ideas are Objects/Communication is Sending Ideas from One Mind-Container to Another:* This metaphor entails an emphasis on top-down instruction, where teachers are expected to deposit information and "fill in the gaps" in students' knowledge.
- *Thinking is Perceiving/Paying Attention is Looking At/Directing Attention is Pointing:* This metaphor system leads to specific behavior norms, including expectations that students must look directly at their teacher to show respect or understanding. The cultural invisibility of these expectations means many students are disciplined because they are unaware that their own cultural norms (to look away in deference to adults) do not match teacher expectations.
- *Ideas are Food:* It is also common to conceptualize thinking in terms of cooking, swallowing as accepting, chewing as considering, and understanding as digesting. This metaphor system legitimizes the thinking behind colonialist equations that consider a lack of formal education as a

lack of nourishment. Deficit theories are based on the assumption that someone without intellectual nourishment (access to books, standard language models, or discourse practices) is "lacking" or "impoverished."

These embedded metaphorical structures all contribute to "closing the achievement gap" initiatives where interventions for "at-risk" students are designed to "fill the gap" or "feed the minds" of students who have not received "adequate" language models. The term "gap" itself is a metaphorically imagined distance between a desired endpoint, based on a Western normative notion of proficiency.

One of the predominant metaphors of schooling—the "banking style of education"—imagines students as empty containers to be filled by educators. This metaphor was first described by philosopher and critical educator Paulo Freire. "Education is," Freire writes,

> an act of depositing, in which the students are the depositories and the teacher is the depositor. Instead of communicating, the teacher issues communiqués and makes deposits which the students patiently receive, memorize, and repeat.... In the banking concept of education, knowledge is a gift bestowed by those who consider themselves knowledgeable upon those whom they consider to know nothing.... The more students work at storing the deposits entrusted to them, the less they develop the critical consciousness which would result from their intervention in the world as transformers of that world (1970, pp. 58, 60).

Freire calls into question the notion that teachers are the knowing subjects, the authorities who "deposit knowledge." He critiques the sonority of traditional teacher-narration, where teachers repeat *"four times four is sixteen"* over and over again. Students may memorize and repeat these words without understanding what four times four really means. In Freire's view, even solving an algorithm like four times four is not a neutral task, but one that creates a "culture of silence." The banking style of education leads, he argues, to passive learners who do not develop the capacity to voice challenges to official knowledge. Countering the banking metaphor of education is difficult, though, as critical educator Ira Shor says,

> after long years in traditional schools, teachers become conditioned to lecture, to assert their authority, to transfer official information and skills.... It is not easy for them to share decision-making in the classroom, to negotiate the curriculum, to pose problems based in student thought and language, to lead a dialogue where student expression has an impact on the course of study (1993, p. 29).

The preference for scripted curriculum mandates and the wide acceptance of centralized curricular control reflects the domestication of teachers accomplished through literacy instruction policy regimes and the cultural invisibility of the foundational metaphors of education.

Literacy Instruction Policy Debates

Historical debates over literacy policy in US educational discourse have been waged within narrow parameters that exclude analysis of the metaphors of schooling, social discourse practices, and other critical cultural theories. Debates over literacy instruction have historically swung on a relatively narrow pendulum arc every few decades between experiential learning approaches and direct instructional approaches. This pendulum swing is evident in the US in the shift from the whole language movement in the1980s, to emphasis on phonetic skill acquisition in the No Child Left Behind legislation of the Bush era in the 1990s, to integration of literacy in thematic units for Common Core alignment in the early 2000s. The trend to centralize educational policy through national mandates is not unique to the US; similar sweeping literacy policy shifts have occurred in the United Kingdom, Australia, and New Zealand. These national policy swings are perpetuated by ahistorical, atheortical approaches to teacher training and a research emphasis on measuring and comparing literacy strategies with individual student achievement rates.

The whole language movement of the 1980s in the US emphasized experience and immersion as key literacy strategies; students were expected to learn how to read primarily through exposure. This approach emphasized personal responses to literature and tried to cultivate students' individual voices as writers. The instructional approach was accompanied, according to critics, by a problematic decrease in explicit instruction in phonics and expository "academic" writing. In the late 1990s, educational policy and practice swung back to direct instructional approaches for decoding and comprehension. Several states in the US passed laws requiring the teaching of phonics for reading instruction in teacher preparation programs. The "Reading First" component of the federal No Child Left Behind Act of 2001 further required "evidence-based, scientific research" to support instructional techniques, narrowing what constituted a "legitimate" literacy practice. Literacy theory and qualitative research outcomes diverged widely from these government-mandated literacy policies and practices. Classroom teachers and school administrators, however, were generally unaware of the substantive theoretical differences between the government-mandated curricula and assessment schemes generated by large publishing houses and the findings of most university literacy researchers (Allington, 2002, 2006; Cunningham, 2002; Stuebing et al., 2008).

The US National Institute of Child Health and Human Development formed a National Reading Panel to "bring order" to the field of reading research knowledge. As one federal policymaker observed at a reading research conference, the multiple definitions of literacy being discussed by academics sounded like "chaos" (Meacham, 2000–2001, p. 182). The Panel claimed that it had developed criteria to establish "objective" and "credible" results, promoting an evidenced-based assessment of the scientific research literature:

> In what may be its most important action, the Panel then developed and adopted a set of rigorous research methodological standards.... [to contribute to] a better scientific understanding of reading development and reading instruction.... The evidence ultimately evaluated by the Panel met well-established objective scientific standards.... Unfortunately, only a small fraction of the total reading research literature met the Panel's standards for use.... [Studies were disqualified] if they were not reporting experimental or quasi experimental studies, if they were not published in English, or if they dealt exclusively with learning disabled or other special populations, including second language learners.... (National Institute of Child Health and Human Development, 2000, pp. 5, 27).

By excluding this research, the National Reading Panel ignored many of the most rapidly growing groups of learners in many parts of the US and the world's global cities. These criteria also excluded the large body of qualitative, narrative, and ethnographic research studies conducted by literacy researchers in university-based programs.

The National Reading Panel report determined that there were five areas related to reading instruction that had sufficient quantitative research to warrant instructional recommendations: (1) phonemic awareness, (2) phonics, (3) fluency, (4) vocabulary, and (5) comprehension. These became known as the five "pillars" of reading instruction. Educators and textbook publishers interpreted the National Reading Panel findings to mean that the "five pillars" were the most important areas—indeed the only areas—to address in reading instruction; they were subsequently embedded in the federal Reading First funding and codified for the elementary grades.

The narrowing of literacy instructional areas to five pillars led to the rejection of many historically, widely accepted reading pedagogies, such as independent reading. According to literacy researcher Curt Dudley-Marling,

> Although there is an abundance of correlational evidence... supporting independent reading... this practice has been banished from many classrooms because the National Reading Panel identified no scientific research supporting it. As one member of the Panel put it, "if it isn't proven to work through [scientific] research, you can't count it toward instruction" (2005, p. 273).

The circumscribed notions of "scientifically-based" research that emerged from the National Reading Panel were further used to limit the professional discretion of teachers. As Dudley-Marling argues, "The move toward standardized approaches to the teaching of reading... reflects an underlying absence of trust that teachers can or will do what is best for their students... reducing teachers to technicians" (2005, p. 275). Curriculum mandates, pacing guides, and test-driven curricula shifted the focus in teachers' professional development and evaluation to fidelity to "research-based" practices. Teachers are, for example, evaluated on their adherence to publisher's pacing guides rather than the relevance of instruction to students. The effect both deskills teachers and diminishes their capacity for real-time assessment or monitoring of student performance. As educational researcher Sheila Valencia and associates note:

> It appears that when the curriculum material is comprehensive..., when instruction is... prescribed, and when school expectations for fidelity are high, there is little need for teachers to think through their practice and limited flexibility for them to meet the varied needs of their students. This combination of factors seems to direct teachers toward materials and particular teaching strategies rather than toward their students and the effects of their teaching (2006, p. 114).

Though claiming to be "evidence-based" the scientistic discourse accompanying the No Child Left Behind federal legislation was neither "value-free" nor "objective." Literacy researcher P. David Pearson argues that it was part of a larger agenda:

> for the past 30 years, a conservative lobby has been trying to manipulate several policy levers (standards, assessment, professional development, and evidence-based practice) to shape a national reading policy that privileges basic skills for students and limits teacher education to training rather than educative practices. The case... could be characterized as a sort of 'skill the kids and de-skill the teachers' approach (2004, p. 231).

Eight years after the National Reading Panel was first released, the US Department of Education's research institute, the Institute of Education Sciences, found that while schools using NCLB's Reading First programming did devote significantly more time to teaching the "five pillars," the percentage of students engaged with print, both fiction and nonfiction, was reduced. The Institute also found that students in Reading First-supported schools were no better at drawing meaning from what they read than students at other schools. Thus, research did not support the "research-based" NCLB Reading First program. Despite continuous research in the 20th and 21st centuries, literacy debates have yet to be empirically resolved, though a focus on quantitative scientific methods remains.

Adhering to the historical trend in policy swings, the US began in the early 2000s to shift away from NCLB mandates toward adoption of the Common Core Standards. The Common Core Standards, a project sponsored by the Council of Chief State School Officers and the National Governors Association, was adopted across the nation by 2012, including forty-five states, the District of Columbia, four territories, and the Department of Defense Education Activity. The Common Core standards spell out what students should learn from kindergarten to the end of high school. Changes called for in the transition to Common Core Standards include integrating reading instruction in other disciplines; reading is no longer the sole province of the language arts teacher. Teachers of math, science, social studies, and other subjects are expected to teach literacy skills unique to their disciplines. The Common Core Standards focus on informational texts, primary sources, essays, speeches, articles, biographies, and other nonfiction texts, and the development of explicit writing. According to Pearson,

> these standards have the potential to lead the parade in a different direction: toward taking as evidence of your reading ability, not your score on a specific skill test—or how many letter sounds you can identify or ideas you can recall from a passage— but the ability to use the information you gain from reading (qtd. in Gewertz, 2012, p. 1).

The effect of predictable, periodic pendulum swings in literacy policy, argues English professor Thomas Newkirk, does not serve students well. He suggests that the Common Core's bias against narrative means students will learn to argue, interpret, and inform at the expense of being able to distill emotion, convey experience, and tell stories: "The world is much more narrative than the standards suggest" (Newkirk, qtd. in Gewertz, 2012, p. 21). The dismantling of past instructional strategies in favor of new ones is common in these policy swings. The belief that "newer" is better contributes to the uncritical acceptance of new curriculum mandates in school districts. Adoption of the Common Core may lead, argues Maureen McLaughlin, the president of the International Reading Association, to the loss of all the strategies, developed in the years since the National Reading Panel, for reading and comprehension, as well as metacognitive factors that contribute to reading success, such as attention and motivation. There is, she argues,

> a gap between the standards and school curriculums, because typically when [previous] state standards were developed, they basically became the curriculum.... If the states that adopted the Common Core say to their school districts, 'This is the curriculum,' and teachers feel they must teach to the test, the curriculum as it exists

would not include the metacognitive strategies, the writing-process strategies... and that's a problem (qtd. in Shanahan, 2012, p. 12).

Despite all the money and effort devoted to developing the Common Core Standards ($16 billion by some estimates to implement), analysis of states' past experience with standards and examination of several years of scores on the National Assessment of Educational Progress standards, suggests that the adoption may have little overall impact on student learning. Even with the shift to interdisciplinary work and thematic applications of literacy skills, Common Core Standards maintain a modernist focus on the individual. The associated "Smarter Balanced" assessments substantially shift the kinds of literacy skills schools measure, but they continue to commodify language and literacy, reinforcing hierarchical rankings based on standard language norms (Loveless, 2012).

The narrow set of parameters that constrain literacy debates produce a normative developmental model, exclusively focused on the individual. The commodification of literacy leads to a rigid system of measurement, where all aspects of comprehension and production of language are subjected to behavioral quantification. Children are tracked throughout their schooling, identified and ranked by their literacy levels. Their reading abilities are turned into commodities through the production of literacy as a quantifiable entity that can be distilled, measured, marketed, and packaged. This approach ignores contextual factors, community practices, and cultural or linguistic complexity. As long as educational discourse excludes social cognition and social constructions of literacy, it will continue to commodify literacy and maintain the systems of measurement that privilege some discourses over others.

Multiliteracies

Instead of commodifiying literacy and distilling it artificially into separable parts (the five pillars), there is an area of scholarship that takes a sociocultural approach to language and literacy, referred to as a multiliteracies approach. In this approach, there is no attempt to resolve the reading debate over phonics and whole language, nor an attempt to blend the two instructionally; multiliteracies studies disavows both modernist approaches. The multiliteracies approach treats literacy as "part and parcel of, and inextricable from, specific social, cultural, institutional, and political practices. Thus, literacy is, in a sense, 'multiple'" (Gee, 1999, p. 356). A multiliteracies approach, Gee writes, "argue[s] for a focus... on oral and written language as composed of diverse, closely interrelated 'tools' (mediating devices) for learning, development, and activity within concrete social practices at specific, sociocultural diverse sites like schools, homes, communities, and workplaces" (1999, p. 358; Cope & Kalantzis, 2000).

From a multiliteracies perspective, there are many representational resources and multimodal practices involved in reading. Representational resources include linguistic, visual, audio, gestural, and spatial modes. Thus, the definition of a "text" includes "lifeworlds"—structured spaces, contexts, and discourse communities as texts to be read. With this broader view of what constitutes a text, recognizing and deciphering cultural, historical, ideological, spatial and other dimensions become key parts of reading practice. Being a successful reader, then, means acquiring multiple discourses and knowing how to employ various media to navigate among them.

Literacy researcher Anne Haas Dyson argues that print material is not the only medium that impacts literacy development of young children. Students actively make meaning from their exposure to various forms of media and popular culture, integrating it into their literacy development. When children consume and experience electronic media with families and friends, they organize what they see or hear into various genres (for example, stories, raps, inspirational songs, and informational pieces):

> Children appropriate the symbolic stuff of these media genres… and adapt it to their own childhood practices, including storytelling, dramatic play, group singing, and informational display. In this way, children actively participate in the production of popular culture, through their use of the repertoire of commodities supplied by the cultural industry for communal meaning-making practices (Dyson, 2003, p. 329).

Children make use of the media culture that surrounds them to do work using different kinds of symbol systems (written language, drawing, or music), different technologies (video, radio, or animation), and different ideologies or ideas about how the world works. When children tell stories, play collaboratively, or sing, they often borrow, translate, and reframe media material. These borrowing processes, then, often shape children's entry into school literacy. As Dyson notes,

> Children did not approach official literacy activities… as though they had nothing to do with their own childhoods. They made use of familiar media-influenced practices and symbolic material to take intellectual and social action in the official school world. Recontextualizing material across social relations (e.g., unofficial to official), symbolic tools (e.g., audiovisual to written), and ideological values (e.g., joint to individual productions) provided teaching and learning opportunities to help children become more skillful and more sociopolitically astute decisionmakers and communicators in their expanding social world (2003, p. 330).

Though children's experiences with electronic media can be integral to their linguistic development, many teachers retain a negative attitude toward children whose home environments are not deemed to be sufficiently print-centered. Children with insufficient exposure to print texts in the home are generally viewed by teachers as "textually underprivileged."

Research drawing on a multiliteracies approach has found that youth "deliberatively develop and deploy multiple literacies in their out-of-school lives to achieve personal, social, civic, and other goals" (Skerrett, 2012, p. 366). In contrast to the common assumption that screen time is universally a waste of time, there is evidence that many forms of digital media (internet browsing, chatrooms, social media, video games) can provide effective forums for literacy learning. The interactive structure of video games, for example, may help students more readily comprehend textual information than print-based media. "The more exploratory, open mind-set promoted by adventure games," literacy researcher Charles Kinzer and colleagues observe, "helps students understand narrative elements" (2012, p. 270). By gradually increasing difficulty through each level of play, video games also provide scaffolding for players, allowing them to work in their "zone of proximal development" and retrieve information on-demand. Vygotsky's term *zone of proximal development* refers to a level slightly above a learner's independent working level. "Instruction is good," Vygotsky argues, "only when it proceeds ahead of development. Then it awakens and rouses to life an entire set of functions which are in a state of maturing, which lie in the zone of proximal development" (1934, p. 222).

Video games are effective learning forums, Gee argues further, because they provide opportunities for players to take on various social roles and identities both within the context of the game and in affinity groups with other players. "Video games recruit identities and encourage identity work and reflection on identity in powerful ways... All deep learning—that is active and critical learning," he writes, "is inextricably caught up with identity in a variety of different ways" (2003, pp. 50, 59).

Other forms of digital media also provide learners access to the social contexts necessary for acquisition of language skills and literacy. Reading and writing fan fiction online, for instance, provides English Language Learners access to affinity groups, where they find motivation to engage in advanced writing tasks, as literacy researcher Allison Skerrett writes,

> These youth composed and interacted in multiple genres and social registers, they offered sophisticated reviews and meta-analyses of fictions, they found opportunities for rhetorically conducting themselves as successful authors, and they enjoyed high levels of interactions with their online community (2012, p. 366).

Lam and Rosario-Ramos (2009) found that digital media not only provide access to forums for practicing reading and writing skills, but also the built-in scaffolding learners need to acquire a secondary discourse. Among ESL students they found,

> there was an eagerness and intentional effort to seek out opportunities to learn and practice English online... Besides reading online on a range of topics including movies, songs, video games, and current events, many of these students pointed out the use of chat to improve their conversational fluency, vocabulary, and writing skills (Lam & Rosario-Ramos, 2009, p. 182).

The use of text-based online chats allowed language learners the additional composing time and dictionary access they needed to become conversational partners, while also serving as a venue to build social relationships. One 16-year-old, who had left her home in Peru at six to come to the US, expressed that she liked emailing and IM-ing with her family and friends in Peru because,

> It makes me understand how they talk, like their slang... cuz the way they sometimes cut the word out, sometimes I don't understand what they are saying... I tell them to write the entire thing out... I learn a lot of things like the equal sign is 'igualmente' and 'porque' is 'pq' or 'px' or something (Lam & Rosario-Ramos, 2009, p. 182).

Duncan-Andrade points out that students enter the classroom already possessing many of the skills that teachers expect to teach them, based upon their extensive interactions with digital media. They can analyze texts, develop and support arguments, and understand concepts of theme, characterization, rhyme, rhythm, meter, and tone. They display these skill sets almost every day, says Duncan-Andrade, in their interactions with peers, media, and popular culture. "Students want a classroom culture that reflects expanded definitions of literacy. They want literacy instruction that emphasizes more meaningful learning activities that allow them to develop academic literacy skills that are transferable to their daily lives" (2004, p. 332).

Instead of tapping students' funds of knowledge (Moll et al. 1992; Yosso, 2005), schools generally ignore the digital multiliteracy experiences, unintentionally hindering their literacy development. Skerrett observes, for example, that transnational students' digital media access helps provide them with rich language repertoires that can be productively used in the classroom. Through exposure to multiple media sources that offer differing accounts of current events, transnational students often gain a bifocality or "dual frame of reference." Online access to the news from their home country allows transnational students to see, for example, the gaps in coverage on the media from their host country. In response to US news coverage one student comments, "Because on TV.... They talk, but they don't give the whole chapter about what's going on in Ecuador... you want to read more about on the internet what's happening" (Lam & Rosario-Ramos, 2009, p. 184). The bifocality and multiliteracy experiences of transnational students are generally an untapped fund of knowledge. These digital multilingual literacy practices are often outside the purview of the school and are thus rarely leveraged in the literacy education of transnational students. Many after school intervention programs for ELLs are designed, perhaps counterproductively, to reduce students' screen time, extending their school day by adding more remedial reading or text-based English-language development (ELD) instruction.

Other multiliteracy practices, beyond digital literacies, are also present in students' identity-building and language development. Visual art and dance, for instance, are not categorized as literacy activities in schools, where "the verbal dominates knowledge management and production" (Heath, 2001, p. 14); art and dance programs are generally physically removed from the school, located in community settings, outside the school day. Yet, educational ethnographer Shirley Brice Heath argues there is substantive literacy work integrated into the production of both visual arts and dance: "When dance appears within a youth arts program it immediately generates other kinds of learning, including new forms of reading and writing, combinations of planful thinking, and integration of media to achieve a plotline or key effect" (2001, p. 13). Art and dance programs may be key sites for language and literacy learning, especially for students left out of academic discourse because of language background, as they are often designed as a community of practice. The mixed-age groups in most community arts organizations give novices legitimate peripheral access to both experienced peers and often professional artists and dancers as role models and instructors (Sánchez, 2007; Rubenstein-Ávila, 2007).

The exclusion of social context from literacy education prevents teachers from leveraging the language and literacy learning that take place in out-of-school experiences—digital spaces, after school enrichment organizations, and student affinity groups. The modernist view of language as an abstract, rule-based system divorces it from this social context. The artificial form/context binary this creates leads to a narrow definition of language and literacy and the promotion of "research-based" practices that measure student achievement based on unquestioned norms of standard language varieties. The ongoing quantification of reading and writing skills contributes to the commodification of language and literacy and the associated deficit-based schooling practices.

7 Discourse and Discipline

One of the most enduring legacies of modernism in the field of education is the privileging of factual, research-based knowledge, presuming that scientific methods offer exclusive access to empirical truths. Any account that claims to be objective, factual, or scientific actually relies, many theorists argue, on metaphors and other fictional, imaginative devices. Truth is not an objective process of deduction; it is, Nietzsche asserts, an imaginative construct that over time becomes normed and accepted as a representation of reality. He defines truth as, "a mobile army of metaphors, metonyms, and anthropomorphisms—in short a sum of human relations, which have been enhanced, transposed, and embellished poetically and rhetorically and which after long use seem firm, canonical, and obligatory to a people" (qtd. in Rorty, 1991, p. 32).

The production of truth, Foucault argues further, is a social, discursive construction. Instead of trying to discover what is scientifically true and what is not, Foucault investigates "historically how effects of truth are produced within discourses which in themselves are neither true or false" (1984, p. 60). Thus, the position of many postmodern theorists is that permanent, lasting, or verifiable truths cannot be established. Instead of conducting research to find these elusive "truths," postmodernists seek to understand and deconstruct the structures that have been put in place for legitimating and enforcing "truths" and the corresponding official knowledge.

Adopting this perspective would mean a shift, in the field of education, from uncritical acceptance of "evidence-based" instructional practices and policies to analysis and deconstruction of normative discourses—processes by which knowledge comes to be accepted as "true." In educational research, this would mean a departure from the privileging of quantitative, experimental methodologies and causal analysis. In teacher training, it would mean less of a focus on "best practices"—the "most effective" instructional techniques and classroom management practices — and more coursework on the histories and theories behind educational polices. In curriculum development, it would mean a departure from decontextualized knowledge and global skill-building, as well as inclusion of students' hybrid funds of knowledge and home discourses. This shift would entail breaking down the scientistic binaries that diminish narrative, social context, popular culture, and other multiliteracies. Instead of aiming to discover universal, empirical truths (on how to best teach reading or support second language acquisition), the aim of educational studies would become the analysis of discourses and disciplinary techniques used in the classroom, in order to illustrate how these normalizing forces work to constitute learners.

Power/Knowledge, Discourse, and Governmentality

Power is not simply a repressive force, Foucault argues, that restricts, policies, and controls behavior. "We must cease once for all," Foucault argues,

> to describe the effects of power in negative terms: it 'excludes,' it 'represses,' it 'censors,' it 'abstracts,' it 'masks,' it 'conceals'... In fact, power produces, it produces reality; it produces domains of objects and rituals of truth (1977, p. 194).

Power, Foucault asserts, is exercised primarily in the production and legitimation of multiple forms of knowledge and "regimes of truth" distributed in the medical and social sciences. A regime of truth, Foucault argues, is

> linked in a circular relation with systems of power which produce and sustain it, and effects of power which it induces and which extend it.... We are subjected to the production of truth through power and we cannot exercise power except through the production of truth.... [T]ruth isn't outside power. Each society has its regime of truth... that is, the type of discourse which it accepts and makes function as true; the mechanisms and instances which enable one to distinguish true and false statements, the means by which each is sanctioned; the techniques and procedures accorded value in the acquisition of truth; the status of those who are charged with saying what counts as true (1980, pp. 93, 131).

Truth, from Foucault's perspective, is thus not something discovered through scientific methods. "By truth," he writes,

> I do not mean the ensemble of truths which are discovered and accepted, but rather the ensemble of rules according to which the true and the false are separated and specific effects of power attached to the true.... [Truth is instead generated through] a system of ordered procedures for the production, regulation, distribution, circulation and operation of statements (1980, pp. 132, 133).

Foucault refers to the mechanisms used to produce such regimes of truth, as "power/knowledge." Power/knowledge operates in the field of education, for example, through the ensemble of rules distributed in manuals of diagnostic criteria for psychological disorders, assessments, and behavioral checklists. These diagnostic tools produce the neurological, biological, and medical "evidence" for establishing categories of learners (ADD, dyslexic, or gifted and talented). These regimes of truth work to naturalize and universalize these categories, hiding their historical origins as invented constructions.

To illustrate how power/knowledge operates, Foucault investigates the ways various institutions—asylums, hospitals, and prisons—discipline subjects through the production of regimes of truth:

> I have tried to see in what ways punishment and power... are effectively embodied in... local, regional, material institutions.... One should try to locate power at the extreme points of its exercise. Where it is always less legal in character (Foucault, 1980, pp. 96–97).

Foucault traces the history of power as it shifted from physical force (the feudal power to seize material goods and the lives of subjects) to the control of subjects through bureaucratic regulation (generally without force). In his historical analysis—what he calls "archeology of knowledge" or "genealogy"—Foucault finds that individuals are constituted as subjects through the power/knowledge created, maintained, and distributed in the discourses of the various institutions and disciplines of the social and medical sciences (biology, psychology, sociology, anthropology, political science, public health, history, among others):

> There are manifold relations of power which... constitute the social body, and these relations of power cannot be established... without the production and functioning of a discourse... In the end we are judged,... determined,... and destined to a certain mode of living or dying as a function of the true discourses which are the bearers of the specific effects of power (Foucault, 1980, pp. 93–94).

Through his investigation of multiple institutions, Foucault describes how "certain texts and storylines get monumentalized into dominant narratives that become authoritative 'history'" (Weems, 2004, pp. 227–228). Foucault uses the term *discourse* to refer to these dominant narratives and more broadly to academic disciplines or any large, codified body of knowledge. His use of the term *discourse* is thus more expansive than its conventional or sociolinguistic use, where it is defined as connected speech or any utterance longer than a sentence. In Foucault's usage, the term describes entire fields of interest, for instance, the discourses of early childhood education, second language acquisition, or special education, among others. A discourse for Foucault encompasses the language, ideology, and rules that comprise a particular field of knowledge or action. As educational theorist Stephen Ball puts it, discourses are "about what can be said, and thought, but also about who can speak, when, where and with what authority" (1990, p. 17).

Through the production and distribution of hegemonic discourses, Foucault relates how institutions have effectively shaped and controlled entire populations. Foucault uses the term "biopower" to refer to the specific administrative forms of power that optimize human capabilities for the benefit of the state. Biopower functions to measure and subjugate individual bodies and control populations. Sex, in particular, became highly regulated, suggests Foucault, allowing the state to harness and distribute the forces of human production and regulate the production of populations. Throughout the 19th century sex, for instance, was medicalized and regulated through political operations, ideological campaigns for raising standards of morality, and economic interventions that encouraged or discouraged procreation. Biopower has historically operated through a diverse range of techniques and regulatory discourses like birthrate, longevity, public health, housing, and migration. This form of administrative power, what Foucault refers to as "governmentality," focuses on generating the capacities of individuals— following the logic of capitalism—rather than impeding them, making them submit, or destroying them.

Governmentality took the place of sovereignty in the 19th century as "the way in which political power now manages and regulates populations and goods... the main way state power is vitalized" (Butler, 2004, p. 51). Governmentality operates through policies and bureaucracies of the state and non-state institutions, and through discourses that are legitimated, philosopher Judith Butler observes, "neither by direct elections nor through established authority" (Butler, 2004, p. 52). The tactics of governmentality operate diffusely to order populations, their practices and beliefs, in relation to specific policy goals. These state policies, along with the discourses of the social and medical sciences, define individuals and work to control their conduct.

Rejecting the Marxist view that subordination is the unidirectional oppression of the working class by elites, Foucault concludes that power is exercised through discourses in a complex, web-like fashion. He writes, "Power must be analyzed as something that circulates... power is employed and exercised through a net-like organization... not only do individuals circulate between its threads, they are always in the position of simultaneously undergoing and exercising this power" (Foucault, 1980, pp. 98–99). This net-like organization of power is apparent in schools, where teachers are both empowered to exercise control over their students and classrooms, and disempowered via administrative constraints, scheduling requirements, the division of academic disciplines, instructional minute matrices, scripted curricula, standards-based assessments, and other forms of power/knowledge.

In contrast to modernists, like Marx, who investigate power in a linear, hierarchical fashion by looking at who holds dominant positions, Foucault analyzes how power operates through the discourses that subjugate individuals:

> Let us not, therefore, ask why certain people want to dominate, what they seek, what is their overall strategy. Let us ask instead, how things work at the level of ongoing subjugation, at the level of those continuous and uninterrupted processes which subject our bodies, govern our gestures, dictate our behaviors, etc. (Foucault, 1980, p. 97).

Schools, Foucault argues, like other "disciplinary institutions" provide "a machinery of control that functions like a microscope of conduct; the fine, analytical divisions that they create formed around men an apparatus of observation, recording and training" (1977, p. 173). This apparatus functions to create and maintain specific kinds of subjectivities, or individuals' perceptions of their own reality and selfhood.

Normalization

Multiple institutions in the West establish how children are viewed, seen to develop, and acted on as subjects. These institutions—schools, pediatrics, parent education forums, juvenile delinquency programs, the toy industry, or media corporations—produce a normative discourse of childhood. This discourse establishes certain arrangements, identities, and relationships as common-sense, natural, or "normal." These normative configurations are enforced through standardized curriculum, assessment packages, classroom management practices, and other school policies that promote conforming behaviors and exclude "abnormal" students by placing them in remedial or intervention programs. The normal/abnormal binary is widely seen as a natural, universal construct, yet Foucault's historical studies of the conceptualization of madness, illness, criminality, and sexuality show vast differences over time in the discourses used to describe these norms.

Through processes of normalization, schools and other disciplinary institutions produce many categories of identity as natural or biological. Gee argues, these identities always gain their force... through the work of institutions, discourse and dialogue... when people (and institutions) focus on them as 'natural' or 'biological,' they often do this as a way to 'forget' or 'hide' (often for ideological reasons) the institutional, socio-interactional, or group work that is required to create and sustain them *as identities* (2000–2001, p. 102).

Gender, for example, is widely perceived as unquestionably stable, fixed, and biological. Schools, among many institutions, divide, calculate, and monitor their populations along static gender lines. The discourses that accompany gender divisions in schools and the media are robust and filled with normative pressure to maintain a strict binary, each with its own attendant roles, themes, and props. There are designated colors, toys, clothes, books, activities, curriculum, and organizations associated with and exclusive to each gender. "Gender figures centrally," argues Heath, "in the images or narratives of the self that all individuals hold and is perhaps the strongest affective 'hook' by which youngsters come to know themselves and become attached to certain behaviors, norms, and evaluative frames" (Heath & McLaughlin, 1993, p. 25).

It is taken for granted in educational discourse that there is a natural division between male and female. Many scholars argue, however, that being female or male is performative, a production of institutions and sociohistorical discourses. As feminist theorist Donna Haraway argues: "there is nothing about being female that naturally binds women together into a unified category. There is not even such a state as 'being' female, itself a highly complex category constructed in contested sexual scientific discourses and other social practices" (1991, p. 155). Butler adds that gender is not a fact of nature, but a performance that has "reality-effects." She writes:

> Gender is not a performance that a prior subject elects to do, but gender is *performative* in the sense that it constitutes as an effect the very subject it appears to express. It is a *compulsory* performance.... It may be that the very categories of sex, of sexual identity, of gender are produced or maintained in the *effects* of this compulsory performance, effects which are disingenuously named as causes, origins, disingenuously lined up within a causal or expressive sequence that the heterosexual norm produces to legitimate itself as the origin of all sex (1993, pp. 315, 318).

Homosexuality, drag, or other subversions of norms, says Butler, work to expose "the causal lines as retrospectively and performatively produced fabrications" (1993, p. 31). Schooling is an intensive rehearsal process for the performative act of gender, defining, naming, and fabricating behaviors based on sex.

Many identities—beyond gender—are assumed in educational discourse to be natural, fixed, or biological. "[T]here is a significant renewal today of claims that people's biology, chemistry, neurons, and/or earlier experiences (e.g. stimulation before 3 years of age) 'determine' their futures in certain very significant respects" (Gee, 2000–2001, p. 120). Learning disabilities, for example, are ascribed to individuals as biologically determined, but as educational theorist Ray McDermott argues "learning disabled (LD)" is a socially constructed identity. It can be actively or passively recruited or resisted, often in unstable, contradictory, or ambiguous ways. The same rapid shifting of attention and high level of motor activity of a student—defined as having "Attention Deficit Hyperactivity Disorder" (ADHD)—may be considered a disability in one setting or viewed as creativity or giftedness in another. An ADHD identity can be actively recruited by affluent students and their families as a way to obtain more time for tests and receive special treatment, or it may be rejected as an unwelcome stigma, often simultaneously.

Occupying, claiming, performing, or being recognized as having a particular identity, such as ADHD is, thus, a product of a set of discourses, institutions, and social systems that work in concert, reinforcing identities by offering an official diagnosis, institutional measures to document and monitor behaviors, and a network of others with similar profiles. "[Learning disabled] LD exists as a category," McDermott writes, "in our culture, and it will acquire a certain proportion of our children as long as it is given life in the organization of tasks, skills, and evaluations in our schools" (1996, p. 271).

Educational discourses produce and regulate many categories of learners through defining and collapsing behaviors into the normal/abnormal binary. Those defined as "abnormal" are studied and generally excluded through special programs, behavior management systems, or counseling treatments. Through observation and diagnostic testing, schools and other medical, psychological, social work, or clinical institutions define and assess normal/abnormal or proficient/at-risk academic and interpersonal skill levels. Based on these standardized measures, educators shape remediation plans to enforce norms of "proficiency."

The ways students' skills are observed and measured in math lessons, for instance, mark some students as "fit" problem solvers and others as "slow," or "math phobic." As critical educational theorist Thomas Popkewitz writes, "A continuum of value is established that differentiates and classifies what the child is and should be and whether the child fits the map" (2004, p. 13). Through standardized assessments, students' performance and recall speed are compared to one another or to a mythical norm. The intense scrutiny of individuals through normative assessments both imposes homogeneity and individualizes, argues Foucault:

> by making it possible to measure gaps, to determine levels, to fix specialties and to render differences useful by fitting them one to another.... [T]he power of the norm functions within a system of formal equality, since with a homogeneity that is the rule, the norm introduces, as a useful imperative and as a result of measurement, all the shading of individual differences (1977, p. 184).

These comparative practices have the effect of positioning teachers as "informed rescuers" of struggling students. Popkewitz sees this "redemptive culture" as problematic, for "any attempt to promote subjectivity through governing thought is neither benign nor neutral" (Popkewitz, 2004, p. 14). The standard practices of monitoring, examining, and measuring students' skills and aptitudes, of dividing and comparing students, thus function to normalize students by applying constant pressure to conform through a system of inclusion and exclusion. "We conform to and contest normalizing practices by policing ourselves in relation to particular classificatory systems" (Weems, 2004, p. 228).

The normalizing, classifying functions of the social and medical sciences have, Foucault argues, taken on the force of law. Governmentality operates primarily, Foucault claims, through institutional processes of normalization, often subverting, transcending, or even replacing existing systems of law; governmentality has colonized the legal system. "Disciplines have their own discourses," he writes, "they engender apparatuses of knowledge and a multiplicity of new domains of understanding.... The code they come to define is not that of law but that of normalization" (Foucault, 1980, p. 106).

Even though laws, for example, may be in place to guarantee equity in educational institutions, the effects of normalization maintain systemic inequities. The federal Title IX legislation in the US, for instance, was passed to prohibit gender discrimination in federally-funded educational programs, including athletics. The normalization of gendered subjectivities, however, naturalizes the idea that girls "prefer" not to play rougher sports such as football, together with the idea that women's teams would be less competitive or would otherwise generate less fan support. Women's sports therefore continue to be underfunded and underrepresented in schools, athletic scholarships, and professional income opportunities. "The procedures of normalization," Foucault concludes, "come to be... constantly engaged in the colonization of those of the law. I believe that all this can explain the global functioning of what I would call *a society of normalization*" (Foucault, 1980, p. 107).

Case in Point: Normalizing Puberty through Corporate- and State-Sponsored Curricula

School curricula often operate to produce the power/knowledge that normalizes and enforces specific student subjectivities, sanctioning certain behaviors and identities. One example of this comes from the corporate- and state-sponsored curricula designed to teach students about the "realities of growing up." Through distribution of curriculum packages aimed at informing and supporting students in their transitions through puberty, schools promote a heteronormative discourse. Heternormativity is defined by critical educational theorist Lisa Weems as "discourses around sex, gender, and sexuality [that]... produce certain identities as 'normative' and others as 'deviant'" (2004, p. 229). Analysis of the "family life" curricula used in US elementary schools shows how schools promote the heteronormative view that there are two distinct genders, each with certain "natural" roles. Through the medicalization of puberty, these curricula operate as regimes of truth, essentializing gender divisions and acceptable/deviant behavior norms.

The family life curricula distributed in elementary schools present a universalized depiction of puberty, obscuring behind its medicalized, scientistic language the commercial and national interests that have constructed this normalized version of growing up. The commercial hygiene industry has had a presence in schools for decades, offering teachers and administrators free educational materials that create a demand for their products (soaps, shampoos, deodorants, mouthwashes, menstrual pads, and tampons). These commodities were scarce at the beginning of the 19th century, but through the expansion of global markets and advertising they were normalized as "basic necessities." As Marx observed, "production not only supplies a material for the need, but it also supplies a need for the material" (qtd. in Clarke et al., 2003, p. 263).

Kotex, one corporate producer of school curricula, offers a complete teacher's kit containing detailed lesson plans, interactive films, classroom posters, and product samples. Providing free curriculum is a profitable investment, as Kotex discovered, making each girl "a confirmed Kotex user... would provide more business in the long-run than convincing a thirty-five year old woman to switch to Kotex" (qtd. in Kennard, 1989, p. 77). Promoting Always, Tampax, and Crest brand products, Procter and Gamble provides similar teacher resources. "The appropriation of an education discourse into the advertising campaign did more than help increase sales...," observes Kennard, "it also enabled the agency to both legitimize the corporation as the best source for information on menstruation and women's health, and to praise the corporation for performing a valuable service to mothers, young girls, and women" (1989, p. 77; Kotex, 2013; P&G School Programs, 2013) .

To promote consumption of their products, corporations disseminate curricula nationally in elementary schools that normalizes fear, worry, and embarrassment about puberty. The first statement in one booklet, for example, states "Puberty can be tough" (Clark, 2000). The *Puberty: What's Normal and What's Not* booklet concentrates on teens' concerns over the way they look and smell: "Most teens feel self-conscious about how their bodies are changing. It's normal to worry." The pamphlets tell teen girls that it's normal to have the following thoughts: "I hate my hair. I'm growing too fast. My feet feel too big. I've got zits. My breasts are different sizes. I'm fat" (Kotex, 2005).

The normalization of adolescence as an anxious developmental period helps not only to cultivate consumers for hygiene and beauty products (by creating a "need" for them), but also makes individuals responsible for their appearance and its corresponding social status. Blame is assigned to the young people themselves, and in response, schools "institute different disciplinary and surveillance structures and regimes" (Besley, 2003, p. 167). The *Always Changing Program for 5th and 6th Grade Girls and Boys* suggests, for example, that a girl change her pad more often than otherwise necessary to avoid "any chance of odor," while boys are encouraged to guard against oily hair, body odor, and oily skin. Girls are instructed to keep a calendar of their periods so that they will not "be caught without a good supply of pads or tampons" and to monitor their bodies, to make sure that they have a normal 28-day cycle. By normalizing hygiene concerns and fear of discovery, hygiene product corporations position themselves as necessary for the protection of girls: "The institutionalization of both state surveillance and patriarchal family ideologies is related to such discourses of protection" (Moallem, 2005, p. 81).

The commercially driven message that girls must track and record their menstrual cycles is based on the presumption that girls would be ashamed if anyone discovered their secret. To promote hygiene products, the educational materials normalize the notion that periods are something that must be hidden. In one example, a booklet states: "Your lab partner is totally hot. Ok, your period is no big deal. But if he found out, you'd change schools. It's a lot simpler to just use Kotex ultra thin maxis and relax. He'll never, ever know" (Kotex, 1992).

The booklets and films are distributed in schools in secretive ways. Girls are separated from boys. Behind closed doors teachers give elaborate introductions about the "sensitive nature of the topic." Permission slips are also solicited from parents, and students are often asked to sign a "ground rules contract" before they can participate. In these contracts, students agree to use medical terminology and refrain from asking teachers any "personal questions."

Teachers' and parents' personal knowledge and experience are disavowed in favor of the scientific accounts provided by schools and corporations. One family life teacher training manual provided across California, for example, prohibits teachers from discussing their own experience (Gardner, 2004). This curriculum explicitly forbids the use of any slang terms, requiring that teachers and students use only medical, scientific language. The information distributed by schools is positioned as offering the "correct" terminology, "naturaliz[ing] educational value as 'accurate,' 'truthful,' 'authentic,' and 'factual'" (Kennard, 1989, p. 90). As Kennard describes in her observations of teacher-student discussions on puberty:

> The female sources of menstrual education rarely spoke from their own experiences as menstruators. Instead they delivered stilted explanations of 'accurate knowledge.' The tension was particularly apparent because the girls asked questions in a frank conversational manner, but the answers that came back were in the language of a textbook (1989, p. 213).

At the end of its medicalized curriculum, Procter and Gamble assures educators that the materials "have been reviewed by the American Association for Health Education and accepted as educationally appropriate." The included glossary of terms includes definitions of anatomy (fallopian tubes, pituitary gland, uterus) and other scientific terms (estrogen, progesterone, hormones), thus legitimizing the commercial product knowledge listed alongside (antiperspirant, period protection). Medical science, as Foucault writes,

> set itself up as the supreme authority in matters of hygienic necessity.... it claimed to ensure the physical vigor and the moral cleanliness of the social body.... in the name of biological and historical urgency it justified the racisms of the state.... it grounded them in truth (1990, p. 54).

Technologies of the Self and Self-regulation

Even the most seemingly neutral tasks like helping students attain proficiency in basic skills involve the constitution, normalization, and subjugation of individuals. The attention in schools to student performance is paired with the constant assessment of individual traits, as teachers help produce learners who participate with classroom materials in "meaningful, productive" ways, engaging in "appropriate" behaviors. Literacy instruction, for example, involves not just teaching reading and writing, literacy researcher Dawnene Hammerberg argues, but "more significantly... managing and training technologies of the self" (2004, p. 360). Foucault's concept, "technologies of the self," refers to techniques and operations that individuals are socialized to apply to their own conduct,

> so as to transform themselves in order to attain a certain state... [Technologies of the self include] certain modes of training and modification of individuals, not only in the obvious sense of acquiring certain skills but also in the sense of acquiring certain attitudes (1988, p. 18).

Hammerberg investigates how technologies of the self are employed in early literacy classrooms in particular to help children become "independent learners." The "center-based" and "print-rich" design of early literacy classrooms is based on the assumption that everyone in the classroom has individual needs. To meet these needs, teachers work one-on-one or in small groups, expecting the rest of the class to be meaningfully engaged in the specifically prepared environment (selecting books from leveled bins, reading with a buddy in a book nook, gluing letters to paper, or journaling). To an outside observer the students in this classroom may appear to be self-directed or acting "independently," but every aspect of conduct is described and trained in minute detail.

Preschool and kindergarten teachers typically spend the first six weeks of school training students in how to use each center, introducing them one at a time and role playing how to use them; reminders on how to behave appro-priately and manage one's body continue throughout the school year:

> Thus, pedagogies rooted in "independent" learning construct a subject whose every tiny action is anticipated, regulated, and made normal before children can be "left on their own" in the learning environment... in time this rigorous training is made in-visible, because the system only works if students have made it "their own" and can maintain themselves "independently." The routines learned through training become technologies of the self that allow individuals to act on themselves (no longer with the help of others) in ways that appear "independent" and "productive" (Hammer-berg, 2004, pp. 364, 366).

Classroom management is predicated on the idea that students come to school with varying attitudes and capacities that determine the extent to which they are able to become "productive, independent" learners. In this system, individuals are defined as responsible/irresponsible, moti-vated/unmotivated, attentive/distracted, or reliable/unreliable.

> A particularized sense of self is... made manifest through a narrow range of descriptors built around management routines, curriculum content, and idealized notions of attitudinal adjustments... it becomes a problem of the student, not the training, nor the demands of a socially constructivist learning environment, if the student does not operate the appropriate mechanisms for self-conduct (Hammerberg, 2004, p. 373).

The problem is not, Hammerberg suggests, that self-regulated independence is "necessarily bad," but that the "techniques used to govern oneself in the learning environment are internalized in such a way that they are described as a part of a private self, as opposed to part of the system." Attributes of individuals are naturalized, instead of understood as socially prepared and organized, making "an individual into an object of case study in terms of psychological norms" (2004, pp. 374, 376).

Those who have mastered technologies of the self, in educational discourse, are often referred to as self-directed, self-motivated, self-regulated, or independent learners. "Children are increasingly expected to be socialized and controlled," educational theorist Ludwig Pongratz writes, "through internalized forms of discipline—hence such terms as "self-regulation" (2007, p. 30). Self-regulation in educational discourse is defined as "being able to control and plan emotions, cognitions, and behaviors" (Willingham, 2011, p. 23).

Self-regulation is measured in the US, for example, on a nation-wide school readiness assessment, the Kindergarten Observation Form, as students' ability to "comfort self, pay attention/stay focused, control impulses, follow directions, play cooperatively, participate in circle time, and handle frustration well" (Applied Survey Research, 2013, p. 4). These self-regulation skills are determined to be the "basic emotion regulation and self-control skills needed to be able to perform well in the Kindergarten classroom" (Applied Survey Research, 2013, p. 4). The importance of self-regulation is reinforced by teacher training and reported research findings that

> good self-regulation in preschool predicts reading and math proficiency in kindergarten, over and above intelligence.... the association of self-regulation and academic achievement continues into elementary and middle school... in teens poor self-regulation is associated with delinquency, drug and alcohol abuse, and risky sexual behavior.... These facts highlight the urgency for teachers to do all they can to help students grow in this area (Willingham, 2011 pp. 23–24).

Thus, paradoxically, self-regulation requires constant training, monitoring, and guidance.

Surveillance

Governmentality functions not only through forces of normalization, but also through surveillance. This form of disciplinary power contributes to the formation of individuals, Foucault argues: "It is a specific technique of power that regards individuals both as objects and instruments of its exercise" (1977, p. 170). The effects of power operate through surveillance or hierarchical observation, which Foucault asserts is embedded in the architecture of many institutions. The design of military camps, for instance, influenced the architecture of these institutions, which were organized to ensure general visibility (like the military commander's tents "erected opposite the streets of their companies"): "For a long time this model of the camp or at least its underlying principle was found in urban development, in the construction of working-class housing estates [projects], hospitals, asylums, prisons, and schools" (Foucault, 1977, p. 171).

The architecture of such institutions was not only built to be seen, but to permit detailed observation and control. The rooms of schools, for example, are generally distributed along corridors with windows that allow supervisors to see into each class. In each classroom, teachers' desks are centrally positioned and taller than student desks, allowing instructors a view of the entire classroom. Even bathrooms are designed to allow surveillance with half-doors that permit school staff to see the legs of students underneath. Many urban middle and high schools now also have entry gates, metal detectors, and no longer have private student lockers, in the name of surveillance and security. Some schools in Asia, likewise, place video cameras in the classroom to enable constant administrator or parental observation. This high-security architecture allows for a single gaze to see everything constantly, making possible what Foucault calls a"panopticon."

The intense, continuous supervision of students is achieved through not only the architecture of schools, but also through classroom management systems that establish a hierarchy of observation. At the top are school administrators supervising credentialed teachers, who direct classified staff (classroom aides, yard duty supervisors). Students, too, are enrolled in this surveillance apparatus, as classroom monitors, teacher's helpers, peer mentors, and conflict mediators. Student surveillance is even built into the curriculum. For instance, in the Guided Language Acquisition Design (GLAD) program, selected students are designated "scouts." Their job is to monitor their peers, passing out "Super Scientist" or "Super Historian" Awards to students who are on task. They are also assigned to monitor student behavior and enforce the GLAD behavior standards to "show respect, solve problems, and make good decisions" (Project G.L.A.D., 2013). Scouts are expected to award their peers certificates acknowledging their adherence to posted guidelines, which include specific body positions (sitting "criss-cross applesauce" or "looking at the speaker"), sanctioned movements ("use walking feet"), and endorsed discourse behaviors ("don't interrupt or blurt-out").

The constant surveillance that students are subject to is illustrated in one fifth-grade student's narrative description of her school day. Asked to write a letter to an incoming second grader about what to expect when she arrives at her new school in California, Evelyn writes:

> Second graders when you line-up you have to be ready for what is coming up. First, we have snack time. Snack time is when you eat a cracker and a juice, but you have to sit ready for snack. That way they could call your table to get snack.

> After snack time we go to the classrooms where we sit in chairs. Then we wait for the teacher to tell us what to do. That is called Learning Lab. After Learning Lab comes recess [and then] we have homework time... After homework we have reading time. Reading time is when you take out a book and read it until it is time to go home.

> After reading time we get our backpacks and wait for the teacher to tell us to line-up. Then when we line-up the teacher will take us out to the bus. In the bus you have to sit down all the time. You can't shout. If you do anything bad you will get in trouble. In the bus there is two boss [bus] monitors. Boss monitors are people who watch you in the bus. If you do something bad and the boss monitors see you they will put your name in a paper. On top of the paper it will say, "Bad List." If you get your name on the list that's a warning. If you get a check that means you have behaved very bad.

> The next day the Boss monitors will give the paper to Mr. S. Mr. S is the person who is in charge.... (Blakely, 2007, pp. 85–86).

For Evelyn, every part of the school day is monitored by some type of authority figure. English is Evelyn's second language, but her substitution of the term boss for bus is a telling phonological error. Almost all of the students' writing samples for this prompt focused exclusively on the rules and routines of the school day. The rules and regulations are, in the students' reflections, much more important for the new second grader to know than the content of instruction. They realize that their success depends on adherence to rules, as one student writes "if you doing a bad job you might get kick out to" (Blakely, 2007, p. 86). Like most of her peers, Evelyn does not discuss the actual content of the lessons. She defines learning as sitting in a chair and waiting for the teacher to tell her what to do. As Foucault writes, "A relation of surveillance, defined and regulated, is inscribed at the heart of teaching, not as an additional or adjacent part, but as a mechanism that is inherent to it and which increases its efficiency" (1977, p. 176).

Through surveillance, disciplinary power becomes an "integrated system... organized as a multiple, automatic, and anonymous power" (Foucault, 1977, p. 176). This power operates through both hierarchical observation (from Mr. S to bus monitors), as well as through a diffused network of relations "from top to bottom, but also," Foucault adds,

> from bottom to top and laterally; this network 'holds' the whole together and traverses it in its entirety with effects of power that derive from one another: supervisors perpetually supervised... and although it is true that its pyramidal organization gives it a 'head', it is the apparatus as a whole that produces 'power' and distributes individuals in this permanent and continuous field. This enables the disciplinary power to be both absolutely indiscreet, since it is everywhere and always alert, since by its very principle it leaves no zone of shade and constantly supervises the very individuals who are entrusted with the task of supervising (1977, p. 177).

In addition to hierarchical observation, disciplinary power also functions, as a result of "normalizing judgments," which bring five distinct operations into play, according to Foucault: 1) it compares individual actions to a whole; 2) it differentiates individuals from one another—in terms of a minimum threshold, an average, and an optimum toward which one must move; 3) it quantitatively measures and hierarchizes the abilities, the level, and "nature" of individuals; 4) "it introduces, through this 'value-giving' measure, the constraint of a conformity that must be achieved"; and 5) it establishes the external limit of the abnormal (Foucault, 1977, p. 183). The perpetual penalty that supervises every instant in disciplinary institutions "compares, differentiates, hierarchizes, homogenizes, and excludes. In short," says Foucault, "it *normalizes*" (1977, p. 183).

Hierarchical observation and normalizing judgment together operate through a specific technique of disciplinary power—the examination. This technique, he argues, has become widespread (from psychology to education), making it possible to extract and constitute knowledge from and about individuals. The examination, Foucault writes, "combines the techniques of an observing hierarchy and those of a normalizing judgment. It is a normalizing gaze, a surveillance that makes it possible to qualify, classify, and to punish" (1977, p. 197). Schools have become sites of uninterrupted examination, making perpetual comparisons; it is a constantly repeated ritual of power. The examination enables teachers, while transmitting their knowledge, to transform the students into an entire field of knowledge. The examination situates individuals in an entire range of documents that encapsulate them, making it possible to capture and fix them. The technique of examination makes each individual into a "case." This case can then be described, judged, measured, compared to others; through this classification students are objectified, and pedagogy, in turn, operates as a science. Examinations thus make possible the calculation of the gaps between individuals and their distribution in a given population (Foucault, 1977).

A letter sent home by one US preschool teacher shows the level of attention devoted to making each student a case, describing, judging, measuring, and comparing individual them. This work supersedes the attention given to academic content:

Hello Parents,

I hope everybody is having a smooth transition into the new year. It is great to have everybody back!! We have created a behavior chart in our classroom that has everybody's name and 4 behavior levels. The four levels are: excellent, good, warning, and bad day. Every child will start the day on good. It is up to them where they end up at the end of the day. Excellent means that they really stood out by having an amazing day. They followed all of the rules, they were good helpers, they shared, etc. Good means that they had a great day as well, just not over the top amazing. We might [have] had to remind them to walk rather than run in the classroom, to share with their friends, or they have had a few warnings, but all in all still a great day. Warning means that we had to talk to them many times throughout the day. They were not following many of the classroom rules, not being respectful to their peers or teachers. Bad day means they really disobeyed the teachers and maybe had to miss out on a fun activity because they were not following the rules and being unsafe. We would love it if you took a look at the chart. Also, we could use your help by encouraging your child to have an excellent day (because if they end up on excellent… they get a sticker at the end of the day)! We believe that this can be a partnership! When you pick up your child, ask them where they ended up on the behavior chart in school. Thank you so much for your help and cooperation. We truly appreciate it! Also, we started with the letter of the week this week and it went great!!! I love all of the "B" words your children brought in for sharing!!!! Thanks!!!

Discipline is routinely exercised through not only systems of surveillance like classroom charts and processes of normalizing and codifying categories of behavior ("excellent, good, warning, bad"), but also through systems of punishment (reminders or loss of "fun activities").

Schools and other institutions are controlled via what Foucault calls "micropenalities" of: "time (latenesses, absences, interruptions of tasks), of activity (inattention, negligence, lack of zeal), of behavior (impoliteness, disobedience), of speech (idle chatter, insolence), of the body (incorrect attitudes, irregular gestures, lack of cleanliness)" (1977, p. 178). What is specific to disciplinary penalty, Foucault says, is non-observance–those behaviors that do not measure up to the rule or that depart from it. The entire domain of non-conforming behaviors is punishable; students commit an "offense" whenever they do not reach the norm or carry out the assigned tasks.

For punishment, a whole series of procedures are used, from tardy slips, warnings, detentions, loss of privileges, enforced public apologies, mandated attendance in counseling, social-skills, anger-management or parent education programs, to suspensions or expulsions. Many more subtle punishments are also deployed:

> By the word punishment, one must understand everything that is capable of making children feel the offence they have committed, everything that is capable of humiliating them, of confusing them... a certain coldness, a certain indifference, a question, a humiliation, a removal (La Salle qtd. in Foucault, 1977, p. 178).

Punishment in schools also includes enrollment in remedial or intervention programs or forced repetition of incorrect or incomplete assignments. Training, as a form of punishment, Foucault argues, is even more primary than forms of punishment meant to make students repent.

In addition to a wide spectrum of punishments, Foucault demonstrates that gratification or awards are also used as disciplinary techniques. Gratification (privileges, recognition, and incentives) play a major role in the process of training and correction (such as the award certificates issued by GLAD scouts, stickers, or a grade of "excellent").

Students' behavior is distributed between a positive and a negative pole; all behavior falls in the field between

> good and bad marks, good and bad points... by play of this quantification, this circulation of awards and debits, thanks to the continuous calculation of plus and minus points, the disciplinary apparatuses hierarchized the 'good' and the 'bad' subjects in relation to one another. Through this micro-economy of a perpetual penalty operates a differentiation... of individuals... their nature, their potentialities, their level of value. By assessing acts with precision, discipline judges individuals 'in truth'; the penalty that it implements is integrated into the cycle of knowledge of individuals (Foucault, 1977, pp. 180–181).

Surveillance is not limited to the monitoring of individuals, but is also a technique of power that is applied to school systems and other broad, institutional practices. Evaluations, standardized testing and other accountability measures in place across the US function as instruments of surveillance, seeking to make transparent the performance of the school for outside observers. Critical educational theorist Pauline Lipman illustrates how surveillance operates, for example, in the Chicago public school system, where there is especially intense state scrutiny of "low-performing" schools:

It is well known among educators... that the best practice is to avoid any controversy that could bring scrutiny from school administrators or district authorities. In short, accountability as a system of surveillance and coercion breeds fear and suppression of dissent and teaches people to silence themselves.... [W]hat is operating here... is surveillance as open coercion. The monitoring eye of the state and its ability to mete out punishment is quite explicit. Education accountability teaches fear and accommodation to repression as a system of "governmentality" that coercively shapes the conduct of persons (Lipman, 2006, pp. 56–57).

School failure rates are used to publicly humiliate schools, teachers, and students as forms of disciplinary control:

[F]ailure is made highly visible while the state intrudes into the lives of teachers and students through intensified regulation and monitoring including holding them accountable to standardized tests, classroom inspections, mandated scripted curricula, and systems of punishment, such as school probation, student retention, and tying teacher evaluations to student test scores. These accountability practices contribute to the legitimation of surveillance and punishment by the state as a normalized practice (Lipman, 2006, p. 55).

The wide-spread acceptance of accountability discourses, argues Lipman, makes surveillance an inevitable, unquestioned part of the way all schools function: "The annual ritual of the publication of standardized test results, state watch lists of schools scoring below state minimums, and... [an] index of failing schools is already routine" (Lipman, 2006, p. 56).

Those frequently most injured by such normalized modes of discipline and surveillance in urban public school systems, Lipman points out, are low-income minority students:

By measuring and sorting students, teachers, and schools and holding them publicly accountable for results on standardized tests, the state brings those who are failing more closely under the gaze of power. Schools and the students designated as failing are overwhelmingly African American and Latino. In these schools, surveillance and punishment have become routine (2006, p. 56).

Equity issues have been appropriated by framing a simple choice between promoting accountability through centralized regulation of schools or continuing the injustices of social promotion, low expectations, and low achievement of students of color. To oppose accountability is, thus, to oppose school improvement. Accountability has accordingly become a closed system; by presenting accountability as the only alternative, official policy becomes a "discourse of containment." Lipman adds that accountability has been turned into "a regime of truth. Education has been redefined as achievement on standardized tests" (2006, p. 57). This "discourse of containment" permits little to no critique, as one Chicago teacher described being met with a wall of silence when she challenged the ethics of high-stakes tests at a teachers' meeting. Though teachers may engage in relatively narrow debates about the level of instructional time spent preparing for standardized tests or the effectiveness of "cultural proficiency" of classroom management systems, it is almost unheard of to examine or critique the overall apparatus of surveillance and its attendant, normalized systems of accountability.

Commodification of Knowledge

In the US, UK, and other Western or Western-influenced nations, widely endorsed accountability systems have resulted in multiple forms of standardization including: national testing regimes that measure student performance at designated ages; regular, ongoing site-visits and inspections or evaluation of school programs; time requirements to set the number of hours students are required to spend on math, reading, and physical education; and district-wide curriculum adoptions linked to national standards. As part of the trend towards accountability and alignment, educational processes routinely reduce production and service to numbers. It is common practice to calculate university rankings, performance indicators, Academic Performance Index (API) scores, and other quantifiable measures of learning outcomes. All of these comprise a kind of commodification of knowledge in schools.

Beginning in the last few decades of the 20th century and continuing into the 21st century, ideas, representations, signs, and symbolic resources have superseded raw materials as a medium of exchange. In this new economy, knowledge has become the principal force of production. Capital growth has shifted away from manufacturing and services to procuring and producing intellectual property (copyrights and patents). "It is conceivable," Lyotard says, "that nation-states will one day fight for control of information, just as they battled in the past for control over territory, and afterwards for control of... raw materials and cheap labor" (1999, p. 5). The status of knowledge has been altered by globalizing forces that have made its possession on a broad level a commercial or national advantage; digital technologies give militaries, for example, strategic advantages in enhancing state security or improving international monitoring (Fleissner, 2009).

Since most economically advanced countries have the overriding objective of building "knowledge economies," there has been enhanced focus on research and education as keys to achieving new knowledge economies. Universities are under pressure to promote the commodification of knowledge produced by faculty and students through university-industry collaboration, promoting innovation, entrepreneurship, and the development of marketable outcomes in the form of knowledge. According to management policy researcher Merle Jacob, "Although universities have always been in the business of producing knowledge, it is now argued that innovation and not more knowledge creation should be a first priority" (2003, p. 126). The terms "academic capitalism" and "the entrepreneurial university" have emerged to describe the impetus for universities to become more deeply involved with industry and government in the development of new knowledge as a marketable commodity. According to policy researcher Henry Etzkowitz and associates,

> There is empirical evidence that identifying, creating and commercializing intellectual property have become institutional objectives in various academic systems. Coming from different academic and national traditions, the university appears to be arriving at a common entrepreneurial format in the late 20th century (2000, p. 313; Valimaa & Hoffman, 2008).

Collaborations between academics at Stanford University and technology businesses in Silicon Valley, for example, combine business interests with university objectives to co-sponsor projects like: the Stanford Computer Forum (to align technology companies with university research); private equity and iPhone app clubs; conferences such as the Silicon Valley Energy Summit; and the Silicon Genesis (oral history project) or the Stanford Silicon Valley Archives. These library archives of the "pioneers of Silicon Valley" comprise the collected works of Silicon Valley billionaires, the founders of HP, Google, Netflix, Pandora, and Instagram, who are all Stanford alumni. Across the US and other developed nations, it is now common for many university courses in business schools and science and technology departments to be taught by "professor-entrepreneurs" who rotate between time in the classroom and business ventures, mentoring students in writing business plans or learning how to patent ideas.

Globalization and the technologies that contribute to time-space compression have led to economic incentives for the ever-increasing speed of production and distribution of knowledge. These conditions have altered educational institutions, turning universities into "theaters of fast knowledge... driven by an ethos of performance in teaching and research conferences that now restrict presentations to bite-sized bits no longer than fifteen minutes" (Peters & Besley, 2006, p. 97). TED Talks, for example, conferences sponsored by the Technology, Entertainment, and Design non-profit organization, aim to "bring together the world's most fascinating thinkers and doers, who are challenged to give the talk of their lives (in 18 minutes or less)" (TED, 2013). In a similar trend to compress and speed up knowledge distribution, microblogging sites, like the online social networking service Twitter, limit text-based messages to 140 characters.

Efficiency is the tacit, central aim of educational policy in many Western nations, where policies are designed according to performative epistemologies to align schools and make them predictable, with calculable outcomes. The standards-based curriculum that has spread throughout public education is "being organized scientifically for efficiency, deriving learning objectives from social and economic needs and casting teachers as managers of the process of producing student achievement scores" (Sleeter & Stillman, 2005, p. 44). This efficiency trend, sometimes referred to as McDonaldization, is apparent, for example, in the US in the standardization of curriculum and assessments on a national level, through the transition to Common Core and Smarter Balanced Assessments, as well as the national focus in professional development on horizontal and vertical alignment. The primary goal of these policies is to standardize classroom management and instructional practices between and across grade levels to maximize efficiency. The result is the advent of machine-graded, multiple choice exams and streamlined, standards-based textbook and curriculum packages. "Rather than asking whose knowledge, language, and points of view are most worth teaching children, teachers and administrators are pressed to ask how well children are scoring on standardized measures of achievement" (Sleeter & Stillman, 2005, p. 44). The focus on standardized testing measures has likewise shifted evaluation from

> what the school does for the student to what the student does for the school... The entire enterprise establishes a new metric and a new set of goals based on a constant striving to win the market game.... under these conditions not only does education become a marketable commodity like bread and cars in which the values, procedures, and metaphors of business dominate, but its results must be reducible to standardized 'performance indicators' (Apple, 1999, pp. 9, 12).

Lyotard predicted that learning would begin to circulate along the same lines as money, instead of for its purported educational value. The pertinent distinction, then, says Lyotard, is "no longer... between ignorance and knowledge, but rather... between... units of knowledge exchanged in a daily maintenance framework ['payment knowledge']... versus funds of knowledge dedicated to optimizing the performance of a project ['investment knowledge']" (1984, p. 7). For such an exchange system to take place, there needs to be a precise system of measurement and accountability. PreK–12 schools have become part of an outputs-driven performance culture. Schools are monitored, audited, and evaluated, so that results or "learning outcomes" can be measured and compared.

"The illusion of measured learning," write Lave and McDermott,

> makes substantial what is not and reifies it into numbers that align children within
> hierarchies that replicate injustices in the distribution of access and rewards.... [I]n a
> system in which success is defined by failure of others, in a system in which every-
> one has to do better than everyone else, there is no way for everyone to achieve
> school success (2002, p. 21).

Accountability systems have led to the emergence of rhetoric and funding to promote "choice" or "free market" structures in education, including charter schools and performance-based waivers that allow select, informed families to transfer out of failing schools. As educational researchers Trevor Hussey and Patrick Smith put it, "education has become a commodity, and the 'products' it offers to its 'customers' have had to be commodified: divided into distinct, measurable quantities or modules each capable of being 'bought' by prescribed units of assessment" (2002, p. 220). In many communities, for instance, it is expected that parents will go "Kindergarten shopping" to find the right school for their child. This trend continues through higher education with organized tours of college campuses and annual rankings published by *US News and World Report* that quantify everything from academics to campus life.

The specification of learning outcomes and criteria of assessment are mandatory in this performative structure. The state requires transparency; school districts must publish their scores on standardized assessments for public review. In this outputs-driven context, learning is, Lave and McDermott argue, not simply about the production of knowledge, but about the

> production and distribution of assessed knowledge. The learner produces not for
> himself, but for his or her place in the system. It is no longer sufficient for him to
> simply learn. The only learner who is productive is one who produces test scores for
> the school... (2002, p. 44).

There is an over-reliance on assessment and accountability systems, argue Hussey and Smith:

> while learning outcomes can be valuable if properly used, they have been misappro-
> priated and adopted widely at all levels within the education system to facilitate the
> managerial process. This has led to their distortion. The claim that they can be made
> precise by being written with a prescribed vocabulary of special descriptors so as to
> serve as objective, measurable devices for monitoring performance, is fundamen-
> tally mistaken, and they may be damaging to education when used in this way
> (2002, p. 220).

With the commodification of knowledge, teachers have been required to develop only those learning objectives that are observable and measurable. Many districts in the US, for example, have adopted policies that require teachers to develop "SMART goals" that are "Specific, Measurable, Attainable, Realistic, and Time-Bound." These goals are used to specify exactly what skills or knowledge students will have attained by the end of a distinct period of learning. Assessments are then derived from these objectives to measure what students can do, making the entire process explicit, transparent, and auditable.

In this outputs-driven culture, a learning objective like "students will understand..." is not an acceptable (SMART) goal, since "understanding" cannot be observed nor directly measured. The accepted descriptors for developing more specific learning outcomes, such as "name," "recall," "explain," or "illustrate" or adding phrases such as "in detail" or "fully" fail to make the objectives sufficiently precise because all these terms require interpretation. "The meanings of these terms are just as relative to the situation, subject matter or level... they will remain ambiguous whatever descriptors are used" (Hussey & Smith, 2002, p. 225).

SMART goals or other presumably measurable learning outcomes give the impression of precision, but even when they are stated as simply as "will count to ten without errors," they are difficult to measure precisely. Some students will perform this counting task easily, others hesitatingly. They may count "with or without understanding." "To make [learning outcomes] applicable [teachers] need to specify knowledge, understanding, skills, and abilities, rather than simple behavioral responses, and to indicate the quality or standard of these" (Hussey & Smith, 2002, p. 225).

Concrete criteria for measuring academic success are an illusion. Their clarity, explicitness, and objectivity are spurious, argue Hussey and Smith. Any term requires interpretation "in the light of a prior understanding of what quality or standard is appropriate in a given subject at a given level — yet this is what the learning outcomes are supposed to be stating with precision" (Hussey & Smith, 2002, p. 227). For learning outcomes to be informative or useful, they must be understood within the context of students' experience and prior performance. Thus, it is often useless, Hussey and Smith argue, to frame them in advance. Establishing learning outcomes, Hussey and Smith conclude, may have value

when properly conceived and used in ways that respect their limitations... but they are damaging to education if seen as precise prescriptions that must be spelled out in detail before teaching can begin and which are objective and measurable devices suitable for monitoring educational practices (2002, p. 222).

The focus on alignment across US districts exacerbates this problem, since enforcing "shared language" across entire grade levels or school districts further decontextualizes learning outcomes. Asking educators to align their instructional practices and curriculum standards horizontally within each grade level and vertically across the K–12 span presumes that every group of students and every teacher should have the same set of approaches. The enforcement of the same curriculum, policies, and class-room management practices does not take into account contextual factors — students' funds of knowledge, teacher-student relationships, or any other local considerations. Setting learning objectives in absence of this localized information, Hussey and Smith argue, is impossible because "the quality of the skills and capacities can only be grasped from the context" (2002, p. 229).

Context is generally ignored, however, in teacher preparation where the focus remains on providing educators the tools to implement "best practices." Through the commodification of knowledge, teacher preparation has in many instances become little more than marketing of approved products for instruction and remediation: "The operational assumptions are that the right method, textually encoded into a particular commodity and then decoded and remediated into a normalized set of behaviors around the text/commodity constitute an optimal educational practice and experience" (Luke, 2004, p. 1434). As a result, educational research has been reduced to product testing, and teacher training has become a form of marketing educational policies as commodities (standards-aligned textbooks, instructional techniques, class-room management systems). This leads to the recasting of educational policy as commodity testing, endorsing, and purchasing. In this context, teacher and administrator credentialing has become the main way to verify that educators have acquired the normative practices, discourse, and disciplines that ensure fidelity to state-adopted curriculum packages. Commodification of knowl-edge leads to deskilling of teachers, narrowing of curriculum and pedagogi-cal choices, decontextualization, neglect of social relations and students' funds of knowledge, and maintenance of colonial/modernist hierarchies.

A classroom job chart shows who is assigned to each role for the current week. Two students are selected to be the class "Scouts." Their job is to function as a panopticon, keeping their eyes on all students, monitoring their behavior, and awarding points or prizes to those in compliance with class rules.

A classroom bulletin board presenting ranked lists of rewards and consequences, making visible a system of gratification-punishment for behavioral management.

References

Abu El-Haj, T. R. (2007). "I was born here, but my home, it's not here": Educating for democratic citizenship in an era of transnational migration and global conflict. *Harvard Educational Review, 77*(3), 1–2.

Alim, H. S., Ibrahim, A., & Pennycook, A. (Eds.), (2009). *Global linguistic flows: Hip hop cultures, youth identities, and the politics of language.* New York, NY: Routledge.

Allington, R.L. (2002). *Big brother and the national reading curriculum: How ideology trumped evidence.* Portsmouth, NH: Heinemann.

——(2006). Reading lessons and federal policy making: An overview and introduction to the special issue. *The Elementary School Journal, 107*(1), 3–15.

Alonso, A. & Arzoz, I. (2003). *Basque cyberculture: From digital Euskadi to* CyberEuskall-herria. Reno, NV: Center for Basque Studies, University of Nevada, Reno.

Altschuler, G.C. (2003). *All shook up: How rock 'n' roll changed America (Pivotal moments in American history).* New York, NY: Oxford University Press.

Altshuler, S.J. & Schmautz, T. (2006). No Hispanic student left behind: The consequences of "high stakes" testing. *Children and Schools, 28*(1) June, 5–14.

Anderson, B. (1991). *Imagined communities.* New York, NY: Verso.

Anzaldúa, G. (1999). *Borderlands/La frontera: The new Mestiza.* San Francisco, CA: Aunt Lute Press.

Appadurai, A. (1986). *The social life of things: Commodities in cultural perspective.* Cambridge, MA: Cambridge University Press.

——(1996). *Modernity at large.* Minneapolis, MN: University of Minnesota Press.

Appell, G. & Hemphill, D. (2005). *American popular music: A multicultural history.* New York, NY: Thomson-Schirmer.

Apple, M. (1979). *Ideology and curriculum.* London: Routledge & Kegan Paul.

——(1999). Rhetorical reforms: Markets, standards, and inequality. *Current Issues in Comparative Education, 1*(2), 6–18.

——(2001). Comparing neo-liberal projects and inequality in education. *Comparative Education, 37*(4), 409–423.

Applied Survey Research. (2013). *Kindergarten observation form. The ASR school readiness assessment model.* Claremont, CA: Applied Survey Research.

Aronowitz, S. (1995). Literature as social knowledge: Mikhail Bakhtin and the reemergence of the Human Sciences. In A. Mandeker (Ed.), *Bakhtin in contexts: Across the disciplines.* Evanston. IL: Northwestern University Press.

Auman, M. (2008). *Step up to writing primary teacher's manual and classroom reproducibles, second edition*. Longmont: Sopris West Educational Services.

Bakhtin, M. (1981). *The dialogic imagination: Four essays*. Austin, TX: University of Texas Press.

Ball, S.J. (1990). *Politics and policy making in education*. London: Routledge.

Banks, J. A. (1991). The dimensions of multicultural education. *Multicultural Leader, 4*, 5–6.

——— (1993). Multicultural education: Historical development, dimensions, and practice. *Review of Research in Education, 19*, 3–49.

———(1994). *Multiethnic education: Theory and practice, third edition*. Boston, MA: Allyn & Bacon.

——— (2007). Approaches to multicultural curriculum reform. In J.A. Banks & C.A. McGee Banks (Eds.), *Multicultural education: Issues and perspectives*. Hoboken, NJ: John Wiley & Sons.

Barber, M. & Mourshed, M. (2007). *How the world's best-performing school systems come out on top*. New York, NY: McKinsey and Co.

Barthes, R (1981). The discourse of history. *Comparative Criticism, 3*, 7–20.

Basch, L. et. al. (2008). Transnational projects: A new perspective and theoretical premises. In S. Khagram & P. Levitt (Eds.), *The transnational studies reader: Intersections and innovations*. New York, NY & London: Routledge.

Baudrillard, J. (1988). *Jean Baudrillard: Selected writings*. Stanford, CA: Stanford University Press.

———(1994). *Simulacra and simulation*. Ann Arbor, MI: University of Michigan Press.

Baugh, J. (1995). The law, linguistics, and education: Educational reform for African American language minority students. *Linguistics and Education, 7*, 87–105.

Baumann, Z. (1998). *Globalization: The human consequences*. New York, NY: Columbia University Press.

Bazron, B., Osher, D., & Fleischman, S. Creating culturally responsive schools. *Educational Leadership, 63*(1) (Sept., 2005), 83–84.

Berry, J. W., Poortinga, Y. H., Segall, M. H., & Dasen, P. R. (1992). *Cross-cultural psychology: Research and applications*. New York, NY: Cambridge University Press.

Besley, A.C. (2003). Hybridized and globalized: Youth cultures in the postmodern era. *The Review of Education, Pedagogy, and Cultural Studies, 25*, 153–177.

Bhabha, H. K. (1994). *The location of culture*. New York, NY: Routledge.

Bianchini, J.A. & Cavazos, L.M. (2007). Learning from students, inquiry into practice, and participation in professional communities: Beginning teachers' uneven progress toward equitable science teaching. *Journal of Research in Science Teaching, 44*(4), 586–612.

Blakely, E.M. (2007). *Interrupted narratives: Cultural invisibility in the classroom*. San Francisco, CA: San Francisco State University.

Blassingame, J. W., (Ed.), (1971). *New perspectives in black studies*. Urbana, IL: University of Illinois Press.

Blauner, R. (1969). Internal colonialism and ghetto revolt. *Social Problems*, 393–408.

Bloome, D., Katz, L., and Champion, T. (2003). Young children's narratives and ideologies of language in classrooms. *Reading and Writing Quarterly, 19*(3), 205–223.

Bourdieu, P. (1991). *Language and symbolic power*. Cambridge, MA: Harvard University Press.

Bowers, C.A. (1995). *Educating for an ecologically sustainable culture*. Albany, NY: SUNY Press.

Bowles, S. & Gintis, H. (1976). *Schooling in capitalist America: Educational reform and the contradictions of economic life*. New York, NY: Basic Books.

Boyd, H. (2010). Gender Differences. www.education.com/magazine/article/Gender, accessed 6-10-11.

Brizendine, L. (2010). *The male brain*. New York, NY: Broadway Books.

Bruch, P., Jehangir, R., Jacobs, W., & Ghere, D. (2004). Enabling access: Toward multicultural development curricula. *Journal of Developmental Education, 27*(3), 12–19.

Buras, K. L. and Motter, P. (2006). Toward a subaltern cosmopolitan multiculturalism. In M.W. Apple & K.L. Buras (Eds.), *The subaltern speak: Curriculum, power, and educational struggles*. New York, NY: Routledge.

Burns, J.F. (2011). Cameron criticizes 'multiculturalism' in Britain. *New York Times,* February 5, 2011, http://www.nytimes.com/2011/02/06/world/europe/06britain.html, accessed 3–20–11.

Butler, J. (1993). Imitation and gender insubordination. In H. Abelove, M.A. Barale, & D.M. Halperin (Eds.), *The lesbian and gay studies reader*. New York, NY: Routledge.

——(2004). *Precarious life: The powers of mourning and violence*. London: Verso.

Cahoone, L. (2003). *From modernism to postmodernism: An anthology*. Cambridge, MA: Blackwell Publishing.

California Department of Education. (1998). *History-social science content standards for California public school, kindergarten through grade twelve*. Sacramento, CA: California Department of Education.

Carmichael, S. & Hamilton, C. V. (1967). *Black power: The politics of liberation in America*. New York, NY: Vintage.

Carnoy, M. (2000). Globalization and educational reform. In N.P. Stromquist & K. Monkman (Eds.), *Globalization and education: Integration and contestation across cultures*. Lanham, MD: Rowman and Littlefield.

Castells, M. (1996). *The rise of the network society*. New York, NY: Blackwell.

——(1997). *The power of identity*. New York, NY: Blackwell.

Chomsky, N. (1975). *The logical structure of linguistic theory*. New York, NY: Plenum Press.

Clark, K. (2000). *Puberty: What's normal/what's not*. Santa Cruz, CA: ETR Associates.

Clarke, D.B., Doel, M.A., & Housiaux, K.M.L. (2003). *The consumption reader*. London: Routledge.

Clifford, J. (1988). *The predicament of culture: Twentieth-century ethnography, literature, and art*. Cambridge, MA: Harvard University Press.

——(1997). *Routes: Travel and translation in the late twentieth century*. Cambridge, MA: Harvard University Press.

Cohen, L. and Cohen, A. (Eds.), (1986). *Multicultural education: A sourcebook for teachers*. London: Harper and Row.

Coleman, D., & Pimentel, S. (2011). *Publishers' criteria for the Common Core State Standards in English Language Arts and Literacy, Grades 3–12*. Washington, DC: CCSSO & NASBE.

Coloma, R. S. (2009). 'Destiny has thrown the Negro and the Filipino under the tutelage of America': Race and curriculum in the Age of Empire. *Curriculum Inquiry, 39*(4), 495–519.

Common Core State Standards Initiative. (2012). http://www.corestandards.org/about-the-standards, accessed 10-25-13.

Cook, L. A. (1947). Intergroup education. *Review of Educational Research, 17*, 267–278.

Cope, B. & Kalantzis, M. (Eds., for the New London Group), (2000). *Multiliteracies: Literacy learning and the design of social futures*. London and New York, NY: Routledge.

Cortazzi, M. & Jin, L. (2001). Large classes in China: 'Good' teachers and interaction. In D.A. Watkins & J.B. Biggs (Eds.), *Teaching the Chinese learner: Psychological and pedagogical perspectives*. Hong Kong: Comparative Education Research Center, University of Hong Kong.

Cuban, L. (2004). Assessing the 20-year impact of multiple intelligences on schooling. *The Teachers College Record, 106*(1), 140–146.

Cunningham, J.W. (2002). The National Reading Panel Report [A Review]. In R.L. Allington (Ed.), *Big brother and the national reading curriculum: How ideology trumped evidence*. Portsmouth, NH: Heinemann.

Darling-Hammond, L. (2010). *The flat world and education: How America's commitment to equity will determine our future*. New York, NY: Teachers College Press.

Davis, A. (1998). *Blues legacies and black feminism*. New York, NY: Pantheon Books.

Derman-Sparks, L., & Ramsey, P. (2006). *What if all the kids are white: Anti-bias multicultural education with young children and families*. New York, NY: Teachers College Press.

Delpit, L. (1995). *Other people's children: Cultural conflict in the classroom*. New York, NY: New Press.

Dillard, J.L. (1972). *Black English*. New York, NY: Random House.

Dirlik, A. (1999). Is there history after Eurocentrism? Globalism, postcolonialism, and the disavowal of history. *Cultural Critique, 42*, 1–34.

Disney Studios. (2001). *Disney's American legends*. Burbank, CA: Walt Disney Studios.

DuBois, W.E.B. (1935). *Black reconstruction in America*. New York, NY: Harcourt Brace.

Dudley-Marling, C. (2005). Disrespecting teachers: Troubling developments in reading instruction. *English Education, 37*(4), 272–279.

Dulay, H., & Burt., M. (1974). A new perspective on the creative construction process in child second language acquisition. *Language Learning, 24*(2), 253–278.

Duncan-Andrade, J. M. R. (2004). Your best friend or your worst enemy: Youth popular culture, pedagogy, and curriculum in urban classrooms. *The Review of Education, Pedagogy and Cultural Studies, 26*, 313–337.

Duncum, P. (2001). Visual culture: Developments, definitions, and directions for art education. *Studies in Art Education, 42(3)*, 101–112.

Duranti, A. (Ed.) (2001). *Linguistic anthropology: A reader*. Malden, MA: Blackwell Publishing.

Dussel, E. (1998). Beyond Eurocentrism: The world-system and the limits of modernity. In F. Jameson and M. Miyoshi (Eds.), *Cultures of globalization*. Durham, NC: Duke University Press.

Dyson, A.H. (1997). *Writing superheroes: Contemporary childhood, popular culture and classroom literacy*. New York, NY: Teachers College Press.

———— (2003). Welcome to the jam: Popular culture, school literacy, and the making of childhoods. *Harvard Educational Review, 73*(3), 328–361.

Ellsworth, E. (1989) Why doesn't this feel empowering? Working through the repressive myths of critical pedagogy. *Harvard Educational Review, 59*(3), 297–325.

Erickson, F., & Gutierrez, K. (2002). Comment: Culture, rigor, and science in educational research. *Educational Researcher, 31*(8), 21–24.

Etzkowitz, H., Webster, A., Gebhardt, C., & Cantisano Terra, B. R. (2000). The future of the university and the university of the future: Evolution of ivory tower to entrepreneurial paradigm. *Research Policy, 29*, 313–330.

Fackler, M. (2013). In textbook fight, Japan leaders seek to recast history. *The New York Times*, December 28, 2013, http://www.nytimes.com/2013/12/29/world/asia/japan-fights-a-political-battle-using-history-texts.html, accessed 1–9–14.

Faruqi, S.S. (2011, June 29). Decolonising our universities. *Star*. Malaysia.

Fine, G.A. & Mechling, A. (1993). Child saving and children's cultures at century's end. In S.B. Heath & M. McLaughlin (Eds.), *Identity and inner-city youth: Beyond ethnicity and gender*. New York, NY: Teachers College Press.

Fleissner, P. (2009). The "commodification" of knowledge in the global information society. *Communication, Capitalism, and Critique, 7*(2), 228–238.

Floyd, S. (1995). *The power of black music: Interpreting its history from Africa to the United States*. New York, NY: Oxford University Press.

Foucault, M. (1965). *Madness and civilization: A history of insanity in the age of reason*. New York, NY: Vintage Books.

—— (1972). *The archeology of knowledge and the discourse on language*. New York, NY: Pantheon Books.

—— (1973). *The birth of the clinic: An archaeology of medical perception*. New York, NY: Vintage.

—— (1977). *Discipline and punish: The birth of the prison*. New York, NY: Pantheon.

—— (1980). In C. Gordon, (Ed.), *Power/Knowledge: Selected interviews and other writings, 1972–77*. New York, NY: Pantheon Books.

—— (1984). Truth and power. In Rabinow, P. (Ed.), *The Foucault Reader*. New York, NY: Pantheon Books.

—— (1988). *Technologies of the self: A seminar with Michel Foucault*. Martin, L. H., Gutman, H., & Hutton, P. (Eds.). Amherst, MA: University of Massachusetts Press.

—— (1990). Right of death and power over life. *The history of sexuality, vol. 1* New York, NY: Vintage.

Fraenkel, J., Wallen, N., & Hyun, H. (2012). *How to design and evaluate research in education*. New York, NY: McGraw-Hill.

Franklin, V.P. (2002). Introduction: cultural capital and African-American education. *The Journal of African-American History, 87*, 175–181.

Freire, P. (1970). *Pedagogy of the oppressed*. New York, NY: Continuum.

Fry, E. (1977). *Elementary reading instruction*. New York, NY: McGraw-Hill.

García Canclini, N. (1995). *Hybrid cultures*. Minneapolis, MN: University of Minnesota Press.

—— (2001). *Consumers and citizens: Globalization and multicultural conflicts*. Minneapolis, MN: University of Minnesota Press.

Gardner, H. (Ed.), (1993). *Multiple intelligences: The theory in practice*. New York, NY: Basic Books.

Gardner, S. (2004). *Family life education: Teacher training: Elementary*. San Rafael, CA: Marin County Office of Education.

Gay, G. (2004). Beyond *Brown*: Promoting equality through multicultural education. *Journal of Curriculum and Supervision, 19*(3), 193–216.

Gee, J.P. (1990). *Social linguistics and literacies*. Bristol, PA: Falmer Press.

—— (1993). *An introduction to human language: Fundamental concepts in linguistics*. Upper Saddle River, NJ: Prentice Hall.

—— (1999). Critical Issues: Reading and the New Literacy Studies: Reframing the National Academy of Sciences Report on Reading. *Journal of Literacy Research, 31*(3), 355–374.

—— (2000–2001). Identity as an analytic lens for research in education. In W.G. Secada (Ed.), *Review of research in education*. Washington, D.C.: American Educational Research Association.

—— (2003). Opportunity to learn: A language-based perspective on assessment. *Assessment in Education, 10*(1), 27–46.

Geertz, C. (1973). *The interpretation of cultures*. New York, NY: Basic Books.

—— (2012). Common standards drive new reading approaches. *Education Week,* November 14, 2012, 1–5.

Gewertz, C. (2012). Scales tip toward nonfiction under common core. *Education Week,* November 14, 2012, 18–22.

Giroux, H. & Penna, A. (1979). Social education in the classroom: The dynamics of the hidden curriculum. *Theory and Research in Social Education, 7*(1), Spring 1979, 21–42.

—— & Simon, R. (1989). Schooling, popular culture, and a pedagogy of possibility. In H. Giroux & R. Simon (Eds.), *Popular culture, schooling and everyday life*. Granby, MA: Bergin and Garvey Publishers.

González, N. (2005). Beyond culture: The hybridity of funds of knowledge. In N. González, L.C. Moll, & C. Amanti (Eds.), *Funds of knowledge: Theorizing practices in households, communities, and classrooms*. Mahwah, NJ: Erlbaum.

Good, R.H., Kaminski, R.A., Simmons, D., & Kame'enui. E.J. (2001). *Using dynamic indicators of basic early literacy skills (DIBELS) in an outcomes-driven model: Steps to reading outcomes*. Eugene, OR: Oregon School Study Council.

Gordon, M. M. (1964). *Assimilation in American life: The role of race, religion, and national origins*. New York, NY: Oxford University Press

Grewal, I. (2005). *Transnational America: Feminisms, diasporas, neoliberalisms*. Durham, NC: Duke University Press.

—— & Kaplan, C. (Eds.), (1994). *Scattered hegemonies: Postmodernity and transnational feminist practices*. Minneapolis, MN: University of Minnesota Press.

Grossberg, L. (1994). Bringin' it all back home—pedagogy and cultural studies. In H. Giroux & P. McLaren (Eds.), *Between borders: Pedagogy and the politics of cultural studies*. New York, NY: Routledge.

Gu, M.Y. (2001). *Education in China and abroad: Perspectives from a lifetime in comparative education, CERC Studies in Comparative Education 9*. Hong Kong: Comparative Education Research Centre, University of Hong Kong.

Gutiérrez, K. D., Baquedano-López, P., & Tejeda, C. (1999). Rethinking diversity: Hybridity and hybrid language practices in the third space. *Mind, Culture, and Activity, 6*(4), 286–303.

Habermas, J. (1971). *Knowledge and human interests*. Boston, MA: Beacon Press.

Hall, S. (Ed.), (1996). *Representation: Cultural representations and signifying practices*. London: Sage Publications.

—— (2002). Notes on deconstructing the popular. In S. Duncombe (Ed.), *Cultural resistance reader*. London: Verso.

Hammerberg, D.D. (2004). Technologies of the self in classrooms designed as "learning environments": (Im)possible ways of being in early literacy instruction. In B.M. Baker & K.E. Heyning (Eds.), *Dangerous coagulations? The uses of Foucault in the study of education*. New York, NY: Peter Lang.

Haraway, D. (1991). *Simians, cyborgs and women: The reinvention of nature*. New York, NY: Routledge.

Harding, S.G. (1992). After Eurocentrism: Challenges for the philosophy of science. *PSA: Proceedings of the biennial meeting of the philosophy of science association, vol. 2: Symposium and invited papers*, 311–319.

—— (1998). *Is science multicultural? Postcolonialisms, feminisms, and epistemologies*. Bloomington and Indianapolis, IN: Indiana University Press.

Harvey, D. (2000). Time-space compression and the postmodern condition. In D. Held & A. McGrew (Eds.), *The global transformations reader: An introduction to the globalization debate*. Cambridge, MA: Polity Press.

Heath, S.B. (1982). *Ways with words: Language, life, and work in communities and classrooms*. New York, NY: Cambridge University Press.

—— (2001). Three's not a crowd: Plans, roles, and focus in the arts. *Educational Researcher, 30*(7), 10–17.

—— & McLaughlin, M.W. (Eds.), (1993). *Identity and inner-city youth: Beyond ethnicity and gender*. New York, NY: Teachers College Press.

Hemphill, D. (1992). Thinking hard about culture in adult education: Not a trivial pursuit. *Adult Learning*. May, *3*(7), 8–12.

—— (1999). The blues and the scientific method. *Proceedings, adult education research conference*. De Kalb, IL: Northern Illinois University.

Hirsch, E.D. (1987). *Cultural literacy: What every American needs to know*. Boston, MA: Houghton Mifflin, 1987.

Ho, I.T. (2001). Are Chinese teachers authoritarian? In D.A. Watkins & J.B. Biggs (Eds.), *Teaching the Chinese learner: Psychological and pedagogical perspectives*. Hong Kong: Comparative Education Research Center, University of Hong Kong.

Hsu, M. (2000). *Dreaming of gold, dreaming of home: Transnationalism and migration between the US and China, 1882–1943*. Stanford, CA: Stanford University Press.

Hussey, T. & Smith, P. (2002). The trouble with learning outcomes. *Active Learning in Higher Education, 3*(3), 220–233.

Jacob, M. (2003). Rethinking science and commodifying knowledge. *Policy Futures in Education, 1*(1), 125–142.

Jones, L. (Amiri Baraka). (1963). *Blues people*. New York, NY: Morrow.

Joseph, G. G. (1997). Foundations of Eurocentrism in mathematics. In A.B. Powell & M. Frankenstein (Eds.), *Ethnomathematics: Challenging Eurocentrism in mathematics education*. Albany, NY: SUNY Press.

Katzew, I. (1996). Casta painting: Identity and social stratification in colonial Mexico. In *New world order: Casta painting and colonial Latin America*. New York, NY: Americas Society Art Gallery.

Kennard, M.E. (1989). *The corporation in the classroom: The struggles over meanings of menstrual education in sponsored films, 1947–1983*. (Doctoral dissertation: The University of Wisconsin, Madison.)

Khagram, S. & Levitt, P. (Eds.), (2008). *The transnational studies reader: Intersections and innovations*. New York, NY and London: Routledge.

Kinzer, C.K., et al. (2012). Examining the effects of text and images on story comprehension: An eye-tracking study of reading in a video game and comic book. In P.J. Dunston, et al. (Eds.), *Literacy Research Association Yearbook, 61* (pp. 259–275). Chicago, IL: LRA.

Kotex. (1992). *Becoming aware educational kit: Puberty kit for girls & their mothers.* Kimberly-Clark Corporation.

——(2005). *It's a girl thing.* www.kotex.com. Kimberly-Clark Corporation.

——(2013). The U by Kotex: Puberty teaching resources. http://www.teachers.ubykotex.com.au/section/Home/Teachers_Resources, accessed 11–26–13.

Kovecses, Z. (2002). *Metaphor: A practical introduction.* New York, NY: Oxford University Press.

Kraidy, M.M. (2002). Hybridity in cultural globalization. *Communication Theory, 12*(3), 316–339.

Krashen, S. (1982). *Principles and practice in second language acquisition.* Oxford: Pergamon.

Kromidas, M. (2011). Elementary forms of cosmopolitanism: Blood, birth, and bodies in immigrant New York City. *Harvard Educational Review. 81*(3), Fall 2011, 581–605.

Kuhn, T.S. (1969). *The structure of scientific revolutions.* Chicago, IL: University of Chicago Press.

Labov, W. (1972). *Language in the inner city: Studies in the black English vernacular.* Philadelphia, PA: University of Pennsylvania Press.

Lakoff, G. & Johnson, M. (1980). *Metaphors we live by.* Chicago, IL: University of Chicago Press.

—— (1987). *Women, fire, and dangerous things: What categories reveal about the mind.* Chicago, IL: University of Chicago Press.

Lam, W.S.E. (2004). Border discourses and identities in transnational youth culture. In J. Mahiri (Ed.), *What they don't learn in school: Literacy in the lives of urban youth.* New York, NY: Peter Lang.

—— (2006). Chapter 6: Culture and learning in the context of globalization: Research directions. *Review of Research in Education, 30*, 213–237.

—— & Rosario-Ramos, E. (2009). Multilingual literacies in transnational digitally mediated contexts: An exploratory study of immigrant teens in the United States. *Language and Education, 23*(2), 171–190.

Lave, J. (1988). *Cognition in practice: Mind, mathematics, and culture in everyday life.* New York, NY: Cambridge University Press.

——(1996). Teaching, as learning, in practice. *Mind, Culture, and Activity, 3*(3), 149–164.

—— & McDermott, R. (2002). Estranged labor learning. *Outlines. Critical Practice Studies, 4*(1), 19–48.

—— & Wenger, E. (1991). *Situated learning: Legitimate peripheral participation.* New York, NY: Cambridge University Press.

Levitt, P. & Schiller, N.G. (2008). Conceptualizing simultaneity: A transnational social field perspective on society. In S. Khagram & P. Levitt (Eds.), *The transnational studies reader: Intersections and innovations.* New York, NY: Routledge.

Lindsey, D.B. et al. (2009). *Culturally proficient learning communities: Confronting inequities through collaborative curiosity.* Thousand Oaks, CA: Corwin Press.

Lipman, P. (2006). The politics of accountability in a post-9/11 world. *Cultural Studies ↔ Critical Methodologies, 6*(52), 52–72.

Lipsitz, G. (1990). *Time passages: Collective memory and American popular culture.* Minneapolis, MN: University of Minnesota Press.

Loveless, T. (2012). *The 2012 Brown Center Report on American Education: How Well Are American Students Learning? With Sections on Predicting the Effect of the Common Core State Standards, Achievement Gaps on the Two NAEP Tests, and Misinterpreting International Test Scores, 3*(1). Washington, DC: Brookings Institution.

Luke, A. (2004). Teaching after the market: From commodity to cosmopolitan. *The Teachers College Record, 106*(7), 1422–1443.

——— & Luke, C. (2000). A situated perspective on cultural globalization. In N.C. Burbules & C.A. Torres (Eds.), *Globalization and education: Critical perspectives.* New York, NY: Routledge.

Luria, A.R. (1976). *Cognition and development: Its cultural and social foundations.* Cambridge, MA: Harvard University Press.

——— (1979). *The making of mind: A Personal account of Soviet psychology.* Cambridge, MA: Harvard University Press.

Lyotard, J. (1999). *The postmodern condition: A report on knowledge.* Minneapolis, MN: The University of Minnesota Press.

Mabardi, S. (2000). Encounters of a heterogeneous kind: Hybridity in cultural theory. In R. DeGrandis & Z. Bernd (Eds.), *Critical Studies, Vol. 13: Unforeseeable Americas— Questioning cultural hybridity in the Americas.* Atlanta, GA: Rodopi.

Madaus, G.F. & Clarke, M. (2001). The adverse impact of high stakes testing on minority students: Evidence from 100 years of test data. In G. Orfield & M. L. Kornhaber (Eds.), *Raising standards or raising barriers? Inequality and high stakes testing in public education.* New York, NY: The Century Foundation.

Maira, S. and Soep, E. (Eds.), (2005). *Youthscapes: The popular, the national, and the global.* Philadelphia, PA: University of Pennsylvania Press.

Marx, K. (1971). *Capital: Vol I. A critical analysis of capitalist production.* Moscow: Progress Publishers. (Original publication, 1887).

McCarthy, C. (1993). Multicultural approaches to racial inequality in the United States. In L. Castanell & W. Pinar (Eds.), *Understanding curriculum as racial text.* Albany, New York, NY: SUNY Press.

McClintock, A. (1995). *Imperial leather: Race, gender and sexuality in the colonial contest.* New York, NY: Routledge.

McDermott, R. P. (1996). The acquisition of a child by a learning disability. In S. Chaiklin & J. Lave (Eds.), *Understanding practice: Perspectives on activity and context.* New York, NY: Cambridge University Press.

McGraw-Hill. (2000). *McGraw-Hill world atlas for intermediate students.* New York, NY: Macmillan/McGraw-Hill.

Meacham, S.J. (2000–2001). Literacy at the crossroads: Movement, connection, and communication within the research literature on literacy and cultural diversity. *Review of Research in Education, 25*, 181–208.

Merkel, A. (2010). http://www.guardian.co.uk/world/2010/oct/17/angela-merkel-germany-multiculturalism-failures, accessed 10–29–10.

Michaels, S. (1981). "Sharing time": Children's narrative styles and differential access to literacy. *Language in Society, 10*(3) (December), 423–442.

Mignolo, W. (2000). *Local histories/Global designs: Coloniality, subaltern knowledges, and border thinking.* Princeton, NJ: Princeton University Press.

Moallem, M. (2005). The civic body and the order of the visible. *Between warrior brother and veiled sister: Islamic fundamentalism and the politics of patriarchy in Iran.* Berkeley, CA: University of California Press.

—— & Boal, I. (1999). Multicultural nationalism and the poetics of inauguration. In C. Kaplan, N. Alarcón, & M. Moallem (Eds.), *Between woman and nation: Nationalisms, transnational feminisms, and the state.* Durham, NC: Duke University Press.

Moll, L.C. & Greenberg, J. (1990). Creating zones of possibilities: Combining social contexts for instruction. In L.C. Moll (Ed.), *Vygotsky and education* (pp. 319–348). Cambridge, MA: Cambridge University Press.

——, Amanti, C., Neff, D., & Gonzalez, N. (1992). Funds of knowledge for teaching: Using a qualitative approach to connect homes and classrooms. *Theory into Practice, 31,* 132–141.

Morrell, E. (2002). Toward a critical pedagogy of popular culture: Literacy development among urban youth. *Journal of Adolescent and Adult Literacy, 46*(1) (Sept., 2002), 72–77.

Morris, J. (2004). Can anything good come from Nazareth? Race, class and African-American schooling and community in the urban south and Midwest. *American Educational Research Journal, 41*(1), 69–112.

Murray, A. (1996). *The blue devils of nada: A contemporary American approach to aesthetic statement.* New York, NY: Pantheon Books.

Murrell, P.C. (2007). *Race, culture, and schooling: Identities of achievement in multicultural urban schools.* New York, NY: Lawrence Erlbaum Associates.

Myers, I.B. with Myers, P.B. (1980, 1995). *Gifts differing: Understanding personality type.* Mountain View, CA: Davies-Black Publishing.

National Institute of Child Health and Human Development. (2000). *Report of the National Reading Panel. Teaching children to read: An evidence-based assessment of the scientific research literature on reading and its implications for reading instruction.* (NIH Publication No. 00–4769). Washington, DC: US Government Printing Office.

Norton, B. (2000). *Identity and language learning: Gender, ethnicity, and educational change.* Harlow, UK: Pearson Education, Ltd.

Nuñez, J. (2006). *The impact of Colombia's educational reform on students with post-traumatic stress disorder.* San Francisco, CA: San Francisco State University.

Ogbu, J. (1994). From cultural differences to differences in cultural frames of reference. In P. Greenfield & R. Cocking (Eds.), *Cross-cultural roots of minority child development.* Hillsdale, NJ: Lawrence Erlbaum.

Olsen, L. (1997). *Made in America: Immigrant students in our public schools.* New York, NY: The New Press.

Omi, M. & Winant, H. (1993). On the theoretical concept of race. In C. McCarthy & W. Crichlow (Eds.), *Race, identity, and representation in education.* New York, NY: Routledge.

Ong, A. (1999). *Flexible citizenship: The cultural logics of transnationality.* Durham, NC: Duke University Press.

Onwuegbuzie, A.J. and Daley, C.E. (2001). Racial differences in IQ revisited: A synthesis of nearly a century of research. *Journal of Black Psychology, 27*(2), 209–220.

P&G School Programs. (2013). *Puberty materials: Always changing program for 5th and 6th grade girls and boys.* http://www.pgschoolprograms.com/programs.php?pid=1, accessed 11-26-13.

Palmer, R. (1995). *Rock and roll: An unruly history.* New York, NY: Harmony Books.

Pearson, P.D. (2004). The reading wars. *Educational Policy, 18*(1), January and March, 216–252.

Peters, M. (1999). (Posts-)modernism and structuralism: Affinities and theoretical innovations. *Sociological Research Online, 4(3),* http://www.sourceonline.org.uk/4/3/peters.html.

—— & Besley, A.C. (2006). *Building knowledge cultures: Education and development in the age of knowledge capitalism.* Lanham, MD: Rowman & Littlefield, Publishers, Inc.

Pollock, M. (2005) Race bending: 'Mixed' youth practicing strategic racialization in California. In S. Maria & E. Soep (Eds.), *Youthscapes: The popular, the national, and the global.* Philadelphia, PA: University of Pennsylvania Press.

Popkewitz, T. (2004). The alchemy of the mathematics curriculum: Inscriptions and the fabrication of the child. *American Educational Research Journal, 41*(1), 3–34.

Poster, M. (1988). Introduction. In J. Baudrillard, *Selected writings.* Stanford, CA: Stanford University Press.

Pongratz, L. (2007). Freedom and discipline: Transformations in pedagogic punishment. In M. Peters & A.C. Besley (Eds.), *Why Foucault? New directions in educational research.* New York, NY: Peter Lang.

Pratt, R.H. (1973). The advantages of mingling Indians with Whites. In *Americanizing the American Indians: Writings by the "Friends of the Indian" 1880–1900.* Cambridge, MA: Harvard University Press

Project G.L.A.D. (2013). http://www.projectglad.com/, accessed on 1-10-14.

Quijano, A. (2000). Coloniality of power and Eurocentrism in Latin America. *International Sociology, 15*(2), June 2000, 215–232.

—— (2007). Coloniality and modernity/rationality. *Cultural Studies, 21*(2–3), March/May 2007, 168–178.

Ramírez, M. & and Castañeda, A. (1974). *Cultural democracy, bicognitive development, and education.* New York, NY: Academic Press.

Reinke, L. (2004). Globalization and local indigenous education in Mexico, *International Review of Education, 50*(5–6), 483–496.

Rice, G.E. (1980). On cultural schemata. *American Ethnologist, 7*(4) (Feb. 1980), 152–171.

Robinson, A. L., Foster, C. C., & Ogilvie, D. H. (Eds.), (1969). *Black studies in the university.* New York, NY: Bantam.

Rogoff, B. (2003). *The cultural nature of human development.* New York, NY: Oxford University Press.

Rorty, R. (1991). Objectivity, Relativism, and Truth: Philosophical Papers. New York, NY: Cambridge University Press.

Rosaldo, R. (1989). *Culture and truth: The remaking of social analysis.* Boston, MA: Beacon Press.

—— (1994). Cultural citizenship and educational democracy. *Cultural Anthropology, 9*(3) (August 1994), 402–411.

Rouse, R. (1996). Mexican migration and the social space of postmodernism. In D. Gutierrez (Ed.), *Between two worlds.* Wilmington, DE: Scholarly Resources.

Rubenstein-Ávila, E. (2007). From the Dominican Republic to Drew High: What counts as literacy for Yanira Lara? *Reading Research Quarterly, 42*(4), 568–589.

Said, E. (1979). *Orientalism.* New York, NY: Vintage Books.

Sánchez, P. (2007). Urban immigrant students: How transnationalism shapes their world learning. *The Urban Review, 39*(5), 489–517.

Sapir, E. (2004). *Language: An introduction to the study of speech*. Mineola, NY: Dover Publications, Inc.

Sarkar, M. & Winer, L. (2006). Multilingual codeswitching in Quebec rap: Poetry, pragmatics, and performativity. *International Journal of Multilingualism, 3*(3), 173–192.

Sassen, S. (2002). The repositioning of citizenship: Emergent subjects and spaces for politics. *Berkeley Journal of Sociology, 46*, 4–25.

Saussure, F. (2011, 1959). *Course in general linguistics*. New York, NY: Columbia University Press.

Schein, L. (1998). Importing Miao brethren to Hmong America: A not-so-stateless transnationalism. In P. Cheah & B. Robbins (Eds.), *Cosmopolitics: Thinking and feeling beyond nation*. Minneapolis, MN: University of Minnesota Press.

Schlesinger, A. (1992). *The disuniting of America: Reflections on a multicultural society*. New York, NY: W.W. Norton.

Scribner, S. & Cole, M. (1981). *The psychology of literacy*. Cambridge, MA: Harvard University Press.

Shanahan, T. (2012). We were setting expectations of such a modest level. *Education Week*, November 14, 2012, 9–12.

Shohat, E. & Stam, R. (Eds.), (2003). *Multiculturalism, postcoloniality, and transnational media*. New Brunswick, NJ: Rutgers University Press.

Shor, I. (1993). Education is politics: Paulo Freire's critical pedagogy. In P. McLaren & P. Leonard (Eds.), *Paulo Freire: A critical encounter*. New York, NY: Routledge.

Skerrett, A. (2012). Languages and literacies in translocation: Experiences and perspectives of a transnational youth. *Journal of Literacy Research, 44*(4), 364–395.

Skinner, B.F. (1957). *Verbal behavior*. New York, NY: Appleton-Century-Crofts.

Sleeter, C. & Stillman, J. (2005). Standardizing knowledge in a multicultural society. *Curriculum Inquiry, 35*(1), 27–46.

Smith, L.T. (1999). *Decolonizing methodologies: Research and indigenous peoples*. London and New York, NY: Zed Books Ltd.

Solórzano, E. & Solórzano, R. (1995). The Chicano educational experience: A proposed framework for effective schools in Chicano communities. *Educational Policy, 9*, 293–314.

Spivak, G. (1988). Can the subaltern speak? In C. Nelson & L. Grossberg (Eds.), *Marxism and the interpretation of culture*. London: Macmillan.

Strathern, P. (2009). *Napoleon in Egypt*. New York, NY: Random House, Bantam.

Stuebing, K.K., et al. (2008). A response to recent reanalyses of the National Reading Panel Report: Effects of systematic phonics instruction are practically significant. *Journal of Educational Psychology, 100*(1), 123–134.

Sue, D. W. (2004). Whiteness and ethnocentric monoculturalism: Making the "invisible" visible. *American Psychologist, 59*(8), 761.

Taba, H., Brady, E.H., & Robinson, J.T. (1952). *Intergroup education in public schools*. Washington, DC: American Council on Education.

Taylor, C. (1992). *Multiculturalism and the politics of recognition: An essay*. Princeton, NJ: Princeton University Press.

TED (2013). http://www.ted.com/pages/about, accessed 12–3–13.

Tomasello, M. (1999). *The cultural origins of human cognition*. Cambridge, MA: Harvard University Press.

Torres, C. A. (2002). The state, privatisation and educational policy: A critique of neo-liberalism in Latin America and some ethical and political implications. *Comparative Education Review, 38*(4), 365–385.

Toulmin, S. (1990). *Cosmopolis: The hidden agenda of modernity.* Chicago, IL: The University of Chicago Press.

Touraine, A. (1994). *Qu'est-ce que la démocratie?* Paris: Fayard.

Tu, W.M. (1996). Confucian traditions in East Asian modernity. *Bulletin of the American Academy of Arts and Sciences, 50*(2) (Nov., 1996), 12–39.

Tyack, D. (1974). *The one best system: A history of American urban education.* Cambridge, MA: Harvard University Press.

Valdés, G. (2001). *Learning and not learning English.* New York, NY: Teacher's College Press.

Valencia, S.W., Place, N.A., Martin, S.D., & Grossman, P.L. (2006). Curriculum materials for elementary reading: Shackles and scaffolds for four beginning teachers. *The Elementary School Journal, 107*(1), 93–120.

Valimaa, J. & Hoffman, D. (2008). Knowledge society discourse and higher education. *Higher Education, 56*(3), 265–285.

van den Broek, P. (2010). Using texts in science education: Cognitive processes and knowledge representation. *Science,* 328, 453–456.

Verdery, K. (1996). *What was socialism and what comes next?* Princeton, NJ: Princeton University Press.

Vygotsky, L. S. (1981). The instrumental method in psychology. In J.V. Wertsch (Ed.), *The concept of activity in Soviet psychology.* Armonk, NY: Sharpe.

Walters, J. & Gardner, H. (1986). The theory of multiple intelligences: Some issues and answers. In R. Sternberg & R. Wagner (Eds.), *Practical intelligence: Nature and origins of competence in the everyday world.* New York, NY: Cambridge University Press.

Warren Little, J. (2002). Locating learning in teachers' communities of practice: Opening up problems of analysis in records of everyday work. *Teaching and Teacher Education 18,* 917–946.

Waters, M. C. & Jimenez, T. R. (2005). Assessing immigrant assimilation: New empirical and theoretical challenges. *Annual Review of Sociology 31,* 105–125.

Weems, L. (2004). Troubling professionalism: Narratives of family, race, and nation in educational reform. In B.M. Baker & K.E Heyning (Eds.), *Dangerous coagulations?: The uses of Foucault in the study of education.* New York, NY: Peter Lang.

Wertsch, J. V. & Kanner, B. G. (1992). A sociocultural approach to intellectual development. In R.J. Sternberg & C.A. Berg (Eds.), *Intellectual development.* New York, NY: Cambridge University Press.

Westwood, S. (2000). Ruptures—decentered nations: Transnationalism and the nation in Latin America. In S. Westwood & A. Phizacklea, *Trans-nationalism and the politics of belonging.* London: Routledge.

White, H. (1990). *The Content of the form: Narrative discourse and historical representation.* Baltimore: Johns Hopkins University Press.

Willingham, D.T. (2011). Can teachers increase students' self-control? *American Educator,* Summer, 22–26.

Witkin, H. A. (1967). A cognitive style approach to cross-cultural research. *International Journal of Psychology, 2*(4), 233–250.

—— , Moore, C.A., Goodenough, D.R., and Cox, P.W. (1977). Field dependent and field independent cognitive styles and their educational implications. *Review of Educational Research, 47*(1) (Winter 1977), 1–64.

Yosso, T.J. (2005). Whose culture has capital? A critical race theory discussion of community cultural wealth. *Race Ethnicity and Education, 8*(1), 69–91.

Zúñiga, V. & Hamann, E.T. (2009). Sojourners with U.S. school experience: A new taxonomy for transnational students. *Comparative Education Review*, 53(3), 329–353.

Index

Studies in the Postmodern Theory of Education

General Editor
Shirley R. Steinberg

Counterpoints publishes the most compelling and imaginative books being written in education today. Grounded on the theoretical advances in criticalism, feminism, and postmodernism in the last two decades of the twentieth century, Counterpoints engages the meaning of these innovations in various forms of educational expression. Committed to the proposition that theoretical literature should be accessible to a variety of audiences, the series insists that its authors avoid esoteric and jargonistic languages that transform educational scholarship into an elite discourse for the initiated. Scholarly work matters only to the degree it affects consciousness and practice at multiple sites. Counterpoints' editorial policy is based on these principles and the ability of scholars to break new ground, to open new conversations, to go where educators have never gone before.

For additional information about this series or for the submission of manuscripts, please contact:

Shirley R. Steinberg
c/o Peter Lang Publishing, Inc.
29 Broadway, 18th floor
New York, New York 10006

To order other books in this series, please contact our Customer Service Department:

(800) 770-LANG (within the U.S.)
(212) 647-7706 (outside the U.S.)
(212) 647-7707 FAX

Or browse online by series:
www.peterlang.com